Electing the President, 2004

Electing the President, 2004

The Insiders' View

EDITED BY
KATHLEEN HALL JAMIESON

PENN

University of Pennsylvania Press

Philadelphia

10   9   8   7   6   5   4   3   2   1

Published by
University of Pennsylvania Press
Philadelphia, Pennsylvania 19104-4112

Library of Congress Cataloging-in-Publication Data

Electing the president, 2004 : the insiders' view / edited by Kathleen Hall
Jamieson.
        p.   cm.
    ISBN-13 : 978-0-8122-1938-8
    ISBN-10 : 0-8122-1938-4 (pbk : alk. paper)
    Includes bibliographical references and index.
    1. Presidents—United States—Election—2004.   2. Political campaigns—United
States—Case studies.   I. Jamieson, Kathleen Hall.
JK526 2004 .E44   2006
324.973′0931–dc22   2005042371

Contents

Preface

Beginning in 1992, the Annenberg School for Communication has held election debriefings after each general election presidential campaign. First in tape form and starting in 2000 in transcript form as well, we have shared this event with the scholarly community.

We open with a timeline of election year events and with charts drawn from the data of the National Annenberg Election Survey. These materials were prepared for and distributed at the debriefing.

In some sense the 2004 election was a rematch between key consultants on each side, with Bob Shrum and Bill Knapp among those returning for the Democrats and Matthew Dowd, Mark McKinnon, and Alex Castellanos returning for the Republicans.

As the program outline indicates, the first day of the debriefing, held at the school in Philadelphia, focused on the Bush-Cheney and Kerry-Edwards campaigns. A brief biography of each presenter appears in the text before that person's first presentation.

After a weekend break, the second day, which focused on the major 527s, was held at the National Press Club in Washington, D.C. The consultants who attended the first event did not attend the Washington one, nor did the 527 representatives attend the event in Philadelphia. We had hoped to create a debriefing that happened across two consecutive days in one location but schedules did not permit us to do so.

As in the past, we asked the consultants on each side to prepare half-hour presentations. We then opened the floor to questions. In Philadelphia, where the event was closed to the press, the questions were asked primarily by the consultants in the audience. In Washington, the questions came largely from reporters. That half-day was carried by C-SPAN.

The goal of the debriefing was to capture the insights of these individuals for examination by scholars and students in the coming months and years. After we transcribed the presentations and discussion, I removed some of the peculiarities of oral speech and added punctuation and bracketed information for context. We then sent the edited version to the participants for correction of spelling and transcription errors. (For example, in the process "youth" had become "use" in one sentence.)

We are grateful to the consultants who, election cycle after election cycle, have helped the scholarly community better understand their take on what happened. I am particularly indebted to Annenberg Public Policy Center staff members Joyce Garczynski and Jennifer Ernst for superintending the events in Philadelphia (thank you, Joyce) and Washington (thank you, Jennifer) and for shepherding the edited transcripts back and forth to our guests. Brooks Jackson, who heads APPC's FactCheck .org, moderated the Washington Debriefing. Annenberg doctoral student and senior National Annenberg Election Survey analyst Kate Kenski moderated the day in Philadelphia. Kyle Cassidy took the photos for the book. The audiences for both days included Annenberg School and Penn political science faculty, APPC staff, and graduate and undergraduate students from Annenberg classes, along with a few special friends of the school and policy center. These included Richard Johnston of the University of British Columbia and Michael Hagen from Temple University, each of whom played an indispensable role in creating the National Annenberg Election Survey, and Margaret and Hank Kenski, who, like Richard and Michael, are distinguished political scientists, but who, unlike Richard and Michael, are Kate Kenski's parents.

Introduction

In the 2004 post-election period, the Democratic consultants cast the election as close—theirs but for fifty thousand or so votes gone the other way in Ohio. The Republicans cast it as an election that was theirs to lose. They anticipated and got a 2- to 3-point victory in a contest that, as both sides anticipated, came down to the outcome in Ohio. In larger terms, in the heady post-election days the Republicans cast the election as a mandate for the Bush agenda of Social Security reform, tax simplification, tort reform, and the like.

When all the votes were in, the numbers, mercifully, showed that unlike 2000 the same person had carried both the electoral and popular vote with the final Electoral College spread 286–251.[1]

It had been sixteen years since a presidential candidate won a majority of the national popular vote. The final vote in the November 2004 presidential election gave incumbent president George W. Bush 60,693,281 votes to Senator John Kerry's 57,355,978,[2] a 2–3 percent margin of victory and popular vote majority for the Republicans. Unlike the situation in 2000, independent candidate Ralph Nader played no role in the outcome.

Importantly, as one assesses the effects of the election on governance, 2004 elected Republicans beyond the presidential ticket. The Texas son of a former president was the first Republican incumbent since Calvin Coolidge to gain a second term and net seats in the House and in the Senate at the same time.

This was an election in wartime. Five times in the history of the U.S. a wartime president has sought reelection and five times the wartime president has been reelected. Was the outcome decisively shaped by September 11 or more specifically the public's willingness to amalgamate the war in Iraq to the war on terror? Senator John Kerry thought so. On *Meet the Press*, January 30, 2005, he told moderator Tim Russert that "9/11 was the central deciding issue of this race." As the debriefing attests, the Republicans worked persistently to reinforce the public perception that September 11 was the decisive event of the Bush first term and also to drive the public's inference that Senator Kerry wasn't up to the job.

The 2004 election was shaped by geography as well. The last non-

Southern Democrat to win the presidency was Massachusetts Senator John Kennedy. In 2004, the only Southern state in which the Democrat was competitive was Florida, and there he fell short of winning.

Did the economy matter? In Florida, where the economy was doing well, Bush pulled comfortably ahead of Kerry and outstripped his own 2000 performance. But in Ohio, where job losses were comparatively high, both sides thought Kerry had a chance.

Could Senator John Kerry have won? The deficit was at a record high. More than half the country reported as the election neared that the country was on the wrong track. Presidential approval hovered around 50 percent. The stock market had lost value on Bush's watch and as Election Day approached it looked likely that the incumbent would, as the Democrats were fond of noting, be the first president to lose net payroll jobs since Herbert Hoover. Importantly, as well, the war in Iraq had not gone as forecast, with its costs and casualties higher and its end not clearly in sight on Election Day.

On the plus side for the Republicans was the fact that by a number of key indicators the economy was improving. Indeed the standard political science models forecast a Bush victory. And the turnover of authority to the provisional government in Iraq in late June moved headlines damaging to Bush that before had dominated the front page onto the inside pages of the nation's newspapers.

The 2004 election turned some conventional wisdom on its head. High turnout is supposed to benefit the Democrats. However, in 2004 a precinct-level turnout machine staffed by volunteers gave the Republicans a turnout advantage. Importantly, for the first time in recent memory the number of self-identified Republicans who voted equaled the number of people saying they were Democrats. As Democratic pollster Mark Mellman observed, "In the 70s and 80s, Democrats on Election Day had 15-point margins. By the time we got to the 80s, those were 2- and 3- and 4-point margins. It is right to say that today this was the first election where the exit polls showed parity."

In the presidential race, voter turnout was up substantially from 2000. Bush won by about 10.2 million more votes than he had in 2000. Still, Kerry could claim more ballots than any other Democratic contender in history, about 6.4 million more than Gore gathered in 2000.[3] In Ohio, a state in the Republican column in every major race in which a Republican has won the presidency, both parties increased the number of votes they gained over 2000. "Bush countered Kerry's gains in the metropolitan precincts by boosting his margin in exurban and rural counties from 57 to 60 percent, eking out a 118,457-vote victory," Thomas B. Edsall and James V. Grimaldi reported in the *Washington Post*.[4]

The Bush campaign also took on conventional wisdom by risking attacking the Democrat early and often while running relatively few ads burnishing Bush's image and credentials. Before the nomination was even officially Kerry's, the Republicans had bashed him in over $60 million dollars of ads, giving lie to the common belief that high levels of attack will fatally damage the attacker.

After a decade of forecasts that the upcoming election would be the one in which the Internet would become a force to be reckoned with, both sides agree that 2004 was the election in which it did. Among its functions, in 2004 the Internet served as a fundraising vehicle, a mobilizing tool, an informational channel, and a way for bloggers to make their views known and their insights felt. It also enhanced the impact of the 527s that built webpages around their ads and used the web to appeal for money to stay on the air.

Whether communication mattered is always open to debate but the unprecedented level of paid communication was not in dispute. During election season more than 630,000 ads aired.

However, contrary to expectations that Republicans will outspend Democrats, one side didn't decisively win the race for dollars. In the end, reported Edsall and Grimaldi, "John F. Kerry and his Democratic supporters nearly matched President Bush and the Republicans, who outspent them by just $60 million, $1.14 billion to $1.08 billion."

How that money was deployed may however have made a difference. Edsall and Grimaldi conclude, "Democrats simply did not spend their money as effectively as Bush. . . . In a $2.2 billion election, two relatively small expenditures by Bush and his allies stand out for their impact: the $546,000 ad buy by Swift Boat Veterans for Truth and the Bush campaign's $3.25 million contract with the firm TargetPoint Consulting. The first portrayed Kerry in unrelentingly negative terms, permanently damaging him, while the second produced dramatic innovations in direct mail and voter technology, enabling Bush to identify and target potential voters with pinpoint precision."

The campaign by the so-called Swift Boat Veterans for Truth will undoubtedly elicit intense scholarly scrutiny in the coming years. Because of the rules governing when a candidate received federal matching funds and with them a cap on how much he could spend, Kerry fought a general election with fewer dollars to spend per day. In what may have been a strategic error, his campaign conserved its funds in August while it was hammered by a small media buy by the so-called Swift Boat Veterans for Truth. Arguably that first half million dollars or so SwiftVet ad buy, amplified by free airing on cable talk shows, was the most effective small dollar ad purchase since the national Security Political Action Committee added "Willie Horton" to the political lexicon in 1988.

The 527s cut both ways in 2004, however. The pro-Kerry 527s may have thwarted the Republicans' effort to derail the Kerry candidacy in the post-primary season. Days after Super Tuesday locked up the Democratic nomination for Massachusetts Senator John Kerry, the Bush team was on the air with a $40 million six-week assault. Since the Kerry camp was effectively out of money, the pro-Kerry 527s moved into the gap with anti-Bush messages. Were it not for their efforts, described in the debriefing by representatives from The Media Fund and MoveOn, the Bush effort might have effectively ended Kerry's prospects before he was even nominated.

In the category of "what might have been" are many questions as well as significant disputes about the answers. Should Kerry have accepted the $75 million in federal funding and the attendant spending caps that came with it when he accepted the nomination a month before George Bush did?

Is a Senator with decades of votes on the record always a more vulnerable candidate than a governor or incumbent president?

Why did Kerry receive a smaller bounce from his convention than the Republican consultants had expected and the Democrats had hoped?

What if any was the importance of the ballot initiatives in 11 states that defined marriage as the union of a man and a woman?

Did the exit poll that showed moral values as a prime motivator for Bush votes get it wrong?

Did the Democrats suffer an insurmountable strategic disadvantage? In place for President Bush with years of planning time on their hands was the campaign team that had eked out a victory in 2000 and now had the added advantage of plenty of time to find the votes that would give their candidate both an electoral and popular vote victory. The Republicans were blessed as well by the fact that the incumbent was unchallenged in the primaries. Moreover, within his own party, Bush was popular. Republicans traditionally have high loyalty from their party supporters.

The Republicans began running for reelection in 2004 before Governor Bush had been inaugurated in 2000. In the weeks after his election in 2000, his representatives buffered their standard-bearer from bad economic news. George W. Bush has inherited a recession from Clinton, they argued even before he had been sworn in. While the Democrats and the economic indicators said it was not a recession until months into the first Bush term, no one seriously disputed that the downturn had begun before he was in office. After September 11, the Bush team pinned the faltering economy on the terrorist attack.

Did Kerry focus too intensely on his time in Vietnam during the Democratic convention? The Democrats argue that only 6 percent of his acceptance speech focused on Vietnam. The Republicans argue that media coverage created a greater focus. I would add that the notion that the Democrat's acceptance speech was all Vietnam all the time was fueled by a Republican communication team that was relentlessly on message.

Were there decisive moments that could have turned the election for the Democrat or shoved it out of reach for the Republican? How important were the Kerry gaffes including the words that would live on in Republican ads and speeches, "I actually voted for the $87 billion before I voted against it." Or the moment that Kerry decided to windsurf off Nantucket in August within view of photographers who in effect handed the Republican 527s and the Bush campaign a visual metaphor incarnating their claim that Kerry was unmoored from principle, a flip-flopper, out of touch with mainstream values.

Did Bush's petulant performance in the first debate open the possibility that the electorate would rethink its sense of the incumbent? Did the debates benefit Kerry but not enough or too early in the process to affect the final outcome? The Democrats think they did where the Republicans see little net effect. Both teams agree that the debates should be seen as a whole. The Democrats wish they had occurred closer to Election Day.

How did the Republicans close the gender gap? The Republican consultants disclose that they succeeded in finding the 3 points they needed to move from the tie in 2000 to the victory in 2004 from women. As Bush pollster Matthew Dowd put it, "We thought the biggest majority from which we were going to get that 3 points was women, predominantly white women. In the end, if you look at the exit polls, two-thirds of the margin came from white women. We didn't do any better among men on Election Day."

Has the gender gap that closed in 2004 become a marriage gap? The *Washington Post*'s David Von Drehle observes, "In nine states, there are equal numbers of households headed by married and unmarried people. Sure enough, Bush and Kerry split them evenly, four for Bush and five for Kerry—and by middling margins, too: an average 16 points where Bush won, 11 points where Kerry won. Of the 11 states, plus the District of Columbia, where married couples form a minority of all households, Kerry won seven, by a jaw-dropping average of 24 percentage points. Bush won five, by the relatively skimpy average margin of 9 points. The District, with the lowest percentage of married folks, gave Kerry his biggest win: 90 to 9."[5]

Finally, was this an election in which world events such as the 9/11 Commission hearings, the Abu Ghraib scandal, news from Iraq, terrorist attacks around the world, and the last minute Osama tape pushed public perception of the incumbent and his electoral chances more than any imaginable communication by the Kerry campaign could have?

From the debriefing, we learned how the more famous ads from 2004 came to be—from Kerry's on-camera ads to "Wolves," "SwiftVets," and "Ashley." We heard the debate strategies on each side. We learned what the internal polling numbers said and when they said it, what the strategies of the various consultants were, whether they thought they worked, and how and why the strategies changed. We also learned where they think the press and the scholarly community get the story wrong, from polls based on national samples instead of samples in the battleground states to misunderstandings of the effects of individual debates rather than debates taken as a whole. And we learned that increasingly mass communication exists alongside and may be in the process of being displaced by Internet communication and micro-targeting.

Notes

1. http://www.archives.gov/federal-register/electoral-college/2004/election_results.html (U.S. National Archives and Records Administration Office of the Federal Register Website)

2. http://www.archives.gov/federal-register/electoral-college/2004/election_results.html (U.S. National Archives and Records Administration Office of the Federal Register Website)

3. http://www.fec.gov/pubrec/2000presgeresults.htm (Federal Election Commission Website) and http://www.archives.gov/federal-register/electoral-college/2004/election_results.html (U.S. National Archives and Records Administration Office of the Federal Register Website)

4. "On Nov. 2, GOP Got More Bang for Its Billion, Analysis Shows," *Washington Post*, Dec. 30, 2004, A01.

5. "The Red Sea: Want to Know Why George Bush Won? Set Sail into the Crimson Heart of America," *Washington Post Magazine*, Jan. 16, 2005, W12.

Campaign Timeline and Charts

Methodology

The National Annenberg Election Survey (NAES) is a survey conducted each presidential election by the Annenberg Public Policy Center of the University of Pennsylvania. The 2004 NAES telephone interviews began October 7, 2003 and concluded on November 16, 2004. During this period, 81,422 adults in the United States were interviewed.

In addition to its large sample size, the NAES is distinctive because it employs a rolling cross-section (RCS) design. With this method, random samples of respondents are interviewed each day of the presidential campaign period in such a way that the samples are comparable from one day to the next. Daily interviews can thus be used to identify trends and points of change in the public's reactions to political events as they unfold over the course of the presidential campaign.

The RCS design is a series of repeated cross-sections collected with a rigorous sampling plan. This sampling plan works to ensure that each of the repeated cross-sections is composed of randomly selected members from the population under study. In the case of the NAES, the design is used to gather cross-sections of randomly selected adults in the United States during the presidential campaign. Because the composition of each cross-section is random, researchers can treat the date of interview as a chance event. Researchers can analyze the data as a single cross-section or a time series.

The sample of telephone exchanges called was randomly selected by a computer from a complete list of thousands of active residential exchanges across the country. Within each exchange, random digits were added to form a complete telephone number, thus permitting access to both listed and unlisted numbers. Within each household, one adult was designated by a random procedure to be the respondent for the survey. The interviewing was conducted by Schulman, Ronca, Bucuvalas, Inc.

The analyses illustrate several campaign dynamics from the 2004 presidential race. Results are aggregated from the daily RCS data. The daily results are then smoothed using 15-day centered moving averages, meaning that each day represents an average of that day's results plus the seven days prior and seven days after that point in time. Underlying patterns can be obscured by sampling variation. By averaging results across several days, campaign dynamics are detected more easily.

2004 Presidential Campaign Timeline

Date	Event
1/6	Democratic Debate, Des Moines (Radio Debate-NPR)
1/11	Democratic Debate in Iowa (Brown and Black Forum)
1/10	Sen. Harkin (Iowa) endorses Howard Dean
1/11	*Des Moines Register* endorses John Edwards
1/17	*Concord Monitor* (N.H.) endorses John Kerry
1/19	Kerry wins Iowa caucus; Edwards close 2nd; Dean finishes 3rd and gives memorable "Scream Speech"
1/20	Richard Gephardt drops out of the race
1/20	President Bush gives State of the Union speech
1/22	WMUR New Hampshire Debate
1/25	David Kay says case couldn't be made for WMD in Iraq
1/27	Kerry wins New Hampshire primary; Dean 2nd, Clark 3rd, Edwards 4th, Lieberman 5th
2/3	Kerry wins 5 of 7 primaries and caucuses: Missouri, Delaware, Arizona, New Mexico, North Dakota; Edwards wins South Carolina; Clark wins Oklahoma; Lieberman drops out
2/4	Massachusetts highest court clarifies order to legislature to allow same-sex marriages (civil unions not enough)
2/7	Kerry wins Michigan primary and Washington caucus
2/8	Bush goes on *Meet the Press* to defend record and military service; Kerry wins Maine caucus
2/10	Kerry wins Virginia and Tennessee primaries; Edwards 2nd in both
2/12	First gay marriage takes place in San Francisco
2/14	Kerry wins Nevada and D.C. caucuses
2/17	Kerry wins Wisconsin; Edwards a close second
2/18	Dean drops out
2/22	Ralph Nader announces he's running as an Independent
2/24	Bush announces support for constitutional amendment banning gay marriage
2/24	Kerry wins Utah primary and Hawaii and Idaho caucuses
3/2	Kerry wins 9 of 10 Super Tuesday contests
3/3	John Edwards drops out; Bush begins ad campaign
3/5	Bush campaign begins showing ads with 9/11 images

3/9	Kerry wins Florida, Louisiana, Mississippi, Texas—general election campaign begins
3/11	Bush ad campaign continues with contrast ads; Kerry counters
3/11	Terrorist bombings in Madrid kill 200; Al Qaeda implicated
3/14	Ruling party in Spain defeated in national election; supported U.S. and Iraq war; new party in power vows to withdraw Spanish troops from Iraq
3/21	Richard Clarke charges Bush was interested in going into Iraq before 9/11 and pushed him to find a link afterward: general failure in fighting terrorism
3/22–23	9/11 Commission Hearings: Madeleine Albright, Colin Powell, Donald Rumsfeld, Richard Clarke, Richard Armitage, Sandy Berger, and George Tenet testify
4/20–30	U.S. troops killed on daily basis; April deadliest month in war
4/28	*60 Minutes II* shows photos of Iraqi prisoners being abused by U.S. soldiers
4/29	9/11 Commission questions President Bush and Vice President Cheney for over 3 hours in historic Oval Office meeting
5/4	Kerry $25M ad campaign begins in 18 battleground states plus Colorado and Louisiana
5/6	Bush apologizes for Iraqi abuses
5/17	Massachusetts becomes first state to allow same sex marriages
5/24	Gasoline prices climb over $2.00 per gallon nationally
6/1	New Iraqi Governing Council selected to take over June 30
6/3	George Tenet resigns from CIA
6/5	Ronald Reagan dies
6/25	Michael Moore's *Fahrenheit 9/11* opens
6/28	U.S. hands over power to new Iraqi government two days ahead of schedule
7/6	John Kerry picks John Edwards to be his VP running mate
7/22	9/11 Commission Report released
7/26	Democratic Convention begins; Clintons speak
7/27	Teresa Heinz Kerry, Howard Dean, and Ted Kennedy speak at convention
7/28	Kerry officially nominated; Edwards speaks
7/29	Kerry accepts nomination in convention speech
8/5	Swift Boat Ads shown attacking Kerry
8/30	Republican Convention starts: John McCain and Rudy Giuliani speak, focusing on Iraq war
8/31	GOP Convention night 2: Arnold Schwarzenegger and Laura Bush headline

9/1   GOP Convention night 3: Zell Miller goes on the attack; Cheney gives acceptance speech

9/2   GOP Convention night 4: Bush gives acceptance speech; Kerry gives speech in Ohio at midnight (9/3) to rebut attacks

9/8   More documentation comes out suggesting Bush didn't fulfill his National Guard obligations

9/9   CBS airs report on Bush's National Guard service; turns out to include a forged document

9/13   Assault Weapons Ban expires

9/30   Foreign policy debate between Kerry and Bush—polls and pundits give Kerry clear win

10/5   VP debate between Edwards and Cheney—split decision

10/8   Second presidential debate—town hall polls and pundits call it even—later polls give edge to Kerry

10/8   Duelfer report comes out saying that Iraq definitely did not have WMD and may have destroyed weapons in '91

10/13   Third presidential debate—polls and pundits call it a Kerry win; NRA endorses Bush

10/14   Kerry makes reference to Cheney's lesbian daughter at debate on 10/13—criticized by Cheneys for doing so

10/17   *New York Times, Boston Globe, Minneapolis Star-Tribune* endorse Kerry; *Chicago Tribune, Denver Rocky Mountain News, Dallas Morning Star* endorse Bush

10/18   Early voting begins in Florida

10/25   Report comes out that 380 tons of explosives went missing under U.S. control in April 2003

10/29   Osama bin Laden tape shown on Al Jazeera

11/2   Election Day. Bush reelected after Kerry declines to contest Ohio; Bush gets 51 percent of popular vote to Kerry's 48 percent.

CHART 1. VOTE PREFERENCE FOR BUSH AND KERRY OVER TIME

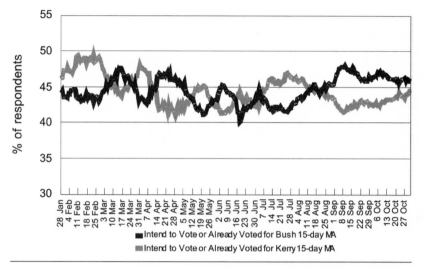

NAES 2004, 1/28/04 -- 11/1/04

■ Intend to Vote or Already Voted for Bush 15-day MA
■ Intend to Vote or Already Voted for Kerry 15-day MA

Vote intentions and behavior were measured in different ways during the course of the survey:

(1/28 to 4/29) Thinking about the general election for president in November 2004, if that election were held today, and the candidates were (ROTATE PAIRS) George W. Bush, the Republican, and John Kerry, the Democrat, for whom would you vote?

(4/30 to 7/20) If the 2004 presidential election were being held today, would you vote for (ROTATE NAMES) George W. Bush, the Republican, John Kerry, the Democrat, or Ralph Nader?

(7/6 to Election Day) If the 2004 presidential election were being held today, would you vote for ROTATE NAMES [George W. Bush and Dick Cheney, the Republicans,] [John Kerry and John Edwards, the Democrats,] or [Ralph Nader and Peter Camejo of the Reform Party]?

(Beginning 9/23, if respondent already voted) In the 2004 presidential election who did you vote for: ROTATE NAMES [George W. Bush and Dick Cheney, the Republicans,] [John Kerry and John Edwards, the Democrats,] or [Ralph Nader and Peter Camejo of the Reform Party]?

CHART 2. BUSH APPROVAL OVER TIME

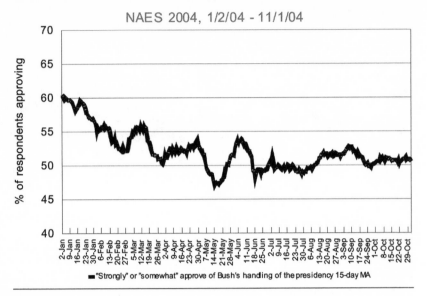

Do you approve or disapprove of the way George W. Bush is handling his job as president?
IF APPROVE: Do you approve strongly or only somewhat? IF DISAPPROVE: Do you
disapprove strongly or only somewhat?

CHART 3. RIGHT DIRECTION/WRONG TRACK OVER TIME

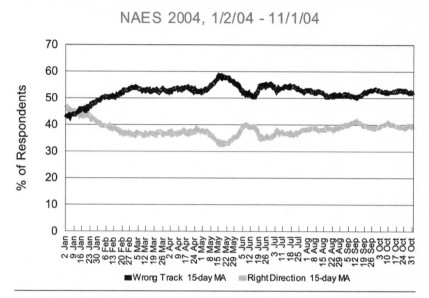

NAES 2004, 1/2/04 - 11/1/04

■Wrong Track 15-day MA   ▦Right Direction 15-day MA

Do you feel things in this country are generally going in the right direction, or do you
think things are seriously off on the wrong track? (Right direction, Wrong track, Don't
know, Refused)

CHART 4. FOLLOWING PRESIDENTIAL CAMPAIGN OVER TIME

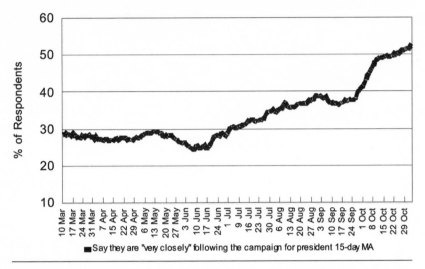

2004 NAES, 3/10/04 - 11/01/04

■ Say they are "very closely" following the campaign for president 15-day MA

How closely are you following the campaign for president? Very closely, somewhat closely, not too closely, or not closely at all? (Don't know and refused also included)

Traits: Presidential Candidates

CHART 5. "STRONG LEADER"

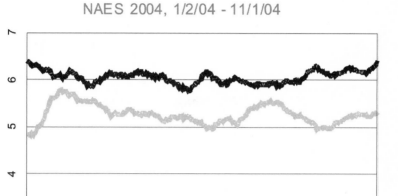

NAES 2004, 1/2/04 - 11/1/04

■Bush 15-day MA   ▨Kerry 15-day MA

I am going to read you some phrases. For each one, please tell me how well that phrase applies to [CANDIDATE]. Please use a scale from 0 to 10, where "zero" means it does not apply at all and 10 means it applies extremely well.

"Strong leader"

CHART 6. "SHARES MY VALUES"

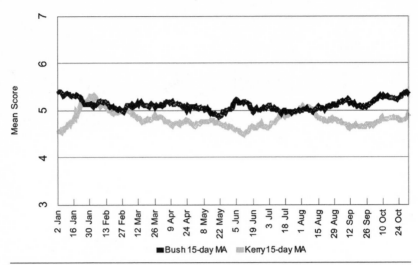

I am going to read you some phrases. For each one, please tell me how well that phrase applies to [CANDIDATE]. Please use a scale from 0 to 10, where "zero" means it does not apply at all and 10 means it applies extremely well.

"Shares my values"

CHART 7. "KNOWLEDGEABLE"

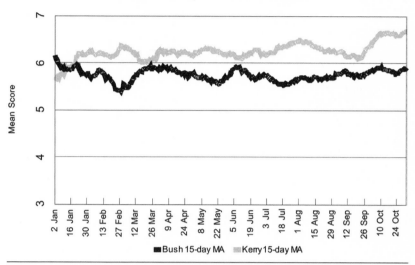

NAES 2004, 1/2/04 - 11/1/04

I am going to read you some phrases. For each one, please tell me how well that phrase applies to [CANDIDATE]. Please use a scale from 0 to 10, where "zero" means it does not apply at all and 10 means it applies extremely well.

"Knowledgeable"

CHART 8. "STEADY"

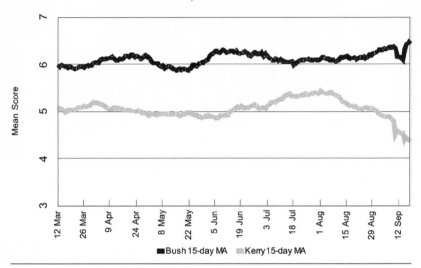

I am going to read you some phrases. For each one, please tell me how well that phrase applies to [CANDIDATE]. Please use a scale from 0 to 10, where "zero" means it does not apply at all and 10 means it applies extremely well.

"Steady"

CHART 9. "SAYS ONE THING BUT DOES ANOTHER"

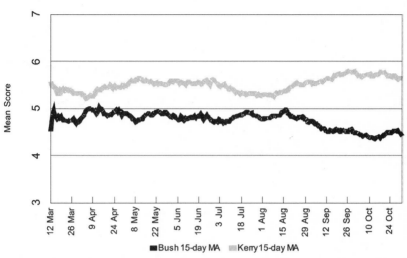

NAES 2004, 3/12/03 - 11/10/04

■Bush 15-day MA   ▨Kerry 15-day MA

I am going to read you some phrases. For each one, please tell me how well that phrase applies to [CANDIDATE]. Please use a scale from 0 to 10, where "zero" means it does not apply at all and 10 means it applies extremely well.

"Says one thing but does another"

CHART 10. "HAS THE RIGHT KIND OF EXPERIENCE TO BE PRESIDENT"

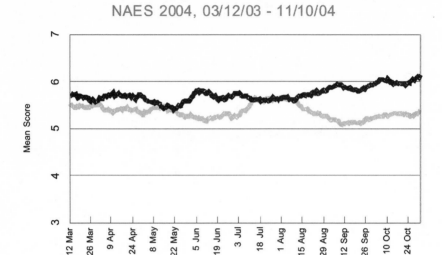

I am going to read you some phrases. For each one, please tell me how well that phrase applies to [CANDIDATE]. Please use a scale from 0 to 10, where "zero" means it does not apply at all and 10 means it applies extremely well.

"Has the right kind of experience to be president"

Chapter 1

Campaign Organization and Strategy

Matthew Dowd

Chief campaign strategist for Bush-Cheney 2004, **Matthew Dowd** *has served as senior advisor to the Republican National Committee and, in 2000, on the Bush for President Campaign as director of polling and media planning. Before joining the Bush campaign in June 1999, Dowd was president and founding partner of Public Strategies, Incorporated, an international public affairs firm. During this time, Dowd served as former Texas Lieutenant Governor Bob Bullock's chief campaign consultant in his two successful runs for lieutenant governor. In 1987 and 1988, Dowd served on the Senate and the campaign staff of former U.S. Senator Lloyd Bentsen (D-Texas).*

For us, the 2004 race started in the immediate aftermath of 2000. We did a lot of analysis of the results of the 2000. As a result of that research we approached the 2004 election differently both from 2000, and I think from a lot of other previous presidential campaigns.

The first thing that we noted was that motivation was as important as persuasion in 2000, and motivation was going to be as important as persuasion in the 2004 race. We concluded that 92 or 93 percent of this country were going to be in the position in which their minds were made up. Very few people were true swing voters or true split ticket voters in this country. That [phenomenon] has been building since the early 80s but really is now at a point where the percentage of people in this country that really are available on Election Day to either side is a very small number. Persuasion and motivation became equal for us. . . .

We basically decided that we were going to split our resources and our time long in advance of 2004 between motivation and persuasion, and that [decision] changed a lot of tactics and what we did approaching the election. [We concluded] . . . that we had to do as a party and as a candidate a much better job of person-to-person contact. Republicans had always relied on direct mail and phone banks as drivers for turning out people, and we realized through what happened in 2000, but also through some really good testing that we did, that we had to change that, and that influenced the resources that we spent on the campaign in 2000.

The other big thing is that an incumbent race is very different . . . We were going to have to suffer the good and bad of whatever the current events were. There's not a lot of an effect we can have on that, and after 9/11 and then the wars [Afghanistan and Iraq], there was a whole series of other issues that were going to impact this race, especially for us, that we had no control over. That was one part of it.

The other part was having the White House, which is another power center. [In] 2000, the power center was all within the campaign. When you do a reelect, the power center is divided, there's the campaign and then there's the White House. We had done a lot of research on previous reelects. It was going to be a different race because we were the incumbent. For good and for bad. There were some good parts of that and there were some bad parts.

In 2000, the Internet was really just starting to blossom into politics. We forecast that it was going to be a big deal in 2004. In the 2000 campaign we had 400 or 500,000 email addresses, which was more than anybody else had. When we ended this campaign we had seven million. And that changes the nature of contact; that changes the nature of message delivery. It changes the nature of how people seek information. Though it won't have that growth rate in the next election, I think that will have an effect in the coming years. So we knew as we organized the campaign, the Internet was going to be a big part of that, and we sought to build that [presence] in the course of the three years leading up to 2004.

In 2000 we got roughly 48 percent of the vote, so we asked: how are we going to get the 3 points to get us to 51? And that was a big part of everything that we did—where were those 3 points going to come from to get us from 48 to 51 percent? It was going to come from a variety of places. We've talked about this; this wasn't something that we hid. It was going to come from women, it was going to come from keeping our numbers among men, it was going to come from Latino voters, it was going to come to some degree among African American voters, and then finally it was going to come, our hope was, in increasing the number of Republicans that existed on Election Day, which was in our minds the most important thing that we were going to be able to do on Election Day.

In a presidential campaign, this is a lesson we all learn, but we learn it over and over again. [That lesson] is what effect free media has and what effect it has [in combination] with paid media. Also the number of cable channels and all the [resulting] discussion. Free media obviously is the dominant way people receive information in a presidential race,

Matthew Dowd

and paid media only works as it feeds the free media message, or as they each work off each other.

When we looked at the field and at the Democratic primary process, we thought the Democratic nominee would be chosen fairly quickly, by the end of February or early March. We assumed that long out, eight, nine months out. We didn't think it would be a protracted battle, and we thought that nominee would probably be very popular when that process was over. In a lot of races, but especially in a challenger race against an incumbent, the challenger gets a big bump. . . . The answer we didn't know was how vetted they would be when the primaries were over.

I think the good news from our perspective was that the process was truncated in 2004 and with what happened with Dean, and Kerry securing the nomination so fast, he was, in our minds, a very unvetted candidate for a vast majority of this country. This was good news for us. He was popular but his popularity was extremely soft because they didn't know much about him. They didn't know his record in the Senate, they didn't know a lot about what you meant when you said he's from Massachusetts. A whole series of things were unexplained to the public that we thought we should tell in March and April. And so though the [Democratic] nomination was secured early, which I think the Democrats saw as an advantage, I think there was a disadvantage: an unvetted candidate who had not, over nine months of campaigning, set his record and set who he was. As a result, he was open to the discussion that happened over the course of the next six to eight weeks.

There was a lot of discussion about approval ratings, reelect numbers, and right direction-wrong track. Our assumption was that approval rating mattered a lot, that your approval rating is going to be roughly within 1 or 2 points of what you end up with on Election Day—we thought that from day one. We didn't think right track-wrong track mattered. We went back and looked at previous races, we looked at our numbers. A number of people were going to vote for the president who thought the country was on the wrong track. So we were always dismissive of all this discussion about right track-wrong track, and what it means, and the lessons we can learn because basically right track-wrong track has not become something that is important unless it is vastly good or vastly bad. If you're in this sort of in-between ground, people factor a lot of other things into how they're going to vote.

The other thing is that "reelect" has become meaningless. Many people are so cynical in this country and so down. They say, yeah, I want to vote for somebody new. They always say, "I'm not going to vote to reelect" but when you give them the choices or when you say it's x against y or here are the two candidates, those numbers change. . . . In

2002, every single candidate was reelected for governor or for Senate with a reelect at 44 percent or higher. So the idea that if your reelect is below 50 percent that's somehow a bad thing [is wrong]; it's really if your reelect is below 40 percent. You have to be really in the tank.

We knew the approval rating was important. We assumed early on, a couple of years out, because of how polarized the country is, and how Democrats view the president and Republicans view the president, that we wouldn't be either at the point at which every president got reelected or at which every president was defeated. We thought we were going to be in that in-between ground—we always thought that. And because of that, we thought the choice mattered. It wasn't just about us. It wasn't just about where the president's standing was. It was about how John Kerry was perceived, what he represented. It was as much about him as it was about us. And we ran a campaign based on that. This is the first time a president has ever been running for reelection since they've been polling, has ever been in that in-between ground running for reelection. Usually a president's defeated or reelected and it's automatic and you pretty much know it long before Election Day. We were in between and therefore we thought the perceptions of John Kerry were going to mat- ter as much or as close to as much as the perceptions of us.

The other thing that I think people missed was the arguments we made about John Kerry, especially the ones about credibility, had as much to do with affecting his ability to make an argument about us as it did with impacting his numbers. I think people missed that. We wanted to put John Kerry in the position where if he said something about us, people would question it. People would say, "Wait a second, I don't know if I can believe that, I don't know if that's true, this is a guy who has a tendency to flip flop," or "he's not really true to himself, and where does he stand, and can I really believe what he's saying about the president." That was as important or more important than affecting his personal ratings because it affected the ability of the Kerry campaign and Kerry to make as a credible argument against us. That was impor- tant to us because we knew if our approval rating had dropped below 46 or 47, we would have a very difficult time, as I was quoted over and over again in paper by the Kerry campaign [saying that]. If we were at that point we basically would have a very difficult time winning. We knew that.

President[ial] elections are always about values. It's very curious that the discussion that's happened post-election is about values, values, val- ues. 2000 was about values. 1996 was about values. 1992 was about values. Presidential elections are always about values. Issues and personality and other things like that, presidential elections are not decided by those things. Those things are indicators to tell people what values you represent—whether or not you're strong and decisive; whether or not you're honest and trustworthy; whether or not you're a tolerant person; whether or not you're compassionate; whether or not you share the values of whatever county or whatever city you live in. Presidential elections are always about values. It's a question on which we led going into Election Day, which is why we thought we were going to win. We had an advantage when you ask people, "Who shares your values?" We had a 4- or 5-point advantage on that question going into Election Day. I guess we'll find out what the Kerry folks had on that question. That was in our internal polls; public polls were out there with the same answer. Moral values are a part of a values election, but presidential races are always values elections. Different than races for senate and different to a degree from races for other offices. It's always a values election for president.

The other assumption that we made is that voters are smart. Voters aren't dumb. Voters figure things out. One advantage I think we had from the president's perspective is that voters might disagree on some policies but they always said, "at least I know where this guy comes from and at least I know where he stands on this." Voters are smart. They're not dumb. They can't be spun. We can't put up a television spot to convince them of something that they don't believe and I think that affected all of our thinking and discussion and how we communicated, whether it was with the press or with other people. We assumed voters were able to take information, factor it in, factor it out, and come to the conclusion in a very smart, intelligent way.

What we did because of those assumptions: much bigger field operation, it was five times as large as 2000. How did we find more Republicans? We called it micro-targeting, a lot of analysis to find unregistered Republicans. We did it using a lot of different data bases and a lot of polling. In the course of this modeling that we did in the 16 target states or 17 target states, we took consumer data bases, we took voter files, and we took 5000 sample polls in each target state. We polled 5000 people in New Mexico. Then through modeling, we could figure out pretty accurately based on whether somebody had a certain magazine, based upon what car they drove, based on their credit card purchases, based on a whole series of things, we could tell whether or not somebody was an unregistered Republican in New Mexico. And we could tell who was a registered potential Republican who didn't vote. And so we did spend a lot of resources and a lot of time before 2002 but a lot in 2003 finding those.

One thing that we realized is 85 percent of Republicans don't live in Republican precincts. And that's a little bit different than Democrats. The Democratic, the base, the vote, has a tendency to be more homogeneous in where they live and where they stay. Republicans don't. In some places like Pennsylvania, 92 percent of Republicans don't live in Republican precincts. So the traditional way of targeting Republican precincts misses these Republicans. More Republicans live in Democratic precincts than live in Republican precincts. And so how do you find those folks? You can't do it through voter files, you can't do it through precincts, you have to do it through consumer data base and modeling, which we think we did very successfully. We mailed them, we phoned them, we had people knock on their doors. In a precinct that might have been a 30 percent Republican precinct in Wisconsin, somebody got a list of 20 names of Republicans who didn't vote last time but were likely to vote this time and they went to those individual doors. So that was different. We didn't do anything like that in 2000.

As I said, the Internet changed the communication. We had a way to reach seven million people fairly quickly—more than 10 percent of the people that were going to vote. If you could have a list of people that's one in ten or one in seven or one in eight or one in nine of people that you need to reach, you're well ahead of the game. It provided a huge advantage to be able to send communications out [through the Internet] because we knew they would talk to their neighbors, and it was instant—you could send it out in one day. Now we didn't raise the money that previous campaigns and the Kerry campaign raised on the Internet, but money-raising on the Internet was not a goal. The goal of building the Internet [contacts] was to communicate and to get the message out quickly and as broadly as we possibly can. We reached a ceiling at about seven million and we could never really get above that seven million. It's a big number and it was very helpful, but I think it's very hard to get much over that. Something we're going to have to answer in the next three or four years is how much are these people connected to the president and how much are they connected to the Republican Party.

Mail and phones. We spent a lot more on direct mail and a lot more on phone banks and a lot more on door to door than we did last time. The media buys, Alex [Castellanos] and Mark [McKinnon] will talk about, we did very differently. First time a national campaign has bought this much cable. People said, "They're buying Fox." We didn't only buy Fox. We bought the Learning Channel. We bought Discovery. And this was because, as we found out, there is a GRP [Gross Rating Points] gap. If we bought TV the same way the Democrats bought TV, they would hit 15 percent or more voters than we did. More Democrat[ic] voters than Republican voters watch news. More Democrats watch spot network than Republicans. We closed the gap in a number of ways including the Golf Channel. We also spent 15–16 million dollars on radio. We bought our spot markets differently and we found certain shows over-perform on Republicans or Independent[s], where others over-perform on Democrats-Independents, based on the partisanship of the audience. How we did it will change the way Republicans approach this [campaign marketing strategy].

Fox News had the largest audience at the Republican convention. It's going to dramatically affect the care and feeding of the nets, because now more and more people are going to other outlets to get the information that they trust, especially on the Republican side, especially on our side. CBS News, for example, has become basically a Democratic network in Republican minds. They don't watch it; whether you agree with it or not, there are a lot of voters out there who think CBS is basically the opposite of Fox News. I think that's going to change the 2008 presidential primary race. It's not about whether you sit down and have a meeting with Dan Rather, who's going to be gone, but Tom Brokaw or whomever; it's going to be what cable show are you able to get onto.

The phases in the campaign [we saw the campaign as six phases]: the post-Democratic primary, the Democratic convention including the VP pick, the post convention (August), the Republican convention, the post-convention phase, and the final ten days. Those were basically the phases of the campaign. We always saw the debates not as one debate, two debates, three debates, but as an accumulation of four debates and the effect that might have on confirming or changing people's biases.

Finally, a lot of the press bought into the presumption that hate was a better motivator than love, that people's dislike for something would motivate them more than their [affection] or love for a person. Ninety percent of our voters voted for us because they liked the president, they liked his policies, and they wanted him there; only 10 percent voted for us because they didn't like John Kerry. I think by a slight majority John Kerry's voters went to the polls because they didn't like the president, they didn't like what he stood for, they didn't like what he did. In turnout, we were at rough parity [with the Democrats] for the first time in a presidential campaign since they've been polling, a fact that suggests that hate or dislike are not necessarily better motivators than love or like. When you have a 93 percent approval rating among Republicans, I'll take that any day of the week. It's higher than Ronald Reagan had in 1984 among Republicans. We thought the best thing about that was that a voter who might not otherwise turn out will turn out because of how much they care for the president.

Mary Beth Cahill

Mary Beth Cahill has spent her professional life in public service, and has established herself as a force in Democratic politics. Most recently, she has served as campaign manager for John Kerry for President. Prior to joining the campaign, she served as the chief of staff to Senator Edward Kennedy and before that as assistant to the president and director of public liaison in Bill Clinton's White House. Recognized as an expert on women and politics, Cahill served for more than five years as executive director of EMILY's List, the nation's largest political action committee, during which the organization's membership doubled from 24,000 to 50,000. She has trained female candidates for political office in Russia, Macedonia, and Ireland.

I have a great appreciation of the value of four years to plan and begin to execute a presidential campaign because the thought that you would have the time and leisure to look at the campaign that far out obviously is an enormous luxury and a planning tool that was not available to us.

I'm going to talk briefly about the primary because the Democratic primary phase took up an enormous amount of time on our side, took an enormous amount of attention, and was very much the precursor to the general election.

John Kerry essentially began running for the presidency in 2002, raising money, building an organization in New Hampshire and Iowa and the other early primary states, trying to assemble a high quality staff, and for a long time in the public and in the minds of Democratic elites, he really was the frontrunner. He declared his candidacy in September of '03 and that was for him an extremely big moment.

But another thing was happening within the Democratic primary electorate that was really much bigger than what the campaigns were doing, and that was growing opposition to the president's position and policies in Iraq. Governor Dean, who was one of the nine people running for the Democratic nomination, took advantage, or was able to capitalize on this enormous strain of opposition to the president and to the president's policies in Iraq. He went almost overnight from being the ninth person in the field to being on the front page of the news magazines, and to being an extremely interesting character in the eyes of the press and in the eyes of Democratic activists across the country. This fundamentally shifted the race and it was in flux for an awfully long time after that. Kerry dropped back, obviously, in the field, during this period. Dean was running a very different campaign based in Vermont, with a lot of information coming out of Vermont [because of] what they were doing innovatively on the Internet.

I agree with Matthew [Dowd] that the big story in the 2004 race is going to be the way the Internet impacted this race. How it's used going forward is actually going to be one of the most interesting stories in the next phase of politics and political technology.

The primary season. From December 4 through March 4, there were 31

Mary Beth Cahill

debates on the Democratic side. There was a debate a week practically. It was a nine-person field. It was extremely difficult to make any headway and as I said the race had shifted fundamentally. The one thing that was going very well for John Kerry was that we had made a very large investment in Iowa early. There we were building an organization that was local office holder by local office holder. We were up against Congressman Gephardt who had enormous labor support and brought a lot of people in from out of state and had strong labor support within the state, and Howard Dean who obviously had a huge number of student activists, people who were very motivated by his candidacy. If you recall that point in time, the American Research Group had a daily poll in which at one point we were 40 points down in New Hampshire. Looking at that, Iowa seemed a pretty good bet for us.

In Iowa, caucus goers are a world unto themselves. Very few news organizations actually bought the 60,000-person list of previous caucus goers, so a lot of the polling in Iowa was completely askew. We thought that a lot of the information that was coming out of Iowa was wrong. So we stuck our flag in Iowa. John Kerry took out a 6.4-million-dollar loan on his house while our fundraising was frankly tanking, and we ran our campaign on that for almost two months.

During that period of time, despite the fact that the Democratic elite and the Democratic conversation had moved decidedly to the left, John Kerry stayed where he was, a moderate in the middle, because he wanted to be in a position to run in the general election. Thus, even though Gephardt was really attacking and pushing on NAFTA, Kerry, who had been a supporter of trade throughout his Senate career, stayed where he was and resisted that pull. He also defended his vote on the war in Iraq from the very beginning regardless what it was Dean had to say about that and regardless of what the Democratic activists were asking of John Kerry.

Money really was the bar for a period of time here. Dean raised almost 40 million dollars over the Internet. That was the other thing that made his campaign so interesting I think, particularly to the press. But we thought that what we were hearing about, what we [were] reading about and what we actually knew about on the ground were two completely different things. And actually, fortunately for us, that was borne out. We came out of Iowa in first place, followed by Edwards, with Dean in third, and the race once again had changed completely. We went on through Super Tuesday, through Wisconsin, and emerged the Democratic victor, the nominee actually, about March 10. Then we were, as Matthew [Dowd] said, on the general election playing field.

From our perspective, 9/11 always was the defining event of the race, giving the president a critical advantage. Voters felt as though they had a relationship with him coming from 9/11. The vision and the image they had of him were very fixed as a strong leader, and regardless of what else they thought about him or what else they thought about his policies, that was their beginning point of any conversation about him. The fact that 9/11 was so large a part of the Bush-Cheney campaign advertising, in particular, was a risk, surprising, and they really struck with it. After the first spot, "Steady Leadership in Tough Times," which showed the sort of iconography of 9/11, there was a real backlash and a very big backlash in the press. But they stuck with it, because obviously they completely understood the same thing that we did, which is that that was the essential part of the relationship between the president and the voters.

Also, with 9/11 as a backdrop, the president was free to attack John Kerry instead of defending his record. This backdrop and security made things like gas prices or a badly managed flu program non-issues. In 1996 or in 2000, those would have been enormous issues. The fact that security was a backdrop also narrowed our ability to have a, "are you better off than you were four years ago?" message, because security was there, it was the elephant in the middle of the room and one always had to navigate around that on both sides.

I agree with what Matthew [Dowd] said about political events and world events impacting this race on a day-to-day basis—terrorism, Chechnya [In early September 2004, Chechen terrorists killed teachers and children in a school hostage massacre in Beslan, Russia], the bin Laden tape [videotaped message from Al Qaeda leader Osama bin Laden that aired on October 29, 2004]. It is very hard to overstate the role that real outside events played on this campaign. While, as an incumbent, you own those events and they get in the way of the carefully laid out strategy, as a challenger, when there are real world events that are so much at the forefront of the voters' minds, it's almost impossible to change the subject, to take it where you want to go, to change the terms of debate.

Throughout this whole race, voters wanted a change in policy, and it was clear to us, not necessarily a change in leadership. We had to work very hard on an ongoing basis to try to get economic and domestic concerns into the mix for John Kerry to get a real look from the voters. One problem with that was that the economy was improving and the "wrong direction" was not growing to the historically significant level that we really needed it to be at. In November, consumer confidence was at its highest level in almost a year. October was the single largest job growth within nine months. So there was enormous dissatisfaction on the Democratic side and among a large segment of the voters with the Bush policies, but there was comfort with him. There was not the overhanging 1992 sense of economic doom that would have made a change a necessary thing in the eyes of the voters.

Also, President Bush was a wholly known individual. Voters felt as though they knew him and they really accept him both with his flaws and with his strengths. There was very little new that we could tell voters about him. They knew that he mispronounced words; they thought that he was a strong leader; they thought that he communicated his emotion and that he felt what he believed and they accepted that in him. So there was no possibility really of redefinition for us of President Bush.

And finally, an essential part of the landscape was the electoral map advantage that Republicans enjoyed. If we had won every state that Al Gore had won—he got 260 electoral votes—we would have to get 266, and so things had changed enough so that the bar was a little bit higher for us.

We came out of the primaries really needing to introduce John Kerry again. He was not a fully defined person. Almost one half of voters did not know that he had served in Vietnam. However, we came out of Wisconsin [on February 17, 2004] absolutely flat broke. We would do what primary campaigns do—we would figure out on Tuesday what we had left from the last week, we would figure out what [we] thought we could raise, the always terrible number was what we thought we needed, and how we were going to get through the next week, the next primary, the next series of television ad buys.

On March 10 we had 2.3 million cash on hand, and the Bush campaign had 114 million dollars. So they did precisely what you thought they would do. They used that opening to try to define John Kerry. We stayed on television at a subsistence level and we moved the campaign to almost completely a fundraising machine. We had 28 [fundraisers] over the course of the month of April.

We greatly enhanced our Internet capacity. We had started in December to really try to build that up. We thought it was going to be extremely important to us. We knew that we had a lot of appeal within the Democratic Internet community. So, for example, the day after the Iowa caucuses, we raised $365,000 online, which for us at that point in time was an enormous amount of money. We sent out an email, we got that money back; that was for us a remarkable thing.

So we were on television at a fairly low level. We needed to introduce him. We introduced him through a series of bio ads that outlined a lifetime of service and strengths and that introduced the record of Kerry as a principled fighter. We made an attempt to reassure voters on terror about John Kerry's strength through his biography and his record.

We attempted in our second phase, "Stronger at Home and Respected in the World," to get domestic issues into this conversation. Also a great many voters were extremely dissatisfied with the way America was viewed in the world as a result of what we referred to [as] the go it alone Bush policies. We attempted in an ongoing fashion to portray Iraq as a mess of Bush's creation and to really tie what voters saw every night on the evening news and the front pages of the papers to the Bush policies. The nation was not antiwar, but a lot of our supporters or people who were going to vote for us were very much anti-Bush policy.

We tried through our advertising to put domestic issues in play by highlighting the real plans that John Kerry talked about on the stump, particularly on the economy and health care—some of the things that were the most persuasive to the voters who were available for us.

Finally, we were always very careful about making a "change" argument. We understood that voters were extremely risk averse. In a time of war, in a time of real international difficulty and in a time when Americans were feeling very patriotic, how we made that argument was an extremely delicate matter. We had to build on it incrementally and we had a pretty small window in which to do that.

As I said, we spent March and April attempting to raise money to communicate about John Kerry and about his biography and plans for the country. When I think about key moments of the campaign, I think that period between March and June is critical, the point at which we had to hang back while the Republicans were using the resources they had amassed. But we were able to compete; everyone thought whoever the Democratic nominee was would be in extremely difficult shape financially. Kerry was able to unite the party very quickly and able to raise money at a clip that was, I think, a surprise to the press, a surprise to the Republicans, and sometimes early on a surprise to us. But we made it [the ability to compete financially with the Republicans], as I said, a major effort of the campaign.

When we were able to achieve parity, and spend $25 million on the air from May 4 to the first of June that, I think, was when we felt that we were fully in the game with the Bush-Cheney campaign.

I also think a critical moment was the selection of the vice presidential nominee. I think the press and people across the country were looking for cues from the way in which John Kerry carried out this search for his running mate. We had seen previous efforts on both sides where the press would be camped at the bottom of the driveway trying to figure out who was in the car going in. In those cases it was a very public process where people won and lost. Kerry made clear from the very beginning that that was not the way he wanted things to go. He wanted it to be very private and wanted the process to respect the people who were involved. I think this process played out extremely well for him, and I think John Edwards was a very strong and outstanding vice presidential nominee. And the vice presidential rollout worked really well for us. We got very good press during that period. The two of them together portrayed a youthful energetic future, helped in no small part by [Edwards's children] Jack and Emma Claire. My favorite moment in the campaign was in Wisconsin. Jack must have thought that his father was going on too long. With a cheese head on, Jack went up behind his father and butted him. When you watch as much news as I watched over the course of the year, you remember these moments.

The Democratic convention has been rewritten as something that it was not. It really was a highpoint for the Kerry campaign and for John Kerry. Only about six minutes of his speech were about Vietnam. We emerged from the convention with the united party, with people understanding John Kerry's background. When we left Boston we led the race with 51 percent. We did well. We did not get an enormous bump but I think that we all knew on both sides that there was not an enormous bump to get at any point in this race.

If there's one thing that I thought was the major hill that we had to climb over the course of this campaign, it was the five-week hole between our convention at the end of July and the Republican convention at the beginning of September. The fact that we both accepted public financing meant that we were essentially running a thirteen-week campaign while the Bush-Cheney campaign was running an eight-week campaign on precisely the same money. And we were absolutely committed to holding onto our money so we could be there at the end when voters were paying the most attention to this. This was the single biggest obstacle I think that we had to overcome during the entire year.

Also there was the intervention in August of Chechnya, which I think was an enormously large event in this campaign. The backdrop of terrorists, small children, a school auditorium was something that really affected women voters in a really serious fashion. And obviously the Bush attacks also, they were still spending primary money and they were spending it raising our negatives during the month of August.

I think that the debates were a critical moment for us. We also saw this as a series of four debates. In our point of view, we won these four debates. We felt as though we did. We did extremely well with the spin and the post-debate coverage, which we put an enormous amount of time and energy into. We think that when seeing President Bush and John Kerry on the stage it was very difficult to think of John Kerry as the straw man that President Bush had been discussing on the stump. [John Kerry] was a moderate, mature, polite leader. And so in a lot of ways, getting to see those two people side-by-side was extremely helpful to us. The clichés are true; John Kerry rises to a challenge, and there was nothing like the challenge of that first debate. He, from my point of view, did himself extremely proud in this.

Finally, I think the bin Laden tape was an enormous event in the campaign. Just as the voters were looking to make a final decision, this terror reasserted itself in what, to many Americans, is the most frightening form. The tape was the backdrop as they went into the voting booth.

As I said before, when we look back on the impact of 2004 I think the use of the Internet was the single biggest innovation in the campaigns on either side. I think secondly the amount that both campaigns and both national committees spent on field and volunteers is an enormous

Mary Beth Cahill and Matthew Dowd

sea change in political tactics and in terms of emphasis. And finally I think that young voters are another big story coming out of this campaign.

Internet. The Internet became an extremely big part of the Kerry campaign, something we spent a lot of time and a lot of money on. We had some of the nicest, youngest, smartest people involved in the campaign doing this stuff. We drew on a lot of people who made a lot of money in the companies they sold. They moved to Washington to bring that background to try to help John Kerry.

We used the Internet in a number of different ways but obviously fundraising for us was extremely important because we had a huge gap to make up. Out of $231 million that we raised in the primaries, $80 million came from the Internet. In the general election, 40 million dollars was raised directly by johnkerry.com for the DNC. We learned lessons from that. In fundraising on the Internet, real events were the biggest thing to which people reacted. So real events such as the vice presidential selection, a report about to come out, or the convention [elicited the strongest response]. Second, negative attacks [help fundraising]. The Swift Boat attacks in August actually elicited some of the biggest response to emails for fundraising that we had in the course of the campaign. But most important I think is an ongoing dialogue with your Internet supporters. Had we sent them an email every day from

John Kerry they would have known that was [not] from him. They wanted a conversation with the campaign, and usually it was with me. We would be sitting in a meeting at the headquarters and everyone in the room would say, "I just got an email from you." As I got off planes across the country people would say "Oh, I get emails from you." And a lot of that was keeping people in line with what we thought was important. It was also another means of communication outside of the press and very importantly outside of television to tell people what we [thought] was going on.

We also used the Internet very much as an organizing tool. We recruited almost 750,000 volunteers over the Internet. We used volunteers in the blue states to help us in the red states. A lot of people who went to phone banks in Pennsylvania or Ohio on Election Day were actually recruited by somebody in New York or Massachusetts. We set up an innovative call center where you could go in, you could pull the names of ten possible volunteers, you could call them, you could report back and you could give them the information on where the closest phone bank was.

We also organized almost 40,000 events over the Internet. People had their own fundraising house parties. We also posted both information on how to attract donations and FEC forms, so it really became another way for us to increase our reach without hiring many more people.

And finally I think the Internet really began to give us the sort of echo chamber that the Republicans have, through Fox, through some of the cable outlets. The Democrat[ic] bloggers—the use of ads on the Internet, the use of video messages on the Internet—really gave us another means of communicating in a very sophisticated fashion with our supporters. More than that, it expanded our numbers of supporters and I think that that is something the Democratic Party is really going to build on in the weeks and the years to come.

Field. On Election Day in 2000 [Democratic Party nominee Vice President Al] Gore had about 100,000 volunteers. We had 250,000. We had 25,000 trained precinct and ward captains that we invested a lot of time and money in along with the DNC that are going to be there over the years to come. Among states that were decided by less than 15,000 votes, we won two: New Hampshire and Wisconsin. We think that the amount of emphasis that we put on the field component of this was really a great investment for the future.

Young Voters. Finally I think the fact that John Kerry won the youngest cohort of voters by 9 points is an extremely strong point for the future. Those voters were among our most passionate supporters. They are extremely tolerant culturally. . . . They were much more responsive to a strong economic message, and they were people we could reach in dif-

ferent ways—once again through the Internet, through Internet advertising and through advertising on other websites. They were some of the
most devoted bloggers. They were people that we tried to reach out to
through our field organizations in every way that we could think of, and
we think of that as a down payment for 2006 and 2008.

Chapter 2
Advertising

Mark McKinnon

Mark McKinnon *is vice chairman of Public Strategies, Incorporated and president of Maverick Media. As chief media advisor to President George W. Bush, McKinnon directed communications and advertising strategy for the 2000 and 2004 presidential campaigns. An award-winning media producer and communications strategist, he has served as principal media advisor for more than 100 corporate and political campaigns in the United States, Latin America, Africa, and Europe.*

Let me just start off with the strategic challenge. The big strategic challenge we faced was ironically completely different than it was in 2000. In 2000 we had the unusual situation where we were really arguing for change in a status quo election. Generally, people felt good about the country and where this country was headed and we were arguing for change.

In 2004 we had just the opposite strategic challenge. We were the status quo in a change environment. So in 2000 we were arguing that things were good so it's time for a change and in 2004 we were saying that things are difficult, stay the course. So a real strategic challenge that we had was how in this very, very difficult environment could we argue for keeping what we described ultimately as steady leadership. The steady leadership idea, by the way, was initially designed for Howard Dean and we had some great Dean spots that we never got to use. We really did believe for a time that it was likely to be Howard Dean. Then, of course, John Kerry ran a terrific primary campaign and emerged the candidate so we had to do some quick reshuffling of the deck.

Very quickly, we determined the idea of steady leadership still held a powerful message for us, certainly on our side, but "steady" in terms of John Kerry is much different than it was for Howard Dean. For Howard Dean it was sort of "steady" versus "crazy." With John Kerry we were going to argue "unsteady" as in "not consistent, politically." Steady meant steady convictions or principles, which we knew people believed about the president. We wanted to articulate the idea that, even if you didn't like this guy you knew where he stood, you knew what he believed, you knew where he was headed.

We did a lot of thinking about our first set of ads, which as Mary Beth [Cahill] mentioned became very controversial. There was a lot of discussion over 9/11 and how we handled 9/11 but we kept coming back to the fundamental notion that this election was really all about 9/11—there was no way we could avoid it. We knew it would be sensitive. We knew it would be controversial. The interesting thing is when we did testing on it, as difficult and as trying a time as that was, people felt it was a collective experience Americans had gone through together. So they thought about it as a very positive experience, not something the president did necessarily, but something that America went through. We came through it together, we're strong, and we're better for it. Ultimately we decided that we wanted the architecture of the campaign to be pinned to that notion. So the ads that we opened with focused on going through 9/11.

Another thing we had always modulated very carefully throughout the campaign was the extent to which things were getting better. Matthew [Dowd] was always pulling us back saying no, no, we can't say things are better, even turning the corner was too much we discovered. We didn't want to say things were bad. We wanted to say they're getting better but it was really a very nuanced pitch. In this first spot, one of the things we wanted to say was, "Let's remember what we've been through folks, this has been a hell of a chapter in American life and history, so remember if you're thinking things are tough, remember how we got here. Remember, we came in with a recession, stock market crash, 9/11." We wanted to set the context of the campaign with this ad.

TV Advertisement—"Safer, Stronger"

PRESIDENT BUSH: I'm George W. Bush and I approve this message.

GRAPHIC: January 2001: The challenge: An economy in recession. A stock market in decline. A dot-com boom . . . gone bust. Then . . . A day of tragedy. A test for all Americans.

GRAPHIC: Today, America is turning the corner. Rising to the challenge. Safer, stronger. President Bush. Steady Leadership in times of change.

As you may recall, within 24 hours this was a firestorm. The press went crazy. The unions went crazy. Everybody went crazy. I'll be interested to

Mark McKinnon

talk to my colleagues on the other side about just how much was engineered and what wasn't. It created an enormous controversy. We felt confident about the strategy. We knew there'd be a blow-up going in. It happened. We got incredible exposure for what we were trying to do but I have to say there were some dark moments there where I thought my hair was really on fire. I thought, maybe we've pushed the dial a little too much here.

We tested and we pre-tested the hell out of this. We post-tested the hell out of it. We discovered in middle America, St. Louis, in a couple of groups, one out of thirty-six really had a truly negative response. Overall it had the powerful collective experience that we were trying to articulate. So we felt very strongly that it was the right thing to do and then stayed pinned to that strategy throughout the campaign.

There's another spot called "Together and Lead," which was much more the president on camera. However, we also knew that our challenge was to make this a choice not a referendum. We didn't want this election to be a referendum on the president. We wanted it to be a choice between two candidates. To the president's credit, he understood that and believed that and so there was no Rose Garden strategy at all. Quickly, after this initial flush of ads, we got to an ad about John Kerry's agenda. And we did it off the 100 days idea. We wanted when we framed Kerry to talk about the flip-flopping that I'll get to in a minute but also wanted to characterize his record on both taxes and the war on terror. We set this up using the 100 days idea as saying not only is he going to do this, but he's going to do this in the first 100 days.

TV Advertisement—"100 Days"

PRESIDENT BUSH: I'm George W. Bush and I approve this message.

ANNOUNCER: A president sets his agenda for America in the first 100 days.

John Kerry's plan: To pay for new government spending, raise taxes by at least $900 billion.

On the war on terror: Weaken the Patriot Act used to arrest terrorists and protect America.

And he wanted to delay defending America until the United Nations approved.

John Kerry: Wrong on taxes. Wrong on defense.

Meanwhile an appropriation for 87 billion dollars in the Congress became a very topical issue. In a Sunday meeting we discovered that

John Kerry was going to West Virginia to talk to an audience of veterans. We believed there was high likelihood that the subject would be the 87 billion. He had been actually articulating a negative message against the president on arming the troops in battle, so we knew it was likely to be a topic given that it was an audience of veterans. We immediately produced an ad on the 87-billion-dollar vote.

Because of technology we have today we could digitally send it down to West Virginia so that it was on the air when he got to West Virginia. This is actually a revised version of the ad. The first version does not have the ending that you'll see on here. The ending you'll see on here was what he said in that audience which we of course argue was one of the most iconic moments in the campaign when he was trying to articulate and defend that vote. So this was the ad that we produced and immediately re-cut with the Senator's reactions and statements to that veteran's audience.

TV Advertisement—"Troops-Fog"

PRESIDENT BUSH: I'm George W. Bush and I approve this message.

ANNOUNCER: Few votes in Congress are as important as funding our troops at war. Though John Kerry voted in October 2002 for military action in Iraq, he later voted against funding our soldiers.

SENATE CLERK: Mr. Kerry:

ANNOUNCER: No.

ANNOUNCER: Body armor and higher combat pay for troops?

SENATE CLERK: Mr. Kerry:

ANNOUNCER: No.

ANNOUNCER: Better health care for reservists?

ANNOUNCER: Mr. Kerry:

ANNOUNCER: No.

ANNOUNCER: And what does Kerry say now?

SENATOR KERRY: I actually did vote for the $87 billion before I voted against it.

ANNOUNCER: Wrong on defense.

A big part of the architecture of our campaign was using that moment and that episode from West Virginia.

"Differences" was another ad about contrast.

During the gas crisis we ran an ad called "Wacky." From a creative point of view it was something a little different to break through the clutter. I like the ad creatively. We also found out from folks that this 50-cent-a-gallon gas tax really stuck like glue. It was one of those [statements] in focus groups that were really sticky. People remembered it. They got it. So I think it was an effective ad at the time although I would say one of the mistakes that I think we made in the campaign was that this ad was up when Abu Ghraib hit [at the end of April 2004]. I realized it was still running about four or five days into the Abu Ghraib deal. We should have pulled it down immediately. So I think this was an ad and a message that probably started at an inappropriate time and had I done it differently I would have pulled it off sooner.

TV Advertisement—"Wacky"

PRESIDENT BUSH: I'm George W. Bush and I approved this ad.

ANNOUNCER: Some people have wacky ideas. Like taxing gasoline more so people drive less. That's John Kerry. He supported a 50 cent a gallon gas tax. If Kerry's tax increase were law, the average family would pay $657 more a year.

Raising taxes is a habit of Kerry's. He supported higher gasoline taxes 11 times. Maybe John Kerry just doesn't understand what his ideas mean to the rest of us.

"Double Speak" was an ad which used some of the editorials talking about John Kerry's saying that even people who knew him had a particular opinion about him. I'll go ahead and show you "Weapons" because from a technological standpoint, I think it was a well-produced ad.

TV Advertisement—"Weapons"

PRESIDENT BUSH: I'm George W. Bush and I approve this message.

ANNOUNCER: As our troops defend America in the war on terror, they must have what it takes to win. Yet, John Kerry has repeatedly opposed weapons vital to winning the war on terror: Bradley Fighting Vehicles, Patriot Missiles, B-2 Stealth Bombers, F-18 Fighter Jets, and more.

Kerry even voted against body armor for our troops on the front line of the war on terror. John Kerry's record on national security: Troubling.

With "First Choice" the central component was really more the title than the ad itself. There had emerged in the press the notion that the Kerry campaign had sought to interest John McCain in the vice presidential selection. So we produced an ad with McCain in it. I'll blow by that for now but the idea was the first choice of the Kerry campaign was John McCain who was endorsing the president.

TV Advertisement—"First Choice"

SENATOR MCCAIN: It's a big thing this war.

It's a fight between right and wrong, good and evil.

And should our enemies acquire for their arsenal the chemical, biological, and nuclear weapons they seek, this war will become an even bigger thing.

It will become a fight for our survival.

America is under attack by depraved enemies who oppose our every interest and hate every value we hold dear.

It is the great test of our generation and he has led with great moral clarity and firm resolve. He has not wavered, he has not flinched from the hard choices, he was determined and remains determined to make this world a better, safer, freer place. He deserves not only our support but our admiration. That's why I am honored to introduce to you the President of the United States, George W. Bush.

PRESIDENT BUSH: I'm George W. Bush and I approve this message.

"Victory" was an ad that we did about the Olympics.

TV Advertisement—"Victory"

GRAPHICS: www.GeorgeWBush.com

PRESIDENT BUSH: I'm George W. Bush, and I approve this message.

ANNOUNCER: In 1972, there were 40 democracies in the world. Today, 120. Freedom is spreading throughout the world like a sunrise. And this Olympics, there will be two more free nations. And two fewer terrorist regimes.

GRAPHICS: Flags of Afghanistan and Iraq

ANNOUNCER: With strength, resolve, and courage, democracy will triumph over terror. And, hope will defeat hatred.

GRAPHICS: Approved By President Bush And Paid For By Bush-Cheney '04, Inc. President Bush. Moving America Forward.

"Windsurfing" was another iconic ad. A couple of things happened during the Kerry campaign—the snowboarding, for example, that caught our attention. The windsurfing certainly did as it was the first day of the convention. When John McCain and Rudy Giuliani were talking about 9/11, John Kerry was out windsurfing. It was just one of those things that said so much to me.

There are not a whole lot of people in Iowa and Wisconsin who are windsurfers. So the moment I saw that I determined we should do an ad on it and the ad sort of made itself. But strategically our idea was to pop this the day before the debates. We had hoped it would just sort of get into your heads. It was never anything we wanted to run a lot of points behind. It got a lot of pop in the press anyway and in fact it didn't get a lot of actual points. But it got a lot of pop and it got a lot of recall.

TV Advertisement—"Windsurfing"

PRESIDENT BUSH: I'm George W. Bush, and I approve this message.

GRAPHICS: www.GeorgeWBush.com

ANNOUNCER: In which direction would John Kerry lead? Kerry voted for the Iraq war, opposed it, supported it, and now opposes it again. He bragged about voting for the $87 billion to support our troops before he voted against it. He voted for education reform and now opposes it. He claims he's against increasing Medicare premiums, but voted five times to do so.

John Kerry. Whichever way the wind blows.

GRAPHICS: Approved By President Bush And Paid For By Bush-Cheney '04 Inc.

The reason we didn't pop it the day before the debate and this, by the way, testifies to the fact that we really didn't coordinate with the 527s. One of the other 527s also did a windsurfer ad, and as soon as that ad came out we realized that we had to get our ad out because it was sort of popping the idea out. That's why we actually executed that ad earlier than we had hoped to.

"Searching" was an ad that we worked on quite a bit and had many different versions of. There was actually an 11-minute version done by the RNC. This ad was an attempt to capture, as best as we could in 25 seconds, Kerry's changing positions on Iraq.

TV Advertisement—"Searching"

PRESIDENT BUSH: I'm George W. Bush and I approve this message.

SENATOR KERRY: It was the right decision to disarm Saddam Hussein, and when the President made the decision I supported him.

SENATOR KERRY: I don't believe the President took us to war as he should have.

SENATOR KERRY: The winning of the war was brilliant.

SENATOR KERRY: It's the wrong war, in the wrong place, at the wrong time.

SENATOR KERRY: I have always said we may yet even find weapons of mass destruction.

SENATOR KERRY: I actually did vote for the 87 billion dollars before I voted against it.

GRAPHIC: How can John Kerry protect us . . .when he doesn't even know where he stands?

One of the things we felt about Kerry's convention was that it was heavy on biography. We knew people didn't have a lot of recall about his agenda coming out of the convention so we worked very hard not only to get that into the president's speech, but we had a very, very aggressive couple of weeks with spots on the president's agenda. Here are a couple of them. We actually did four different spots. We did a health care agenda. Our economic agenda ad was very heavy on content to communicate that the president had a vision for the future.

TV Advertisement—"Economic Agenda"

MALE ANNOUNCER: President Bush and our leaders in Congress have a plan.

FEMALE ANNOUNCER: Strengthen our economy.

MALE ANNOUNCER: Life-long learning.

FEMALE ANNOUNCER: Invest in education.

MALE ANNOUNCER: New skills for better jobs.

FEMALE ANNOUNCER: A fairer, simpler tax code.

MALE ANNOUNCER: Reduced dependence on foreign energy.

FEMALE ANNOUNCER: Freer, fairer trade.

MALE ANNOUNCER: Incentives to create jobs.

FEMALE ANNOUNCER: Comp and flex time for working families.

MALE ANNOUNCER: Strengthen Social Security.

FEMALE ANNOUNCER: Legal reform.

MALE ANNOUNCER: Permanent tax relief.

FEMALE ANNOUNCER: Learn more.

MALE ANNOUNCER: At agendaforamerica.com.

GRAPHIC: Agenda For America: A Plan For A Safer World And More Hopeful America; Agendaforamerica.com

PRESIDENT BUSH: I'm George W. Bush, and I approve this message.

GRAPHIC: Approved By President Bush And Paid For By Bush-Cheney '04 Inc.

"Thinking Mom" is a spot that Alex [Castellanos] produced that was designed to communicate a message to women demographics.

TV Advertisement—"Thinking Mom"

ANNOUNCER: And we'll be checking traffic on . . .

WOMAN: 5:30, gotta get groceries, we're gonna be late.

ANNOUNCER: John Kerry and the liberals in Congress have voted to raise gas taxes ten times.

WOMAN: Ten times? Gas prices are high enough already.

ANNOUNCER: They've also raised taxes on seniors' Social Security benefits. And raised taxes on middle class parents 18 times. No relief there from the Marriage Penalty.

WOMAN: More taxes because I'm married? What were they thinking?

ANNOUNCER: . . . 350 times. Higher taxes from the liberals in Congress and John Kerry.

PRESIDENT BUSH: I'm George W. Bush and I approve this message.

Health care was obviously on the domestic side a strong message for Kerry and the Democrats, so we wanted to poke a stick in that which was done here also with Alex [Castellanos]'s spot.

TV Advertisement—"Complicated Plan"

ANNOUNCER: John Kerry and liberals in Congress have a health care plan for you. A big-government takeover. $1.5 trillion. Rationing. Less access. Fewer choices. Long waits. And Washington bureaucrats, not your doctor, make final decisions on your health.

So if you need treatment, all you have to do is . . .

GRAPHIC: Image of complicated flow-chart

ANNOUNCER: You get the picture. John Kerry and liberals in Congress. Big government-run health care.

PRESIDENT BUSH: I'm George W. Bush, and I approve this message.

GRAPHIC: Paid For By Bush-Cheney '04 Inc. And The Republican National Committee And Approved By President Bush

Ultimately though we wanted the race to conclude on the issue that we'd been articulating all along, which, of course, was the war on terror. We had a whole package toward the end of the campaign that focused on that. Let me talk for just a moment about the "Wolves" spot, which is another spot that Alex [Castellanos] produced that got a lot of attention. This is an ad we worked on for about six months. Alex originally had a metaphysical idea that would represent the threat of the war on terror. He originally did it with the idea of fire. The spot started off with a match and the match lit. But we tested it and people had no idea what we were talking about. Alex said, "Let's test it one more time, come on." As Matthew [Dowd] said, that's why he doesn't like having chefs at the focus groups.

But we really liked the idea. So Alex went back into the kitchen and re-scrambled the works and came back with this idea about wolves, which was really powerful. When we tested "Wolves," people got it immediately. "Wolves, terrorists, we got it, threat, yep." So we thought it was a very powerful spot. We knew it was a spot we wanted to use at an opportune time. We continued to test it and test it and re-tweak it.

It was controversial internally too. There was a little fear about what this spot might do and of course that's what made us think it was probably a good spot. But we kept re-tweaking it, testing it and testing it and testing it and finally airing it toward the end of the campaign at what we thought was a critical time when voters would be making decisions.

TV Advertisement—"Wolves"

ANNOUNCER: In an increasingly dangerous world . . . Even after the first terrorist attack on America . . . John Kerry and the liberals in Congress voted to slash America's intelligence operations. By 6 billion dollars . . . Cuts so deep they would have weakened America's defenses. And weakness attracts those who are waiting to do America harm . . .

GRAPHIC: Several wolves eye the camera, as if preparing to attack.

PRESIDENT BUSH: I'm George W. Bush and I approve this message.

We wanted to close ultimately with the president in a spot that I think worked well because it accomplished two things that you can really do in one spot, which is to articulate and communicate both humanity and strength at the same time.

TV Advertisement—"Whatever It Takes"

PRESIDENT BUSH [Accepting nomination at Republican National Convention]: These four years have brought moments I could not foresee and will not forget.

GRAPHIC: President Bush

PRESIDENT BUSH: I've learned firsthand that ordering Americans into battle is the hardest decision, even when it is right.

I have returned the salute of wounded soldiers who say they were just doing their job. I have held the children of the fallen who are told their dad or mom is a hero but would rather just have their mom or dad. I've met with the parents and wives and husbands who have received a folded flag. And in those military families, I have seen the character of a great nation.

Because of your service and sacrifice, we are defeating the terrorists where they live and plan and you're making America safer. I will never relent in defending America, whatever it takes.

PRESIDENT BUSH: I'm George W. Bush, and I approve this message.

GRAPHIC: Paid For By Bush-Cheney '04 Inc. And the Republican National Committee And Approved By President Bush

And that's how we closed. I'm going to show you one other spot and then I'm going to turn it over to Alex [Castellanos]. This is a spot that didn't air. We really just produced it for fun. Given the environment we were in, we thought it was probably not a good idea [to air it].

TV Advertisement—"Break"   wird ...

GRAPHIC: Fast montage of video and sound clips from different ads rushing forward and off screen

GRAPHIC: Tired of all the Political Ads?

GRAPHIC: So we thought you'd like a break . . .

GRAPHIC: Man and woman sitting on a dock at a lake laughing and kicking water into the air with their feet; and sound lake water and perhaps the subtle engine of a motor boat

GRAPHIC: Dog running slowly through a field of tall green grass; and sound birds chirping

GRAPHIC: Deserted beach cove with a palm tree in the foreground; and sound ocean wave and perhaps a cruise ship horn in the distance

GRAPHIC: George and Laura Bush standing on the porch; they are laughing.

PRESIDENT BUSH: I'm George W. Bush, and I approve this message.

Alex Castellanos

Alex Castellanos, *principal in the media-consulting firm National Media Incorporated, has provided communications and advertising counsel to Fortune 500 companies, leading non-profit organizations, and major trade associations. He has served as media consultant to six U.S. presidential campaigns, most recently to Bush-Cheney 2004. He also has helped elect nine U.S. senators, six governors, and enjoys over two decades of media consulting experience, both in the United States and abroad. A Morehead and National Merit Scholar at the University of North Carolina, he lectures frequently internationally and in the United States.*

I read something a while back in a book about persuasion, an interesting story about Pavlov—a story that formed my thinking about this race. He trained the dogs: rang the bell, brought the food, they salivated. The dogs learned that. And then one day there was a flood. The dogs were in cages. It was a lab and the dogs nearly drowned. At the last minute, [the researchers] came in, opened the cages after the dogs of course had panicked. It was such a traumatic event that the dogs lost all their conditioning. Everything they'd learned they forgot. But they were retrained. In time they became who they had been again. But one day Pavlov took a little trickle of water and poured it under the door and the dogs lost all their conditioning again. The traumatic moment came back. It had seared them. It had changed who they were. I think that was this election. That trickle under the door. The convention for New York. The first spot about 9/11. The last spot about the wolves—just in case bin Laden didn't make a tape. That is, I think, the core of this election.

As a storyteller, spot-maker, this was the most focused campaign I have ever been in, by far. Usually the bigger they get the worse they get and this was just the opposite. I think that came from two things. One is Matthew [Dowd] and Mark [McKinnon] and Sara [Taylor]. We had a team making spots that was incredibly focused. We all had sheet music we could play. I think ultimately that stems from the candidate. We had a candidate who knew who he was and knew what he was about. And I've been in campaigns—Bob Dole's for example—which didn't have the luxury of a candidate who knew who he was and what he was for. It makes all the difference in the world.

Being a southern boy from North Carolina who was actually born in Cuba, I speak Spanish with a southern accent. I actually started working on [Hispanic spots] four years ago doing races in Mexico and Ecuador just to get sharp again.

With the growing Hispanic vote that's of increasing influence here, culture matters. Music matters. Who you are matters. Emotion matters. It is . . . exactly the same electorate that we have here—the Anglo electorate—and in some ways it's very different. It's very much like the Anglo electorate in this sense: we found out that our voters, the voters we wanted to appeal to, Hispanic voters, were homeowners, married, over 35 and if you had some college that was a good thing. Basically you're more likely to be a Republican in those categories.

One thing we found in the research was that this was a persuadable group. We could move 20 points with this group. We were looking at three groups. First the Cuban vote. There was a myth that we were softer with the Cuban[s] than we were. The president started with 69 percent of the Cuban vote and last time I think he got 70 percent. There wasn't that much weakness there.

Alex Castellanos

Then there are Hispanics of Central and South American descent who are a little less likely to be our voters. . . .

The most negative toward the president are the Mexican Americans. But we learned that they empathized with the president as far as who he was as a man. In effect he was daddy bear, a father figure, a strong leader. All those qualities of a strong father, the protector of the family and their values went a long way with this audience. They had a favorable view of the president as a decent family man, and also [believed] that the president understood their family and their economic needs better than Kerry. And I think Kerry's Boston heritage may have been a bit of a challenge that a Southern working class Democrat [wouldn't have faced].

Taxes were an effective issue for us, but ultimately the issues that cut were the same issues that cut in the Anglo audience. Values. Birth control pills to minors. Things like that. The values issues. The Laci Peterson law [to make it a separate crime to kill or injure a pregnant woman's unborn child during an attack on the woman] was an effective message for us with this audience.

One thing that this campaign did that Republicans hadn't done before was go on offense. Kerry was undefined to this audience too. And there's enough flexibility in this audience that we could go grab some votes here. So instead of the usual feel good, fluffy token campaign to Hispanic voters, this was an aggressive campaign with tough, hard-hitting issues advertising. Our goal was to pry votes away from Kerry.

One of the interesting things about the Hispanic vote—they just don't show up. Fifty-eight percent registered to vote (Hispanic) residents do come out to vote compared to 77 percent of all voters. You can see here where we drop off on Republican voters. There's just a lot of work to be done to get people out to vote there.

Percent vote for Republican candidates—exit poll trends in the presidential elections. This (see Chart 11) is looking at the *New York Times* data, and you can see that there has been a trend from '96 to 2000 to 2004—something good is growing here. Hispanic turnout is up for Republicans so we're going to keep working at it—and see if I can lose the southern accent completely when I speak Spanish.

Homeownership is a huge issue to Hispanics. Nine point four percent of U.S. Hispanics plan to buy a home in the next 12 months versus 6.6 percent of non-Hispanics. This is the American dream embodied. Those were voters that we are able to target as Republicans and we looked at these things by market.

If you're a homeowner, if you're a high school grad and have some college, and if you're married you're likely to end up in the Republican box for George Bush.

CHART 11. PERCENT VOTING FOR REPUBLICAN CANDIDATE EXIT POLL TRENDS IN
PRESIDENTIAL ELECTIONS

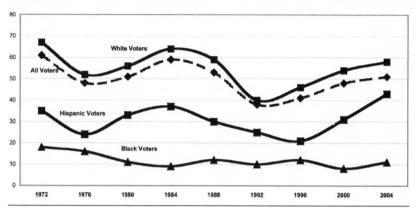

National Media, Inc. analysis of *New York Times* data

Most Hispanic voters got their Republican messaging through Anglo
advertising. That's where they got their news. What we wanted to do with
a lot of the Hispanic advertising then was reinforce the same kind of
messaging in Spanish but also to try to speak to the cultural values. We
wanted to say, "Hey, we get it. We know the language. We understand."
So we used the Hispanic advertising to do something that they weren't
already getting in the Anglo advertising. In all the groups, looking at all
Hispanic adults, the dominant language spoken at home is Spanish. But
if you're a voter, whether a Democrat or Republican, the dominant language at home is English.

Bill Knapp

A managing partner at Squier Knapp Dunn, **Bill Knapp** *has been a senior media
strategist for three U.S. presidential campaigns and dozens of statewide and congressional races. He has helped develop the communications strategy for Senator
Jay Rockefeller, Senate Majority Leader George Mitchell, and Attorney General
Mike Moore. In 1996, with former partner Bob Squier, Knapp was the leader
of the Clinton-Gore reelection and DNC creative teams. In the 2000 presidential
campaign, he served as a senior adviser to the Gore-Lieberman campaign as a
member of the advertising and communications strategy team. More recently,
Knapp served as general consultant to the Kerry-Edwards 2004 campaign, helping develop overall strategy and state-specific advertising for Wisconsin and
Pennsylvania.*

It's a pleasure to be back here, although I'm getting very tired of following Alex [Castellanos] and Mark [McKinnon]. So hopefully four years from now we'll go first. This is the second time they've won and they've been here. I heard their motorcade so I knew they were going to be here.

We thought it would be good to go through a bit of the tale of money. Then Mike [Donilon] is going to go through the strategy, I'm going to add some material, and we're going to show you some of our ads.

What this chart (Chart 12) tries to do is summarize broadly the amount of money that was spent on both sides, the party committees, but also the DNC and RNC IE [Independent Expenditures] as well as the independent groups. In summary there was a fair amount of equality in money but there were differences by periods as to who was spending what. In the pre-convention period, March to July, Kerry-Edwards spent about 80 million dollars in broadcast on television. We clocked Bush-Cheney at $100 million; the Democratic 527s, $54 million, the GOP ones at $4.7, so $134 [million] to $112 [million].

The part I want to pay particular attention to and Mary Beth [Cahill] mentioned this in her discussion was the five-week August period where we spent 406,000 dollars. That was a relatively small buy that we ran cable-oriented to deal with the Swift Boat ads. We held our fire during that month. Bush-Cheney spent 32 million dollars. We felt every dollar of that against us. The DNC IE spent $35 million. They were running ads. The 527s were operating as well. So you see overall there was a difference of between $50 million and $36 million but there was a big difference from the candidate committees. While all the advertising by the third party groups was important and did have some impact, I think voters intuitively understood the difference between an ad from a campaign committee and an ad from a third party.

In the post-GOP convention period, we spent $68 million. Bush-Cheney clocks in at $98 million. Because of the way they targeted and bought, they paid a lot more for their media than we did. Although you see a difference in the total dollar amounts spent, the points put on the board were pretty equal. We were adamant early in our planning we did not want to get outspent in the end. We had to run a general election for thirteen weeks—they ran it for eight weeks. We wanted to make sure we weren't out-pointed at the end. We achieved that. In August we placed our buy for the entire close of the campaign. We added a little as we went along, but we [placed our buy in August] in order to get lowest unit rate, to get the most bang for our buck.

You'll notice there's a little typo in the bottom if you go down two columns where it says hybrid spending 191 million for Bush-Cheney—that should be $88 million. In the post-convention period they spent 10

Bill Knapp

CHART 12. PAID MEDIA SUMMARY

	KE04	BC 04	DNC IE	RNC IE	Dem 527's	GOP 527's	Dem Total	GOP Total
Pre-Dem Conv. (March- late July)	79,644,248	107,343,816	0	0	54,646,481	4,705,290	134,290,729	112,049,106
5 Week August Period	406,055	32,965,265	35,083,692	0	14,759,876	3,097,648	50,249,623	36,062,913
Post GOP Conv.	68,677,468	98,658,218	68,547,573	13,141,958	14,978,632	34,843,224	152,203,673	146,643,400
Totals	148,727,771	238,967,299	103,631,265	13,141,958	84,384,989	42,646,162	336,744,025	294,755,419
Hybrid Spending	37,181,942	191,000,000						
Negative ad spending (estimate)	37,181,942	191,000,000						

million dollars by our account on pure Bush-Cheney advertising. The rest of it was hybrid advertising. [Hybrid advertising is paid for with money from the political party and mentions more than just the candidate, e.g., mentions "Bush and Republicans in Congress" or "Kerry and the Democrats."] We're going to talk a little bit later about the impact of that. So you see in the post-convention period in the close it was $152 million on the bottom right to $146 million so we were pretty competitive. Now Mike [Donilon] will try to explain what we tried to do with the money.

Michael Donilon

Michael Donilon is a partner in the media consulting firm Shrum, Devine, Donilon. He has been involved in some of the most closely followed campaigns in the country. In 2004, Mr. Donilon was a senior advisor to the John Kerry for President Campaign. In 2000, he was the principal media consultant in the campaigns for Senators Mark Dayton, Bill Nelson, Jon Corzine, and Joe Lieberman, and Congressmen Dick Gephardt and Brad Carson. In previous years, he has been involved in the campaigns of Senators including Jack Reed, John Edwards, and Chris Dodd, and Governor Doug Wilder. In 1992, Mr. Donilon was a member of both the Clinton/Gore creative advertising team and the Clinton War Room.

Let me start by saying to Mark [McKinnon] and Alex [Castellanos] and Matthew [Dowd] and others from the Bush campaign, you did a remarkable job and you deserve a lot of credit for it.

In some ways we probably don't know it, but we're really living through some remarkable times in this country. This election was evidence of that. 9/11 really is a searing experience for this country and it really did drive this election from start to finish. I want to start first speaking about a few of the kind of facts of life in the campaign for us, and then talk a little bit about what we were trying to do strategically. Then I was just going to show a sampling of advertising and that should wrap it up.

Obviously 9/11, national security, was the driving issue in this election. That was an enormous asset for the president and he could never be dislodged there. We felt from our side, the key was for Senator Kerry to pass a threshold to be credible on the national security dimension. We believed that happened.

But we also believe in the end that the connection that the president had was personal and I think one of the interesting questions going forward is to what degree this is a personal connection with the president and what degree this is actually a party divide when it comes to 9/11. He obviously had a real rock at the center of his campaign.

The other fact of life for us as a campaign is that we knew from the outset we were going to spend all our money in those battleground states and we had to, in a sense, thread the needle to win. We came, I think, within about 100,000 votes of doing that in two of the toughest states in the country for Democrats, Ohio and Florida. But I think we believed at the outset that was where it would come down to and that is where it came down to.

In many ways, while we talk nationally about this election, what happened in the battlegrounds was in fact very different from what happened nationally. That caused us some trouble. One of the problems it caused us was that national numbers wouldn't necessarily reflect what was happening in the battleground states. There were external pressures brought on the campaign which we had to manage in an ongoing fashion and that was one of them. But we believed it was the only way we could win. I think in hindsight it was still the best strategy to pursue and it was one which came, as I say, very close to doing.

The third thing that Bill [Knapp] mentioned which was a real fact of life in this campaign was that money was a dramatic factor in this race, and it wasn't just a dramatic factor in terms of overall dollars. It was actually a factor in terms of when you had that money available to use in given periods of time. We experienced two very difficult periods of time in the campaign. Early in the spring, as Mary Beth [Cahill] mentioned, right after we won the nomination [on March 2, 2004], we were broke and the Bush campaign came in and started hammering us. That was a very difficult period of time. At that point in time there was fear on our

Michael Donilon

side as well as in the party that we were going to get taken out and get taken out right then and there.

We then, in real ways that we didn't foresee, were able to raise significant amounts of money and fight back and did. You'll see the initial advertising we did, which was really a way of introducing John Kerry the man. We knew from the outset that the basic thrust from the other side was to make it impossible for people to ultimately trust John Kerry as president of the United States. So the opening play was really to survive that opening salvo and to make the case that Senator Kerry was someone who given his experience, substance, seriousness, his presidential caliber, could survive that period of time. He did.

The second period where money mattered a lot was in August when we didn't have it. We didn't have it to spend without risking what was going to happen later. That was a very hard choice. The five weeks between the conventions was an important factor in this election. That was when the Swift Boat [ads] as well as other entities came in. We fought back partly through the advertising, the day-to-day operation of the campaign, but also ultimately the campaign came back, we believe, essentially to a competitive posture, at the first debate [on September 30, 2004]. Bob Shrum will talk about that later, but money was an important factor in this race and it was an important factor to say not only in terms of overall dollars spent but in the periods of time of when it was readily available to be used in an efficient factor.

With that as a backdrop, what we believed we had to do first and foremost was that Senator Kerry had to pass the threshold of people believing he could handle the national security dimension—that he could defend the country in the face of terror and that was going to be an ongoing job. I believe we did that in large measure. I actually believe he passed the threshold of credibility when it comes to whether or not people believed he could defend this country.

The second goal we had was to drive what we believed to be fundamental middle-class values-based issues around health care, around job creation. We knew that while people had, on the one hand, enormous faith in the president around the issue of terror, they had real doubts with respect to his economic plan, with his economic agenda, where he was leading the country, what was happening with health care, on a whole range of domestic concerns that people really felt strongly about.

So we spent a lot of our time in advertising addressing those concerns and did generate substantial margins on those key issues. Most of the exit poll data suggest that when it comes to economic concerns, heath care, etc., Senator Kerry actually won those voters pretty decisively. So that was an ongoing push and pull of the campaign—to continue to survive the attacks, the incoming, to make the case on how we can get over the threshold with respect to terror, and national security, and then to affirmatively push our case.

One of the things that happened through the course of the campaign was that Iraq became more and more a central part of our campaign— the Bush side very much pushed it as a line of attack against Senator

Kerry. We believe that as we pushed back and made the case on it, (you'll see one of the ads I brought today very much did that), it actually worked to our advantage. In fact, if you look at the exit polling on four of the key concerns (terror, Iraq, the economy, cultural concerns), Senator Kerry had pretty decisive advantages on Iraq and the domestic issues.

The Bush campaign had a great asset in that they had the president's record around 9/11, the collective experience that the country had around 9/11. In many ways, they weren't arguing much about what his performance was in office other than that, which really freed them up to take an enormous amount of money and throw it at us. We had to both defend against that incoming and make a case about someone whom the country was just coming to know.

The first ad is a biographical one. You'll see throughout that we very much believed that Senator Kerry speaking in his own voice and Senator Kerry being on the air were important factors for us. One of the things that we found through research was that he was a reassuring presence on television. That became even more important because he was so prominently displayed in the advertising from the other side. [Putting him on camera] was in our view the best response to the character attacks. If you look particularly at the battleground states—you'll see the evidence that Senator Kerry himself was by far the best messenger, and by far the best defender against the attacks that came from the other side. So this was the first ad we ran in the spring.

TV Advertisement—"Commitment"

GRAPHIC: John Kerry

SENATOR KERRY: As president, I'll set a few clear national priorities for America. First, we will keep this country safe and secure. Second, I'll put an end to tax incentives that encourage American companies to ship jobs overseas. And third, we'll invest in education and health care.

GRAPHIC: Keep America Secure; Defend American Jobs; Learn More About John Kerry's Plan for America; JohnKerry .com

My priorities are jobs and health care. My commitment is to defend this country. I'm John Kerry, and I approved this message because together we can build a stronger America.

GRAPHIC: John Kerry; President; JohnKerry.com; Approved By John Kerry And Paid For By John Kerry For President

This actually preceded the bio ad. It was really a basic statement of purpose and values in the candidacy. We thought from the very outset his commitment to defending this country was absolutely essential.

TV Advertisement—"Heart"

GRAPHIC: www.johnkerry.com; John Kerry

SENATOR KERRY: I was born in Fitzsimons Army Hospital in Colorado. My dad was serving in the Army Air Corps. Both of my parents taught me about public service.

GRAPHIC: Father was an Army Air Corps pilot; mother was a community leader

SENATOR KERRY: I enlisted because I believed in service to country. I thought it was important if you had a lot of privileges as I had had, to go to a great university like Yale, to give something back to your country.

DEL SANDUSKY: The decisions that he made saved our lives.

GRAPHIC: Del Sandusky; U.S. Navy; Kerry Crewmate, Vietnam

JIM RASSMANN: When he pulled me out of the river, he risked his life to save mine.

GRAPHIC: Jim Rassmann; U.S. Army Special Forces; Vietnam

ANNOUNCER: For more than thirty years, John Kerry has served America.

VANESSA KERRY: If you look at my father's time in service to this country, whether it's as a veteran, prosecutor, or senator, he has shown an ability to fight for things that matter.

GRAPHIC: Vanessa Kerry

TERESA HEINZ KERRY: John is the face of someone who's hopeful, who's generous of spirit and of heart.

GRAPHIC: Teresa Heinz Kerry

SENATOR KERRY: We're a country of optimists. We're the can-do people, and we just need to believe in ourselves again.

ANNOUNCER: A lifetime of service and strength. John Kerry for president.

SENATOR KERRY: I'm John Kerry, and I approved this message.

GRAPHIC: Approved By John Kerry And Paid For By John Kerry For President

If I could just make a couple of quick points. One, as I say, Senator Kerry speaking in his own voice was an important part of our strategy in the advertising. The second thing was we thought the best way to respond to the charge that Kerry was a flip-flopper, to the attacks on his consistency, was to give a sense that this was a man who throughout his life had demonstrated great purpose, great constancy and had been through some really tough fights. That sense of a lifetime of service and strength to this country was the way to beat back the attacks coming from the other side. The third thing that I just want to mention is the role that Vietnam played in the campaign. Was it too much, too little? Obviously, the Swift Boat [ads] were a factor in this race. But I believe that Senator Kerry's service and his military record were important assets. I think in many ways it made him a competitive choice for the Democratic Party in this election year. So I think it was an important asset all the way to the end.

The next spot is a spot we ran right before the convention, which was on the issue of the war on terror. Again it's Kerry making the case that if we're going to be engaged in this war, we not only have to be tough, we also have to be smart and we have to start thinking about all the ways we can combat terror.

TV Advertisement—"War on Terror"

GRAPHIC: John Kerry

SENATOR KERRY: To win the war on terror, we have to be tough and smart. We have to rebuild our alliances, because that's the best way to find and get the terrorists before they get us. America shouldn't have to carry the burden alone.

And we have to strengthen our homeland security, protect our trains and our ports. We shouldn't be opening firehouses in Baghdad and closing them down in our own communities.

I'm John Kerry, and I approved this message because a strong America begins at home.

GRAPHIC: John Kerry; President; JohnKerry.com; Approved By John Kerry And Paid For By John Kerry For President, Inc.

[handwritten margin note: echoes JFK's focus on domestic to define foreign policy]

As I said, that was what we ran going into the convention. We believe we had an effective and successful convention and one in which Senator Kerry actually had a very strong rating on defending the country, on being commander-in-chief, and on dealing with the central issue of terror.

The next spot I want to show is called "Wrong Choices," which got at the essence of the negative in the case against Bush. The reason I have it on the reel here is because there's an important point in the campaign for us. After August, we had a significant drop in the polling after the Republican Convention. We fought our way back over about a four-week period of time to our even standing with the president—at least in our polling. This was one of [the] turning points in moving those numbers back in the right direction and drove the case about Iraq from our side of the coin.

TV Advertisement—"Wrong Choices"

ANNOUNCER: George Bush. $200 billion for Iraq. In America, lost jobs and rising health care costs. George Bush's wrong choices have weakened us here at home.

The Kerry plan. Stop tax incentives for companies that shift jobs overseas. Lower health care premiums by up to $1000 per family. Reduce the deficit to protect Medicare and Social Security.

Stronger at Home. Respected in the World. John Kerry.

SENATOR KERRY: I'm John Kerry, and I approve this message.

The next two ads I want to run are spots that we did basically in response just to give a sense of how we dealt with some of the incoming. The first spot is called "Never," which basically dealt with the charge that Kerry was going to give a veto over to the UN of our national security. The second spot I want to show is one of the three we did in response to the Swift Boat attacks.

TV Advertisement—"Never"

SENATOR KERRY [at October 4 event]: They're misleading Americans about what I said.

GRAPHIC: John Kerry answers the latest Bush attack

SENATOR KERRY: I will never cede America's security to any institution or to any other country. No one gets a veto over our security. No one.

GRAPHIC: Hampton, New Hampshire; October 4, 2004

SENATOR KERRY [at October 3 event]: I will never take my eye off Osama bin Laden, Al Qaeda, and the terror in Afghanistan.

GRAPHIC: Austintown, Ohio; October 3, 2004

SENATOR KERRY: We're going to hunt down the terrorists, we will kill them, we'll do what's ever necessary to protect America.

GRAPHIC: Approved By John Kerry & Paid For By Kerry-Edwards 2004, Inc.

SENATOR KERRY: I'm John Kerry, and I approved this message.

My basic view about the Swift Boat ads is they hurt us in August. They hurt us partly because they hurt our momentum and prevented us from making a pro-agenda case that we very much wanted to make at that time. But then they dissipated. Their later advertising was less effective. But it did drain our resources because we had to defend against it in an ongoing fashion. So that's sort of a thumbnail view on Swift Boats.

The next spot is actually one that Bill [Knapp] did which addressed how we were dealing with some of the job loss issue in some of the key states around the country. And one of the things I should say and I think maybe it's a little bit different than what the other side did, is we had a whole series of state-specific advertising, which was very much driven by factors in each of the battleground states.

TV Advertisement—"Real Americans"

ANNOUNCER: How out of touch is George Bush with Ohio? Over the last four years, we've lost over 230,000 jobs in our state. Now, George Bush sends his treasury secretary to Ohio to tell us these job losses are a "myth."

GRAPHIC: "denounces 'myth' of job losses"

ANNOUNCER: Do you think it's a myth that we've lost jobs? Over 100,000 Ohioans have lost their health insurance. Family incomes have fallen by $1,500. When is George Bush going to face reality?

SENATOR KERRY: I'm John Kerry, and I approved this message.

GRAPHIC: Approved By John Kerry & Paid For By Kerry-Edwards 2004, Inc.

The next spot is one of the spots we ran on the Hispanic advertising track. Actually Lorena [Chambers] who made these ads is here and you can speak with her as well. I just want to give one example of what we did to deal with the issues that Alex [Castellanos] was talking about in terms of the really competitive environment with the Hispanic voters.

TV Advertisement—"La Graduación/Graduation"

NARRADOR [in spanish]: Apenas la mitad de los jóvenes hispanos se gradúa de la escuela secundaria. John Kerry y los Demócratas desean que más de un millón de estudiantes se inscriban en la universidad. También quieren abrir las puertas de la educación universitaria a todos nuestros hijos y mejorar la educación pública. Para un futuro mejor, vota por John Kerry y los Demócratas.

TRANSLATION:

ANNOUNCER: Barely half of Hispanic youths . . . graduate from high school. John Kerry and the Democrats want . . . to enroll more than a million new students in college . . . They also want to open the doors . . . to a university education for all of our children . . . and improve our public education. For a better future, vote for John Kerry and the Democrats.

Speaking to Hispanic voters about college, education, and hope for the kids. I'm sure Alex [Castellanos] would translate it for us, with a North Carolina (sic) accent.

Let me just show one final spot which is one of our closing ads that really presented what we thought was the choice that people were facing from our side. *framing*

TV Advertisement—"Your Hands"

SENATOR KERRY: Soon the campaign will end, and the election will be in your hands. If you believe we need a fresh start in Iraq. If you believe we can create and keep jobs here in America. If you believe we need to get health care costs under control. If you believe in the promise of stem-cell research. If you believe our deficits are too high and we're too dependent on Mideast oil, then I hope you'll join me, and together, we'll change America. I'm John Kerry, and I approve this message.

GRAPHIC: www.johnkerry.com; A New Direction for America; Kerry Edwards; Approved By John Kerry & Paid for by Kerry-Edwards 2004, Inc.

BILL KNAPP:

We've all done classic races against an incumbent. You spend a lot of time attacking and making it a referendum. Mark [McKinnon] mentioned earlier that they wanted to make this a choice not a referendum on Bush. We knew all along this was going to be a choice. We could not just make it a referendum up or down on him. The stakes here were too big. There was going to be a choice involved. So we set a strategy that we stuck to over the course of the campaign in our communication that made the case that John Kerry was the right choice.

This was not an election, especially early on, where we could yell about change. People were change-averse. They wanted the policies of this administration changed but the leadership was a different issue. In a time of war and uncertainty, we had a hurdle to overcome. So our strategic imperatives were really two. One, we needed to overcome that hurdle, that terrorism-security hurdle. We spent a lot of time and a lot of energy on it. The convention was a big and important part of that. Mike [Donilon] mentioned that we think we cleared that hurdle. It was an important hurdle for us to clear. We had to constantly fight to reassure people that we were going to be good on that dimension. And so that was a big part.

And the second part of our strategy was to focus on a domestic set of issues—on health care, on the economy, oil independence, and to drive those and make them relevant to people. And we did a lot of that in our state-specific media.

In many ways our strategy was the mirror opposite of what Bush's was. They began with some positive on Bush, but they really didn't run very much of it. By my count, at least about 80 percent of the media that they ran was negative, and it served its strategic purpose.

Ours was totally opposite. First we had the DNC IE out there. We didn't know exactly what they were going to run. We didn't know exactly how big their buy was going to be although we monitored it as closely as we could. But they were exclusively negative. In the end they ran 100 million dollars. That freed us up to do strategically what we know we had to do, which was to make us acceptable, an acceptable alternative on terror and to make it clear that on domestic policies, our policies and our positions were better than his. So that was sort of the basic under girding to what we pursued during the course of the campaign.

The Bush campaign had a concerted strategy, at least they stated so in the press, which was in this dark period when we were struggling after the primary, we didn't have money, was to disqualify us and eliminate us. They spent 32 million dollars in that period. It was not clear how much money we could raise. And in that post-primary period, one of the critical events for us was getting back on our legs, raising money, running the 60-second bio introductory spots, which are the ones that Mike [Donilon] and Bob [Shrum] did, and really survive that onslaught and begin to make the case for who we were and what we were about.

That was a period of immense vulnerability for us. There was huge pressure internally to respond to the attacks that Alex [Castellanos] and Mark [McKinnon] were making up and putting on the air. There was a huge desire to do that. All the political bones in our bodies wanted to respond. We wanted to do it, but we knew strategically we had a much more important goal. It was a long campaign. We had to spend the time to introduce our guy.

Mike [Donilon] already spoke about the Swift Boat thing. In August they spent a million bucks. It was probably the most cost-efficient million bucks ever spent in the history of presidential politics short of the [1964 Johnson campaign attack on Barry Goldwater] "Daisy" ad perhaps. They got a disproportionate amount of coverage for it.

There's been a lot of press that we responded too late, etc., etc. The one thing I'll say is that we were aware of it, we monitored it, we watched it. A day and a half after Mark Mellman's poll showed that in fact it was having an impact, we went after it and we went after it viciously. We tried to discredit them, and I think were very successful in discrediting them on one level. When we would go to focus groups, people were dismissive of the attacks, tired of hearing about it. But it distracted us. What happened is, based on the publicity, they were able to raise and spent 17 million dollars in September and October. We had to pull precious resources from our buy and run response ads. [An ad with] Judy Droz [the widow of Lieutenant Donald Droz who was a Swift Boat commander with Kerry in Vietnam] was one of them in response to one of their 60-second ads. There was a second ad that Mike [Donilon] did with Ambassador [Douglas "Pete"] Peterson [former Ambassador to Vietnam] that also responded.

Republican 527s operated in a different plan that it seemed the Democratic 527s did. The Democratic 527s were much more active early. The Republican 527s were much more active later. The Swift Boats were one group; the other was the Progress for America, PFA. They ran, I think by our accounts, 17 or 18 million dollars.

They did a pretty gutsy thing. Toward the end of the campaign they devoted 12 million dollars of that to a 60-second positive ad on Bush that they ran in a selected number of markets. It was a very, very effective spot. It was a story about a girl whose mother, I believe, died in 9/11. The president saw her at one of the rallies and hugged her. That was really the story. It was very emotional and very powerful and it was a girl from Ohio. So they ran it very heavily in Ohio and it was a very effective ad. That was a key moment for us, something to deal with.

The other thing is our strategy was very different from theirs in terms of the paid media. We pursued a very aggressive state-by-state strategy. We ran dozens and dozens of ads targeted by state, sometimes targeted by market. We set out to win a series of statewide races, not to win the national referendum, and I think as Mike [Donilon] pointed out, we came very close to pulling that off.

Discussion

Mark McKinnon:

Alex [Castellanos] had created a great spot called "The Chair," which was really the Oval Office with an empty chair. It's a great narration over the chair describing in eloquent language the power of that office. When Dean appeared to be the nominee, it was this spot that tested off the charts. Basically the notion was that you could not see Howard Dean in the chair of the Oval Office. It didn't work with John Kerry. People could see John Kerry as president of the United States and they did very effectively, through a lot of communications and advertising, push a threshold of credibility to be president. So that is something that we recognized and dealt with as well.

One other thing I wanted to say, as everybody noticed, these were two campaigns on steroids. I think they were certainly haunted by Dukakis in '88 and we took some lessons from '92. And so as many people in the press knew, there were a lot of ads we did for broadcast and ads also to drive press coverage. They did a very effective job of producing ads to drive press and we did that as well. But there was a funny moment I just want to relate. Something happened in news. Nicolle [Devenish] called and said, let's do an ad on X—we want to get it in the news cycle. So we put out the script before we had the spot done. The press is writing about the spot. We're in there producing the spot. My producer calls about two hours later and says they've already cut a response spot to the ad. Should we cut a response to the response? Before the news cycle's even out!

We really struggled with the disclaimer issue throughout. It's obviously something we hated and hated to deal with. We never came to a conclusion about whether or not, particularly in the negative spots, it should be at the beginning or at the end of spots. We had a very divided view of this. Some of us thought very strongly they should be up at the top of the spot because then people would just sort of forget it's a political spot. Others felt like if you put it at the end it would kill your message at the end. So we never came to a consensus view of that. I'm just wondering if you guys had a similar discussion and observation about that.

MICHAEL DONILON:

By the end of the campaign, I think the disclaimer was operating the way no one anticipated it would. I think it gave more attention and credibility to the ads that were being run by the campaigns. In other words, I think it was in a sense a cue to voters that this is coming from Kerry or this is coming from Bush. In some ways I think it served a purpose which was totally unanticipated, which was to identify for the voters the ads which you would sense would have the most credibility. I don't think we ever came to a consensus view about whether it was the top or the bottom. I think we probably had more at the bottom than at the top.

BILL KNAPP:

No, I agree with that. When we were outside the 60-day window we were less restricted and the disclaimer could have some message in it. We ended up putting it at the end as sort of a summary line. Since a lot of your ads were negative we thought you did a good job of getting the disclaimer over with in the beginning and then moving on so that you could have the classic punch at the end, which we felt fairly often.

[Kathleen Hall Jamieson asks Bill Knapp to explain disclaimer laws]

BILL KNAPP:

The disclaimer laws—there were the FEC and the FCC this year, so there were a lot of onerous requirements in terms of the disclaimer. But two of the things you had to do: you had to have your person saying I approve this ad. Now the FEC allowed you to say, at the end, for three seconds or four seconds, "I approve this ad because we need a stronger, better America." But then the FCC came in at the end with different McCain-Feingold requirements saying that you couldn't have the message embedded in it. So when you were in the 60-day window, all of a sudden the disclaimer had to become cleaner.

BILL KNAPP:

I'm sort of curious about the moment or two when you had some uncertainty about what you were doing, the outcome, what was going on because, undoubtedly in any campaign of 280 million dollars, there are

Alex Castellanos and Bill Knapp

those moments of deep uncertainty. So I was wondering when those occurred for you?

MATTHEW DOWD:

We pretty much had a plan of strategic assumptions from the beginning and we were going to stick or try to stick to it as much as possible. I thought we were going to win and I always thought we'd win by three, all things being equal.

Another thing concerning me was, were the battleground states operating differently than nationally? In the end, they didn't. They basically stayed within the national number. There were times when we asked, is the Kerry advertising or what the DNC is doing or what the 527s are doing for the Democrats, are they having an effect because of these numbers? That turned out to be noise momentarily because there were times that we'd fluctuate in any given state.

Then you'd sort of worry, as to our plan. We asked, are you guys having more effect with these state-specific ads, which we constantly talked about. We tested and made the decision early on that we were not going to have state-specific ads because we wanted to run on national security. It doesn't matter if you live in Columbus, Ohio or Des Moines, Iowa or

Santa Fe, New Mexico. This is a president who's going to lead us in a forceful, right way.

We did test a lot of stuff, in states, and it didn't seem to have much effect for us. State-specifics. Most of the worries for us were stuff out of our control that would intercede, completely step on what we were trying to do. The bin Laden tape. I know you all think it had some effect. I think the only effect the bin Laden tape had was to stop the bleeding on the weapons cache. [On October 25, 2004 the *New York Times* reported that nearly 380 tons of explosives were missing from a former military installation south of Baghdad, Iraq.] Honestly. Take out an erroneous story on the weapons cache and add the bin Laden tape, we can argue, it would always get back to its equilibrium point, which was within 1 or 2 points. Fundamentally you worry about all of that, but for us, it was more of a worry about what was going to happen.

In August, we forced the issue on "say yes or no on Iraq—would you have done the same thing—would John Kerry have done the same thing he did on Iraq?" We had a worry internally that John Kerry was going to answer the question, "Yes, I would have done it differently because just like the American public I trusted the president to do this right. In the end it didn't go right. He led us astray. He didn't do the things necessary to do, so if I had to do it all over again . . ." We pressed this question not knowing exactly what the answer was going to be. Our worst-case scenario was he would answer the question and say, "Yes I would have done it differently. Just like the American public I trusted him and like the American public I was led astray, dah-dah-dah-dah (sic)."

How was that debated internally or was it debated internally? Internally we thought that was more important for us in August than the Swift Boat ads.

BOB SHRUM:

He wanted to answer the question. He did answer the question. He answered it in early September at NYU. But his answer, and one of the things about John Kerry that's very interesting is, for all of the grief he took for supposedly having these different positions on Iraq or this complicated position on Iraq, he actually had a position that he believed in, which was you had to support the president on the resolution. It was the only way you could get the weapons inspectors in. So yes, you would vote for the resolution, and no, if he had known that Saddam Hussein had no weapons of mass destruction, of course he wouldn't have gone to war. In fact I believe it was very critical that he answer that question before the first debate or it was going to become a consuming issue in that first debate. He did that in a speech at New York University in early September.

MARK MELLMAN:

You said, and it was quite clear from your campaign, you had some strategic assumptions. You stuck with them all the way. It was also very clear from the beginning that most of the advertising was attack on John Kerry as opposed to defining a new agenda for the president or redefining his four years. At what point did you make that decision—that the bulk of the advertising from the campaign itself was going to be going after the Democrat? Was that a very early decision? Was that something that happened later in the game as you knew who the nominee was?

MATTHEW DOWD:

That decision was made, my guess is at least 12 months out. It was driven by the fact that the president's image for better and for worse was defined. We obviously looked at this. We could run all the positive ads we wanted about the president and it wouldn't move the numbers. People could run a lot of negative ads about the president and it wouldn't move the numbers. He traded in this very small margin which was affected by events. If the economy looked good, his numbers went up. If Iraq looked better, his numbers went up. If those looked worse, his numbers went down.

We decided that the only effective ad strategy was primarily about the opponent because it was black and white and there wasn't much gray on the president. [We made the decision] probably October/November of '03, before we even knew it was John Kerry, when we thought it was Howard Dean. We always thought we were going to have to do that, whoever the Democratic opponent was.

JOE LOCKHART:

I accept that but did you see the same impact from the PFA's [Ashley] ad, the actual ad, particularly in Ohio? I think it was our impression (and that was a wholly positive ad) that at an important point in the campaign it impacted the race?

MATTHEW DOWD:

There's a difference between somebody else testifying as opposed to an ad we would run saying the president's X, Y, and Z, which would be immediately discounted by whatever voter you're trying to move. So that's the first thing. It's different when they're doing an ad without a "Paid for by, I'm George Bush and I approve this ad." That's one.

It was a good ad but our numbers in Ohio just like our numbers in Florida never moved all that much. We were never behind in any significant way in Ohio. It was always within a few points. The ads in the campaign, our[s] and the tests of your all ads, there was very little effect. When you think about it, if you add up these numbers and taking your numbers, there was over 600 million dollars spent on advertising in about 17 states, and those 17 states voted the exact same way as the other 33 states, just as they did in 2000. So, I think the effective ads are the ones that fed a story. Our first ads fed a story, hurt you all because the free press adopted it. Then some ads that you all did fed a story that the press adopted. But by and large, if you look at ad after ad after ad, they didn't have a dramatic effect on the race in this campaign.

MARK MCKINNON:

People did know certain things about the president but what that ad actually did was remind them what they like about the president, which was the human side, the humanity. It was a great ad. I don't know the date on it really—I don't know if you can really accurately tell or maybe you guys have some stuff that did. It's one of those ads that just intuitively really works a lot on us. I saw that and said it's a great ad. It's very emotional. I thought it really struck a chord at a good time when there'd been a lot of flack in the air. So I thought it was very helpful to us.

MARK MCKINNON:

What if Wesley Clark had run in Iowa? Isn't there a good chance that he may have split those votes that came to Kerry, not to get all those votes but to get a good portion of those votes? The votes that went to Edwards would have naturally gone to Edwards. If that had happened, if Clark would have run, then Edwards might have come out running on top in Iowa.

MARY BETH CAHILL:

The period of time where he was ahead in New Hampshire was obviously a very fearful period for us. At that time we had left the field essentially; everybody else was in Iowa. He had New Hampshire all to himself besides Lieberman. He was doing okay when he was by himself. Running for president, as we all know, is a very difficult thing to do and when he actually had to join into a dialogue with the national press or with the other candidates, when he was actually on the stage in a debate—it was a different matter. He was an extremely accomplished person and leader, but the give and take of a political campaign, learned at this level, is very tough. Once everybody else got to New Hampshire and the press really started to pay attention to him, I think that was very hard on him and hard on his campaign.

BOB SHRUM:

I agree with that. The only thing I would add is since we won Iowa by 6 points, if he'd taken 4 or 5 points away from us it would have been basically a tie or 2-point race. But I think it's very hard to know and Mary Beth [Cahill]'s absolutely right. He was, by the way, a very good surrogate for us in the fall and he was a very good candidate at the end of the primaries. He was not a good candidate at the time of Iowa and New Hampshire. The real reason I think he was doing pretty well, at least relative to us in New Hampshire, was as Mary Beth [Cahill] suggests, because no one else was there. People had gone to Iowa.

MARY BETH CAHILL:

And one more thing. He spent a lot more on the air in Boston and in New Hampshire, more in that period than anybody else in the field. We were all concentrating someplace else. That paid dividends for him in a very short period of time, and it went away just as quickly.

ALEX CASTELLANOS:

I don't write movies in Hollywood. I've met some talented people who do. One of the things they say is that there's a moment at the end of a movie, the reverse and reveal, where the hero is tested and you find out what he's really made of. That comes at the end of the movie. You learn, oh, so he's really not the liberal from Massachusetts, he's a Vietnam hero. Some people say that that moment should have been saved for the end. If you do it in act one, then the whole movie is whether he's a hero or not. Did you really have any choice in that? You had to do it in Iowa?

BOB SHRUM:

Unless we wanted it to be a one-act play. (laughter) It was fundamental in my view, to us winning in Iowa. I think what happened strategically in Iowa was a matter of necessity and reality. When your ass is in a crack and there's only one road out, take it. We went to Iowa and did what we had to do. But a critical piece of that was the belief that the voters after January first would actually begin to ask the question: who could and who should be president? And that was a big piece of that. That was a huge contrasting piece with Howard Dean.

Not telling people that about Kerry until the last act, that's a lot easier in a 90-minute movie than it is probably in a several year long campaign. There's a tremendous amount of myth about this. I think Mark [Mellman] has the exact statistics but I believe 6 percent of the acceptance speech dealt with Vietnam and his Vietnam history. The acceptance speech actually had a huge amount of material about what he wanted to do in terms of the economy and health care and a whole set of issues. But look, it was a part of who he was and it was, I believe, one of the reasons that he won the nomination.

MARY BETH CAHILL:

I'd add to that the fact that Jim Rassmann [a person whose life Kerry saved in Vietnam] showed up in Iowa. It was one of those things that fall from heaven that you have no knowledge of. That became a critical part of Kerry's story and we had no idea he was coming. He was in a bookstore in California, saw his name in the Brinkley book, and called us and came out the next day. It led the news that night in Iowa and it was on the national news, one of the first times in a while that we had been there.

MICHAEL DONILON:

Mark [McKinnon], I think you mentioned that it was very controversial how you were going to handle 9/11, be it in advertising or at the convention. (sound dropout) Can you walk us through what you felt were the limits of how you could talk about, where you thought it might go too far, where was it exploitive as opposed to where it was reinforcing for the president? Can you walk us through the discussions you had about how you were going to take this event and, in a sense, not push it too far?

MARK McKINNON:

It was a constant discussion, and it was one that I'd say never stopped until the convention. Your convention, in a way, enabled us to do what we did at our convention. It became part of your dialogue, which naturally I think it had to be, but it empowered us.

The controversy over those ads. Two weeks later, I found a Mondale ad that had an exact same image of flag-draped caskets in it. And there was no controversy whatsoever at the time when that was used. Of course, there was no union for Marines.

MATTHEW DOWD:

First we had to ask, can we use images of this, 9/11, or are people going to think it's exploitive? We found out people didn't think it was exploitive and thought it would be weird if you didn't talk about 9/11. We did a lot of research. They basically said, of course you should talk about 9/11. It's a defining moment in this country. This is a shared experience. Look at what the country's gone through and we all cried and bled together. Taking that to "Look what I did" is when it was a problem.

On the convention, we had a lot of discussion because it was in New York. We obviously knew from the beginning there would be some press about whether or not we were going to go down to the site. We were never going to do that. But we did think, okay, are we going to limit this to one day and one moment at the convention because the press is going to look for this because we're in New York. When the Democrats did the candle thing or the Bic lighter thing or whatever the thing was, I forget what image was used, we thought, we're in New York. This is the president's party. We can now have the images and have the people, whether it's John McCain or Rudy Giuliani or whomever, talk about it as much as they want, because the Democrats celebrated this. Nobody owns this image. We all went through this together. And so we didn't take it in a different direction. We just did it more after the Democratic convention did it.

Part of the problem we had to deal with was not a voter problem, it was a press problem. Voters were fine about it. We asked, how far can you go with this without the press going crazy and you getting hammered on it.

NICOLLE DEVENISH:

How far we took it with the press was an entirely different internal debate from how far we took it as an issue. The decision was made to make the convention about the nation, not about the president in the context of 9/11. So it was never about the president's courage on that day. It was always about the nation's courage—that was our theme Monday. The nation's compassion, land of opportunity. It was never treated at our convention as a story that we told about the presidency or President Bush. It was about what the nation had been through. That was a decision made when the first ads came out.

Ad controversy became an oxymoron. What is an ad controversy? It's your ad being run hundreds of thousands of times—your ad that's been focus grouped and tested that you know works. An ad controversy became something that we kind of laughed about. My favorite ad controversy was driven by *Newsweek* about whether our firemen were really firemen. They ran pictures of the firemen in our ads hundreds of times to determine that they were real firemen. They were volunteer firemen. But the ad controversies were really interesting in the cycle because neither side was running ads that didn't work. So to have an ad controversy was, I think, an example of the press getting duped. I think it's something we can all laugh about together because these ads had the desired effect I think on both sides.

TUCKER ESKEW:

The other thing about 9/11 we haven't touched on is what the campaign was so much about—Iraq. As the prosecutor would say, it gets to motive. The president had to talk about 9/11 because it's so true to who he is and the decisions he made in his presidency. Absolutely fundamental to the decision about Iraq. For all the controversy about WMD or any other stated reason for going into Iraq, the subtext on every aspect was the way he was changed, the way the nation was changed by 9/11. We had to talk about it.

MICHAEL DONILON:

From our view I think the election would be very different if it wasn't for Iraq. I think that made it a much more competitive, difficult situation for the president than otherwise would have been the case. You talk about your controversy on your side. I think from our side, the voters at least in our view had a much clearer view of Senator Kerry's view about Iraq than the press did. The press was prepared to torture him to no end, whereas the voters actually believed with John Kerry there was real promise that change could happen and that could improve in Iraq.

So I actually disagree in that I actually think the move into Iraq, obviously complicated by 9/11 and obviously played in multiple dimensions, made this election significantly closer and more competitive and very different [than it otherwise would have been]. Senator Kerry had a very different view than the president did. There was more hope in what he was offering than a continued path that the president was taking us on.

Could I ask just one final question? I think Matthew [Dowd] it's probably for you. When you look at 9/11 and the president, do you see that event as peculiar to the president or do you see it actually operating along a partisan divide?

MATTHEW DOWD:

It's both peculiar to the president and it's operating along a partisan divide so it's both. I mean it is peculiar to the president because the president was there. He was the president at the time so it is peculiar to him, but the national security issue which 9/11 highlighted and will probably be highlighted for the foreseeable future, breaks in a partisan way. 9/11 is an exclamation point on that, whether you're in a congressional race, a senate race. If terrorism is an issue in a campaign, Republicans have an advantage in it.

Now, can Democrats win races? Obviously they can, but how high and how low that issue is will be more determinative than whether or not a Democrat is good. It's not as much a question of whether a Democrat can equal a Republican on the war on terror than [can he] vis-à-vis 9/11. It is how high is the war on terrorism in the issue discussion. If it's low, the Democrat is better off. If it's high, the Republican is better off. In the presidential race, [it] affected the issue discussion and accrued to the benefit of the Republicans.

Student Questions

University of Pennsylvania students submitted questions to the participants after the debriefing. The participants responded in writing.

FOR MARK McKINNON:

Question: What effect if any did ad-watching have on the specific language of your ads or their content? Did fact-checking or ad-watching prompt you to change any ad content, if so in which ad(s)? (asked by Michael Zubrow)

Response: Focus groups encouraged us to not overstate the condition of the economy; specifically, ad testing helped us a great deal on the "Wolves" spot.

Question: Do positive 527 ads such as the "Ashley" ad make it hard to ban these types of advertisements? (asked by David Burrick) ///

Response: The "Ashley" ad demonstrated that third-party 527 ads can have a positive influence on the process.

Question: We've learned that it's essential that a campaign control the definition of themselves, the opposition, and most importantly, the agenda of the race. I've gathered from what you've said that President Bush benefited greatly from a pre-established definition of himself in the voters' minds, thus being able to immediately jump into defining Senator Kerry and setting the agenda for the election, while the Democrats, instead of simply introducing their candidate, struggled in effect to reintroduce him on their own terms. What advice, if any, could you give to a challenger's campaign to counteract this powerful incumbent advantage? In other words, is there anything the Kerry campaign could have done to run the election on its issues, or was this impossible? Could the best they have done is mold their strengths to those topics determined by the Bush campaign? (asked by Jennifer Reiss)

Response: They should have made a strategic decision in the beginning about whether they were going to run a national security campaign or a domestic economy campaign. Instead, they tried to do both and switched gears in the middle of the campaign. They should have responded to the Swift Boat ads immediately.

For Alex Castellanos:

Question: Does any vestige of the anti-immigration heuristic still surround the Republican Party? If so, how do you work against the heuristic to attract minority, particularly Hispanic, voters? (asked by Alexander Eppstein)

Response: Yes, a vestige of the anti-immigration dynamic still motivates a part of the Republican Party. However, it does not dominate the party. Why? A tale of two governors and two seasons is informative. A few years ago, one Republican governor of a large state took the anti-immigration route, the winter road, and achieved some short-term political success with it. But in doing so, he defined himself and his party as cold, closed, intolerant, mean, petty, and most important pessimistic about the country and its future. He was Pete Wilson. He led his party to ruin in California, from which it is just now recovering. The other governor took a different approach. He thought illegal immigration was illegal and we should therefore enforce the law, all the while remembering that this is a country of immigrants and opportunity, a summer road. This governor remembered that more opportunity for those who choose to come to America can mean more, not less, opportunity for those already here. This second governor was George Bush, who led his party to success in Texas and beyond. That optimistic, summertime view of immigration, enforce the law but don't shut the door, is the majority view of the Republican Party today.

Question: I am interested in the "Wolves" ad and the impact that the included visuals had on test groups. The temporal proximation and the sequencing of the "pack of wolves" followed by Bush's face was troubling for me. Did you consider putting Bush's endorsement of the message at the beginning of the ad in order to avoid the assumption that Bush was a wolf or did this not come up in test groups? (asked by Megan Gompf)

Response: Yes, we originally chose to put the disclaimer at the head of the "Wolves" ad, not the tail. I still believe it might have been better there, but the collaborative decision of the campaign was to put it at the end. Here is my theory on the positioning of disclaimers: If the spot we are creating appeals to the left side, reason side, of the brain, I usually prefer to put the disclaimer at the end. I think a disclaimer up front, in those cases, might turn off some viewers who would be alerted "watch out, political spot coming." I also believe a strongly argued, factual case would not be diminished by an honest disclaimer at the end of the spot: "Here are the facts and we are the people who wanted you to know them." However, an emotional, right side of brain commercial is different. We want emotion to take the viewer away. We want to leave them with that emotion. Therefore, it is usually my preference to put disclaimers at the beginning of spots that appeal more to emotion than reason. A disclaimer at the head of "Wolves" would have been my preference. Interestingly enough, my experience is that after viewers see any spot a few times, the requirements of the commercial, such as the disclaimer, become wallpaper and viewers don't pay that much attention to them anyway.

Question: You noted that the production process for "Wolves" was very deliberate and that the campaign worked very hard on it. At what point and for what reasons did you choose to have a female voice narrating the ad? Obviously you believed a woman's voice would make the ad more effective, but based on what principle of persuasive communication did you decide that? (asked by Ezra Billinkoff)

Response: From March, when I conceived of the spot and put together the first rough cut, until near the end of the campaign, the voice on the rough cut of the spot was mine. I knew what kind of tone I wanted the announcer's voice over of the spot to have. We were targeting women 35 +. And as we tweaked shots and copy, I laid down different scratch tracks of my voice and gradually grew more comfortable reading the copy in a quiet, understated tone. A female announcer was almost always given. However, as we approached the end of the campaign and the spot neared its airdate, we had to make a choice on an announcer. I prepared male and female announcer versions of the spot. The right choice revealed itself. The campaign chose the female announcer and I think that was the right call. In our testing, women responded more powerfully to the message than men did.

Question: When the "Wolves" ad ran, our class discussed the possibility that the visuals were not as strong as they might have been. We did not find the wolves at the end to be intimidating. My question is: Did you experiment with any other shots besides the final one included at the end of the ad? When you tested the ad, did people find the wolves threatening? Alternatively did you intend the wolves to simply function as a metaphor and not invoke visceral fear? (asked by Dan Berstein)

Response: I was trying to make a persuasive ad, not a horror movie. Through repeated focus group testing, we found that our target audience got the message: Terrorists were wolves, renegades, chaotic and unpredictable enemies that lurked in the shadows and could strike any moment. The purpose of the spot was to take the viewer back to a dark moment before a terrorist attack . . . and therefore pose the question, "Who do you want to protect us in this dangerous, shadowy forest in which we now live?" In fact, we darkened the sky of the opening shots to portend the gathering storm and darkened the rest of the shots. We all know wolves are dangerous and scary. I didn't think we had to rub the viewer's nose in that. The last shot seemed to work not because the wolves snarl or, say, rip a college's student's throat and demonstrate how dangerous they are, but because the wolves *are going somewhere. Where are they going and why?* I wanted to leave the end of the spot inconclusive. Testing informed us that women reacted to the spot more strongly than men and that was our intention. The original inspiration for the spot came from a book called *Dante in Love*, which conveyed the thought I might paraphrase as "Innocence is dangerous. Innocence attracts wolves."

Chapter 3

Polling: Decisive Moments and Audiences

MATTHEW DOWD:

We did not think [the post-primary period] was an opportunity to disqualify John Kerry as a president. There was a lot of discussion saying, "Well, you were going to put the boot on their neck and we were going to eliminate him as a possibility and win the race." We never thought that internally. We thought we wanted to get the race back to parity. We were down 5 or 6 points when the Democratic primary ended. Four or five weeks before when the Abu Ghraib scandal hit the race, we were up about 1 point. So we took the race 5 or 6 points in that four- or five-week period of time, six-week period of time. The best that we felt we could hope to do was maybe get up another point or two. We didn't have an opportunity because it was stepped on by the events in Iraq. But that's really what we wanted to do.

John Kerry had a huge favorable/unfavorable advantage. He had about a 63–20 favorability/unfavorability when this was over. We went from a plus 40 to like a plus 17. Here paid assisted free media because John Kerry lost his favorability rating not only in states where we were running ads, but he lost it in states where we weren't running ads. It wasn't just about the ads. It was the free media discussion. The media consultants hate it when I say that.

Abu Ghraib happened. We took a hit from that. We went from being up 1 or so to being down 2 or 3. Then when that cycled off front pages, which took about 30 or 40 days, it was really a never-never land. We acted as if we were conducting a campaign—both sides—but really that [the Abu Ghraib story] was what was driving the news and driving people's perception. And then the race sort of returned, as is wont in this race, to an even race, within 1 or 2 points. It went back to an even race.

We thought the next opportunity was when a VP was picked. We thought the Democrats would do it before the convention. They did. Obviously, I had a question about this, how much others were really seriously considered other than John Edwards. I always thought John Edwards would get picked because of how he ran his race. He was a good speaker. I thought he was effective during the primaries and also I thought because of the support he got it would be hard not to pick him. You'd have to have a real rationale not to pick the guy who finished second especially since he's young and popular and comes from a state to which the Democrats need to send the signal that they're interested in even though it turns out they never competed in North Carolina. So that was the next important phase of it.

Kerry got a little bump from the Edwards pick. It was small but the start of their convention bounce. Then next was the Democratic convention. Kerry got a bounce from that but a smaller one than we expected. I didn't think he would get a 15-point bounce. If you look at the memo that I wrote, it said, if John Kerry meets historical standards, he will get a 15-point bounce. Now, did I think he would get a 15-point bounce? No. I thought he would get a bounce. I thought we would have to go into our convention down 5 or 6 and then we would come out of our convention even, maybe up a point or 2. That didn't happen. I think they came out of their convention 2 or 3 points ahead. Those points were lost in the course of August, which was the next important period. They were lost for a variety of reasons. The seeds for the [Democratic] problems in August were sown in the Democratic convention. Whether it was six minutes in the speech or not, because of the way the media cover the media discussion [the audience thought the convention] said that John Kerry's a senator from Massachusetts and he's a Vietnam veteran. An audience that was close to 30 million people was basically told nothing new about him. That's why I think the bump was smaller and less lasting [than we expected].

What the Swift Boats did is highlight something that voters didn't care about, which is "why are we talking about Vietnam? Why are we talking about whether something is positive or negative for John Kerry? Why are we talking about something 30 years ago and why aren't we talking about Iraq? And why aren't we talking about the economy? And why aren't we talking about the war on terror? Why are we talking about something that we thought was settled?" In the end, [the public] blamed John Kerry for the Vietnam discussion more so than anybody else because they thought he highlighted it.

We went into our convention even when we thought we were going to be 5 or 6 down and we came out of our convention 5 or 6 up, a better position than we thought we'd be in. I think our convention was successful for two reasons. One, it was the first opportunity that we had to showcase people for whom the public had tremendous respect. The speakers in the first two nights were the most popular people in this country, John McCain, Laura Bush, Arnold Schwarzenegger, and Rudy Giuliani. If you

Matthew Dowd

look at the favorability/unfavorability of those people, whatever party you are, those were the four most popular.

On the first two nights of the convention, they talked about how George Bush was the right guy at the right time. That had a big impact because these were people the public sees as above politics. The Democrats didn't have the ability to put comparable people up there. Bill Clinton, while popular among Democrats, is not very popular among the general public. Hillary Clinton is not very popular among the general public. We had four people that were more popular than either candidate in the race giving credit and due to the president.

The other thing that was talked about that we thought was important and affected both the convention and in the immediate aftermath was that [the convention discussion] wasn't just about Iraq. It was about the president's plan for the economy and health care and about his agenda for the future. Our polling in the following weeks showed that [the agenda] did get through to people.

We actually had a big advantage on who had a plan on these things, and the president had an advantage on that post our convention. The debates in total were an important moment [September 30, 2004: first Bush-Kerry presidential debate; October 5, 2004: Cheney-Edwards vice presidential debate; October 8, 2004: second Bush-Kerry presidential debate; October 13, 2004: third Bush-Kerry presidential debate]. One debate by itself wasn't. It was the totality that was important. Before the first debate and after the second debate, the race did not change that much. After the Republican convention, we had us up 5 or 6 points. That lead slowly deteriorated until we got to the first debate. [At the time of the first debate] we were up 3 or 4 points, which was pretty solid. When all the debates were over, we were up 2 or 3 points.

I think the way the press judges the effect of debates is way off from how the public judges it. This is not an academic exercise in which people say, "He made more points" or "he did this or he did that." Who won or lost doesn't matter in the public's mind. The press focuses on it. But in the public's mind, that's not what matters in debate. What matters is whether or not you counter existing biases or preconceptions or you affirm them, whether negatively or positively, and does that change your vote?

In the last ten days there was a lot of [press and pundit] discussion about undecideds. I'd be interested in Mark [Mellman]'s perspective on this and whether or not they accepted the press, the pundits' and the press speculation that undecideds would overwhelmingly go to the challenger. I had discussion after discussion after discussion with press in which I said that there's no historical reason for you to buy into that. Go back and look at the last four presidential races. The average is split when you look at the late-decideds or undecideds. Additionally, if you look at undecided voters in the final days of this race, who are they, how they view the candidates, and who they think is going to win is more determinative than what somebody said happened in 1964 or in 1968 or whatever.

I'll share an interesting discussion on this. Gallup did their last minute poll, and they traditionally allocate undecideds the way they think is appropriate. They called me for comment. They had a poll that came out that had us up 2 or 3 the day before Election Day. I think it was 2. They called me for comment on it. They said, we have the race dead even 49–49. And I said, is that allocated or unallocated? They said "it's allocated." Well, what's in unallocated? You're up 2. Well, how did you allocate undecideds? We gave 90 percent of the undecideds to John Kerry. I said, you're making a huge mistake. In the worst case, you ought to split them. Some think these undecideds aren't even going to show up. I had discussions with CNN and *USA Today* about it before they put the story out. If they had not allocated the undecideds the way they did, their end result would have been almost dead on.

I thought we were up 2 or 3 points in the last 24 hours and we won by 2.7 percent. The states didn't vary much from where we thought they were in the final four days of this race. We thought we were over-performing in Florida. We thought we were slightly, only slightly, under-performing, maybe by a point in Ohio. We thought we'd win Ohio by 2. We won Ohio by 2.4.

I know some people were surprised as I was when I saw the first exit polls. I thought, "Did I completely misread what was going on and what was happening in the country and what happened? And were we total fools on this fool's errand saying we can have the same number of Republican vote[rs] on Election Day as Democrats. Was that a complete fool's errand? Was every strategic premise that we had wrong?" Then I said, "Nah, it can't be right. The exit poll is screwed up." The problem in the exit poll, from my own personal vantage point, should put a nail in the coffin of the exit polls. There's no purpose in them from a voter's perspective. I think we should do what we always did before, which was wait until the votes start coming in. Everybody in this room knows, [leaked exit poll results on Election Day] changed the entire tenor of the coverage. Everybody in our campaign felt it. It was as if Kerry was going to go measure the drapes at the White House that afternoon.

We'd always planned after 2000 to find some place to get 3 percentage points. That was our goal. We needed to move the race from 48 to 51. Where were we going to get those 3 percentage points? Our first goal was to increase the number of Republicans on Election Day and make it as close to parity as possible with the Democrats. And I think we were successful at doing that for a variety of reasons. The president and what he said and did were popular with Republicans. Then mechanically we did a lot of things to help the grass roots. Our advertising, whether on cable, radio, or our spot market was effective.

We thought the biggest majority from which we were going to get that 3 points was women, predominantly white women. In the end, if you look at the exit polls, two-thirds of the margin came from white women. We didn't do any better among men on Election Day. We did slightly better among African Americans, better in some states such as Ohio, but only slightly better. Depending on whose poll you look at, we did 7 or 8 points better among Hispanics, which obviously helped us in places like New Mexico and Florida. But the biggest change was among women.

The biggest driver among women was they felt the president was strong and forceful. They trusted what he said and they thought he would keep them safe. They thought regardless of whether or not I agree with him on this or that specific issue, I trust him. When push comes to shove, I'm going to go with him. The biggest growth for Republicans on Election Day, where we move that number to parity, was primarily among women. More women voted Republican on Election Day than I think at any time since 1984.

So that's significant to us. Finally from an issues perspective, we always felt that this race was about two things. It was about the war on terror, in which we wanted to include Iraq. I think the Democrats wanted to not include Iraq in the war on terror. There was a struggle between the sides over whether Iraq was by itself over here or whether Iraq was part of the war on terror. That's one of the things we consciously were aware of. The second was the economy. Fundamentally that is what Election Day was about. If you look at the results, and we did some post-election polling in the immediate aftermath, we won the economy by 1 point. If you ask people who they trusted on the economy, the president had a 1-point advantage. We had a 10-point advantage on Iraq and we had a 17-point advantage on who the public trusted generally on the war on terror. We lost on issues such as health care and Social Security. We had an advantage on Iraq and we had an advantage on the war on terror. And in the end I think that's why this race was a 3-point race.

No matter who the Democratic nominee was, this race, again to quote something I said at the beginning, it was never going to be a huge victory. What we did was a combination of persuasion and motivation. It was motivating potential Republicans who had not ever voted before. Eleven million more people voted for this president than did in 2000.

When we did focus groups, we never included undecided voters because you couldn't find them. This race basically had 3 or 4 point undecideds total, which means if you go and try to recruit people, you'd have to call a lot of people to get 3 or 4 points, to get 20 people to answer undecided. We never really were worried about someone who was undecided. It was always how do we shore up, motivate soft Republicans, and are there any Kerry defectors that we need to either switch to us or make sure we didn't de-motivate them.

Mark Mellman

Mark Mellman *is a public opinion researcher and communication strategist. He is CEO of The Mellman Group, a polling and consulting firm whose clients include leading political figures, Fortune 500 companies, and some of the nation's more important public interest groups. Mellman has helped guide the campaigns of sixteen U.S. senators, over two dozen members of Congress, and four governors, as well as numerous state and local officials. He served as pollster for John Kerry's presidential campaign. Mellman received his undergraduate degree from Princeton, and graduate degrees from Yale University, where he taught in the Political Science department. He is currently on the faculty of George Washington University's Graduate School of Political Management.*

We've been asked to talk about the major events in the campaign. I'm going to do that. But I first want to issue two caveats. The first one is simple. It buttresses something Matthew [Dowd] said, which is [to] beware of the polls—an odd thing for a pollster to say. This chart (Chart 13) is my favorite chart from the campaign.

Each of these diamonds represents John Kerry's margin in some poll taken on that particular day, some national poll from some polling agency. Now if the social scientists in the room can find more than one or two clear patterns in that data, I will get the media guys to endow a chair for you. It's very, very hard to find. The reality is you can look at

CHART 13. POLLS VARIED DRAMATICALLY

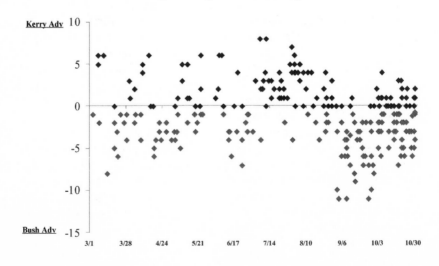

Kerry Advantage in National Polling

Mark Mellman

any two polls at any two points in time in this campaign and tell almost any story you want about any event. Let me give you an example from each of our conventions.

You can take a poll before and after our convention and show John Kerry with an 8-point bounce. You can take a poll before and after and show John Kerry with a 5-point decline. You can take a poll before and after the Republican convention and show George Bush with a 4-point increase. You can take a poll before and after the Republican convention and show George Bush with a 4-point decline. So any story you want to tell about this election can be told by looking at any sets of polls that you happen to choose. So be very careful the stories you choose to tell.

The second caveat I want to offer is a longer one. It is to avoid what the psychologists call fundamental attribution error. Fundamental attribution error consists, as some of you know, of overweighting the significance, the importance of individuals, of personalities, of events, and underweighting the significance, the salience of the structure of the situation of the underlying circumstances. And I want to spend a minute outlining what I think some of those underlying circumstances were as we approached this race. First, as has been noted, there has been a long-term decline of the Democratic plurality in this country. That is not something that happened this year. It's started a long, long time ago. In the '70s and '80s, Democrats on Election Day had 15-point margins. By

CHART 14. TOGETHER, PARTY AND IDEOLOGY ACCOUNT FOR MOST OF THE VOTE

Last Week Of Polling: Party By Ideology			
Kerry - Bush Margin	Liberal	Moderate	Conservative
Democrat	91%	76%	46%
Independent	40%	12%	-43%
Republican	-47%	-75%	-92%

the time we got to the '80s, those were 2- and 3- and 4-point margins. It is right to say that today this was the first presidential election where the exit polls showed parity. But that is not something that we saw [only] in the close of this election. Partisan parity between Democrats and Republicans is something we'd seen in our polling all year long and had seen before this year. Now, together ideology and partisanship count for a lot. If you look at this chart (Chart 14) as sort of the intersection between ideology and partisanship and the margin for John Kerry in each of those boxes, you see that these numbers are mirror images of each other. We had a 91-point margin among liberal Democrats. Bush had a 92-point margin among conservative Republicans.

Bush had a 47-point margin among liberal Republicans. We had a 46-point margin among conservative Democrats. Look at the middle, the people who should swing this election, the moderate Independents. John Kerry actually led those moderate Independents in our data by 12 points. How do you lose an election like this, as we did? The answer is very simple—not very pleasant, but very simple. There are more than twice as many conservative Democrats as there are liberal Republicans. There are about one and one-half times as many conservative Republicans as there are liberal Democrats. So the distribution of voters in this grid (see Chart 15) works to the disadvantage of Democrats.

Second, culture is increasingly replacing class as the central divide in American politics. I'm going to be very clear in agreeing with what Matthew [Dowd] said earlier. This election was not fundamentally about abortion and gay marriage. But there's no question that culture is replacing class as the primary divide in American politics. You can see this if you look at the data by church attendance. In the '70s and '80s, '50s, '60s, there is very little gap. You move to 2000, to 1992, a 12-point gap that expanded to a 20-point gap for Republicans or 20-point margin among frequent church attenders in 2000 and a 22-point advantage this

CHART 15. HOWEVER, CONSERVATIVE REPUBLICANS OUTNUMBER LIBERAL
DEMOCRATS AND CONSERVATIVE DEMOCRATS OUTNUMBER LIBERAL
REPUBLICANS

Last Week Of Polling: Party By Ideology			
Kerry - Bush Margin	**Liberal**	**Moderate**	**Conservative**
Democrat	91% (19%)	76%	46% (9%)
Independent	40%	12%	-43%
Republican	-47% (4%)	-75%	-92% (28%)

time around for people who are frequent churchgoers. Positions on cultural issues do a lot more to help you predict someone's likelihood of
voting one way or another than does, for example, their income. That is
a change in the nature of American politics today.

Look at the key demographic groups in Chart 16.

The horizontal axis here is the size of each group. The vertical axis is
the margin of one candidate over the other. As you can see, there are
three groups that gave about 50-point margins or better to John Kerry—

CHART 16. KEY DEMOGRAPHIC GROUPS IN THE 2004 ELECTION

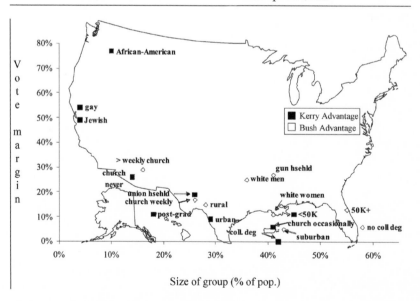

Size of group (% of pop.)

African Americans, gays, and Jews on our side. On the Republican side, one group gave about a 50-point margin or better to George Bush— white, Evangelical Christians. Again, you see the cultural divide there. You also see the fact that blacks, Jews, and gays together constitute about 18 percent of the American electorate. White Evangelical Christians constitute about 23 percent of the electorate, something of an imbalance there as well.

The third point to keep in mind is that incumbents have an advantage. In the last century, incumbents won 75 percent of their races, 66 percent since World War II. Take out the un-elected Gerald Ford, and it goes back to 75 percent. There is an incumbent advantage. Voters have to feel a certain level of pain in order to get rid of an incumbent. It's pretty clear that they didn't feel that level of pain this time around. If you look at the academic models, which I actually do, most of them predicted George Bush getting somewhere around 51–58 percent of the vote. Now one way to look at that is to disdain the models and say that they were wrong. A more sensitive interpretation is to say that voters were not feeling a high enough level of pain either in terms of the economy or in terms of Iraq [to vote out an incumbent]. I think that's what these models tell us.

In the campaign, we talked a lot about trying to spin the fact that the president's approval rating was at 49, 50, 51 percent. Jimmy Carter's approval rating was at 37 percent when he was defeated. George Bush's father was at 33 percent when he was defeated. It takes a low approval rating to actually get someone ousted. When Gerald Ford was defeated by 2 points, his approval rating was at 45 percent, 5–6 points lower than where President Bush was this time around.

We talked a lot about the economy and the level of pain in the economy. Yes, only 47 percent of the public gave the economy a positive rating. In 1992, the last time an incumbent lost, only 19 percent gave the economy a positive rating. In fact, I saw I'd written an article in *The Hill* in December of last year saying that if the president had any reasonable expectation of winning this year, he'd have to create 2 million jobs this year. Well, as of the end of October, the number is 1,920,000 jobs. So, in fact, by historical standards, [the Bush administration] measured up pretty well with respect to the economy.

The issue structure also portended a pretty close race. When we asked people what they cared about personally, health care and jobs come out very high on the list. Terrorism was also on the list but less salient to people on a personal level than things like health care and jobs being outsourced. On the other hand, when we asked people what's the most important job for the president to focus on, terrorism is at the top of this list. Other issues fall a little bit further down. So terrorism was very much on the agenda for this election as everyone has rightly said. And that makes a difference.

Compare this to 2000. This is the exit poll result for 2000. When people came out of the voting booth, 62 percent checked off some issue you would normally say is a Democratic issue; 26 percent checked off some issue that was a Republican issue. On the taxes issue, President Bush won a much larger margin than Gore did on his issues, but still very different. And Gore lost this election anyway. Well, he didn't lose but didn't win the election. Let's put it that way.

In 2004, clearly the issues did change. We had terrorism on the agenda. John Kerry did win overwhelming victories among voters who were concerned about the economy, voters concerned about health care and education; Kerry also won by almost a 50-point margin among those people who said Iraq was the most important issue influencing their vote. The president won a decisive victory among people saying moral values was critical. More about that in a minute. Of course the largest margin for either candidate was among the number who said terrorism was the most important issue influencing their vote.

Nonetheless, and I think it has to be said, John Kerry did better than most other challengers. And I differ here with what Matt [Dowd] said before. John Kerry actually did win the battleground states. If you look at where John Kerry came with respect to other challengers this century, there are only three challengers who got a higher percent of the vote than John Kerry did in 2004. One of those was Franklin Roosevelt in the Depression, so if you take that one out, look at post-World War II, there's really only two challengers to incumbents who did better in percentages of the vote than did John Kerry this time around.

Moreover, as others said earlier, we focused very heavily on the battleground states. We knew our goal was to win 270 electoral votes and we believe that focus paid off. If you look at the 13 states that we were in at the end, John Kerry actually won those states in aggregate, very narrowly, with 50.2 percent. But clearly those voters weren't optimally distributed from our point of view. If we could have moved 100,000 from Michigan and Minnesota to Ohio, we'd have a different conversation here.

They won. They are to be congratulated. But the reality is where the campaigns were really engaged up to the end in those states; it was a different race than it was in the rest of the country. That's not just a function of the different nature of those states. Compare those same states to where they were four years ago. Al Gore did a little bit better in those states than he did nationally but only by 4/10 of a percentage point. This is, as the Annenberg folks said, you had this naturally occurring experiment. This time the difference between the battleground states and the rest of the country is meaningfully larger than it was.

CHART 17. SHARED VALUES IS THE STRONGEST DRIVER OF THE VOTE,
FOLLOWED BY NATIONAL SECURITY

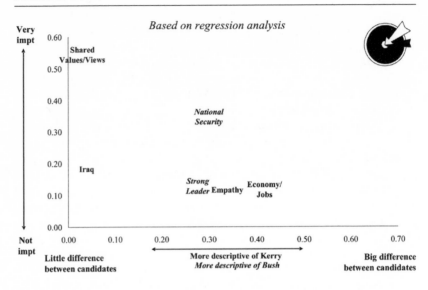

Another way of looking at this is to say for hundreds of millions in advertising, weeks and weeks of campaign visits, tremendous field effort, all
the kinds of things that went to this, for all that you get 1.3 percent of
the vote difference for above and beyond the national news, and the
natural situation in which people find themselves. Some people would
argue whether that's really worth it. If you're on the winning side of this,
it's worth a lot. In any event, there was some difference between the battleground states and the rest of the country.

The values debate, I think, is a very important one because I think
there has been a lot of misinterpretation of it. This (Chart 17) is what
we call a strategic map. This is the analysis we used throughout the campaign to indicate what was really driving the vote. The horizontal axis is
the level of difference between the candidates. The vertical axis is the
level of importance attached to that dimension based on our statistical
analysis to that dimension.

The single biggest determinant of vote throughout this campaign,
every time we did this with this constantly was shared values, the single
most determinant of vote. From our perspective, the candidates were
actually relatively even on that dimension. I think this chart gives you a
pretty good sense of what else was happening in this race. George Bush
had a significant advantage on national security. That advantage was
somewhat less important than shared values. But it was a big advantage

on his part. We had an advantage on economy and jobs, on empathy. Bush has an advantage on strong leadership on Iraq, also very close between us. That was somewhat less important than the overall national security dimension.

But what do people mean by shared values? I submit to you it's not abortion and gay marriage. In fact, the *LA Times* national exit poll, which few people who don't live in LA actually pay attention to, asked people directly: gay marriage and abortion—were those the issues that were important to you? A smaller number of people checked off that box. More importantly John Kerry actually won the vote among those who said gay marriage and abortion were their most important issues. He won those voters by only 4 points. But it's hard to look at these data and say that abortion and gay marriage were the dispositive issues in the campaign. As I said, Bush and Kerry [were] fairly equal on shared values.

What does this concept of shared values mean then? In our research, shared values means something very particular and very simple. Voters have no idea what decisions a president is going to have to make. They have no idea what issues he's going to face. They have no idea what crises are going to develop over the next year, two years, four years. What they want to know is when that president makes that decision, is he or she, he in this case, going to employ the same set of priorities, the same set of principles, bring to bear the same background, the same experience, the same considerations that they would employ were they making that decision in the Oval Office. By that criterion, George Bush and John Kerry were actually fairly even throughout this campaign. That is what people mean by shared values. It's not really about gay marriage and abortion.

Now let me turn to some of the key moments in the campaign, which I arbitrarily and capriciously divided into five sets (see Chart 18). First, the spring: We needed the spring to introduce John Kerry as our ads showed. In this poll, what you see here is our margin.

As you can see, in January we were way down. After Kerry secured the nomination, we headed back toward even and then actually were ahead for a while through Super Tuesday as the Republican campaign kicked off. After Super Tuesday, we started to see a decline in our margin. A lot of events happened during that period. The data moves up and down in no particular order. We had this unprecedented negativity from the Bush campaign, extraordinary for both the volume of the attacks and the liberties they've taken with the truth.

If you look over time, when our campaign started its advertising, those ads start to kick in. You see John Kerry starting once again to take the lead. And then you see Abu Ghraib, other kinds of events happening, President Reagan dies [on June 5, 2004]. You have a big hit for us at

CHART 18. BUSH'S EARLY ATTACKS HELPED HIM SEIZE A SLIGHT ADVANTAGE, BUT EVENTS BUFFETED THE RACE

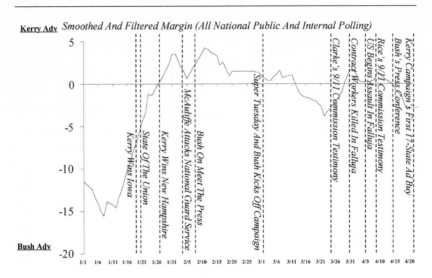

that point. You have again other events until the Edwards selection [on July 6, 2004], the lead-up to the Edwards selection; all of a sudden John Kerry's margin starts to increase again as we get to the Edwards selection. We also saw people's exposure to John Kerry's biography [produce] real movement on their part. We tested people seeing these bio ads, asked them before and after questions and people moved. They were much more likely to think he was tough enough to deal with terrorism. They were much more likely to think that he was a strong leader, that he cared about people like them, would keep America militarily strong. He shared their values, represented their point of view and they were much less likely to see him as a flip-flopper.

Now as I said, these bio ads actually affected people's perception of John Kerry across a wide range of indicators. Bill [Knapp] talked about the key issues that we looked at. I'll pass over that. We also had some weaknesses that we identified with Bush, focusing too much overseas in expense of the home front, too stubborn, credibility problems, policy failures on Iraq and the economy, special interests. We had data to back that up. I'm going to skip over it.

We then had the Edwards selection and the Democratic convention along with the convention. The convention again introduced the theme of stronger at home, respected in the world, redefined the values debate, and passed the national security threshold that Mike [Donilon]

CHART 19. SPLIT FORM ANALYSIS

EVERYBODY HEARD THE FOLLOWING MESSAGE:

President Bush says he provides steady leadership in times of change. To help the economy, President Bush passed a bold jobs and growth package that allows Americans to keep more of their own money and creates jobs. President Bush knows that his most important job is to protect the American homeland and win the War on Terror. President Bush has led the fight against terrorists, working to defeat al Qaeda and the Taliban in Afghanistan, and turning back threats in Iraq. Because of our efforts, Iraq will be a free, independent country, and America and the Middle East will be safer because of it. We need President Bush's steady leadership.

CHART 20. A MESSAGE FOCUSING ON MAKING AMERICA STRONGER AT HOME AND RESPECTED ABROAD WAS EFFECTIVE

HALF OF THE SAMPLE WAS READ:

John Kerry says he will work to make America strong at home and respected abroad. To be strong at home, Kerry says he has an economic plan that will stop rewarding companies for shipping jobs overseas and instead focus on creating good jobs here at home. To make us strong at home, Kerry has a plan to cut healthcare costs for families and businesses while ensuring healthcare is a right, not a privilege. To make us strong at home, Kerry has a plan to use American technology to make us independent of Middle East oil. And for Kerry, "respected abroad" means a strong military, but also America leading strong alliances to help us win the war against terror, instead of going it alone in the world. John Kerry has a plan to make us strong at home and respected abroad.

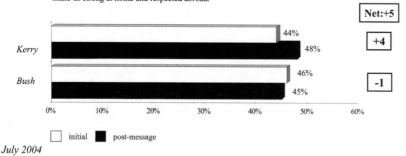

July 2004

talked about. From the convention, from the pick of Edwards on, we had a lead. As we got into the convention, that lead expanded. We put our message, "stronger at home, respected in the world," against the president's message, "steady leadership in times of change." We also talked about John Kerry's message. We defined "stronger at home" with an economic plan—stop awarding companies for shipping jobs overseas, cut health care costs, use American technology to make us independent of Middle East oil. "Respected abroad" means a strong military but also leading strong alliances. When voters were exposed to these positive paragraphs (see Charts 19 and 20) about the two candidates, we moved into a very slight lead. But for people who are used to looking at these kinds of data, it's a pretty small movement.

Here Matt [Dowd] is exactly right. There's not a whole lot of movement we got in this whole race one way or the other. We could marginally move them to our side. They could marginally move them to their side. The arguments had some impact back and forth. We could squeeze out a message that produced a win but it was always within a very close band, always relatively little movement.

The Democratic National Convention history, as people have suggested, has been re-written here. Six percent of the convention speech was about Vietnam. About a quarter of it was about domestic policy. About a fifth was trying to redefine the values debate. Another fifth of it about John Kerry's personal background, who he was as a person. So the reality is there was a very heavy emphasis on the domestic issues and domestic agenda. People did get that at the time. In fact, when you look at people's reported change of attitudes about John Kerry and compare it to Al Gore, with respect to their convention speeches, 49 percent of convention watchers said the convention made them think better of John Kerry. Thirty percent had said the same thing about Al Gore in response to that same question four years before. So by any standard, 49 percent saying they have a more favorable view of John Kerry as a result of the convention is a very positive result.

We saw that in specific traits as well. When we did national polling after the convention, we saw a real increase. There was a real increase in the public's sense that he would keep America militarily strong. They were optimistic that he would deal with terrorism, was a strong leader, that he'd hold down taxes, that he was a good family man, qualified commander-in-chief, cared about people like you, shared your values, a man of faith. We actually did move a lot of people in short order. In August we had the Republican Convention, the Swift Boats, Beslan [September 1–3, 2004, Chechen terrorists killed teachers and children in a school hostage massacre in Beslan, Russia], etc. (see Chart 21).

After the convention, we got up to about a 4-point margin. Naturally after that you get some slide downward with the Swift Boat attacks. Then you get the Republican Convention, which happened at the same time as Beslan and the Chechnya incident that Mary Beth [Cahill] referred to. Chechnya brought the fact of terrorism back to people's TV screens in a very visceral way.

In our statistical analysis before and after the convention, before and after Beslan, the level of importance that women attached to national security went up 50 percent. This didn't necessarily change their perceptions of the candidates but the level of importance that they were attaching to national security issues went up very dramatically.

CHART 21. THROUGH AUGUST, OUR LEAD ERODED, CULMINATING WITH BESLAN
AND THE REPUBLICAN CONVENTION

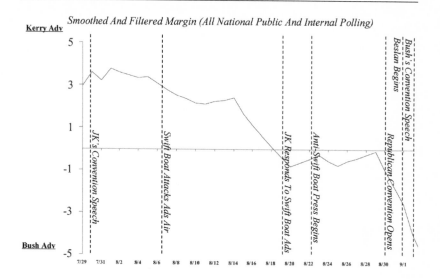

John Kerry really won all three debates, most clearly the first debate and third debate. To have a challenger to an incumbent president beat him toe-to-toe in three debates is an enormous achievement. Bob [Shrum] will talk more about that later. What was also clear is that the more people saw these debates the more likely they were to think that John Kerry had won by an even more decisive margin. The data are pretty clear in saying that those debates, the lead-up to the first debate and the first debate and beyond, moved John Kerry into contention. Going into the first debates after the end of September, we are about 4 or 5 points down. After the first debate we moved to 2 points down. After the second debate Kerry was 1 point down in the aggregated data. Kerry's superb performance in the debates had a very dramatic impact.

Finally, let me talk about the close of the campaign when we were focused on the battleground. Bush maintained a steady lead here (see Chart 22).

In the course of this campaign every week we did two million simulations of the outcome of this election and, again, focusing on the battlegrounds, were able to determine what percent of the times was each of these states pivotal, decisive on the one hand, close on the other. Florida, Ohio, Wisconsin, Pennsylvania would not be surprised at the way this comes out. But these percentages (see Chart 23) gave us a lot of

CHART 22. BUSH MAINTAINED A LEAD GOING INTO ELECTION DAY

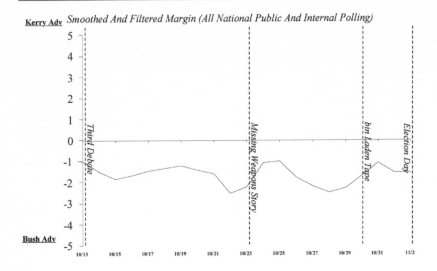

CHART 23. OUR RESOURCES SHOULD BE ALLOCATED IN ROUGHLY THE
PERCENTAGE OF TIMES THE STATE IS PIVOTAL

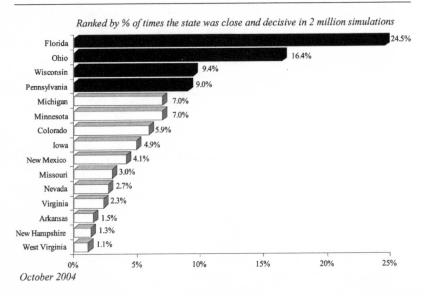

CHART 24. GETTING TO 270

Base:	Strong Kerry:		Lean Kerry:		We Must Win 2 Or 3 Of The Following:	
DC	Maine (total)	2	Michigan	17	Pennsylvania	21
Massachusetts	Maine CD-1	1	Oregon	7	Florida	27
Rhode Island	Washington	11	NH	4	Ohio	20
New York	New Jersey	15	Hawaii	4	PA+FL = 258 EV	
Maryland	**178 EV**	**+29**	**210 EV**	**+32**	PA+OH = 251 EV	
Illinois					FL+OH = 257 EV	
Connecticut					FL+OH+PA=278 EV	
California					**And/Or Some**	
Delaware					**Combination Of:**	
Vermont					Minnesota	10
149 EV					New Hampshire	4
					Iowa	7
					New Mexico	5
					Wisconsin	10
					Nevada	5
					Maine CD-2	1
					270+ EV	

information about how to allocate our resources and target the time of the candidate and the money that the campaign was spending.

We also saw that we could actually win this race while losing the popular vote. In fact, if we got an even national popular vote, our analysis said we had about an 82 percent chance of winning this race, which is pretty good. At this point, we were 1.6 points behind nationally. We only had about a 4 out of 10 chance of winning the race. As has been noted, that John Kerry came pretty close to actually winning the Electoral College while losing the popular vote by a meaningful margin. We knew we had to win at least two of Pennsylvania, Florida, and Ohio, and/or, depending on exactly which ones, some combination of this set of other states. It's really those states that were on the farther end of this chart (Chart 24) that we were most focused on throughout this campaign.

For most of this chart (Chart 25), the right track/wrong track number is really driven by the Iraq number. The ocular test will show you that and you can see that there's a relationship between perception of Iraq and overall right track/wrong track.

However, toward the end of October, the economy really starts to drive that overall right track/wrong track number. The first Blackberry email I got on election morning was from ABC. With polling done the day before the election, its consumer confidence numbers were at the

CHART 25. FOR MUCH OF THE FALL, NEGATIVE PERCEPTIONS OF IRAQ HELPED
DRIVE THE NATIONAL MOOD, UNTIL THE ECONOMY TOOK OVER IN THE CLOSE

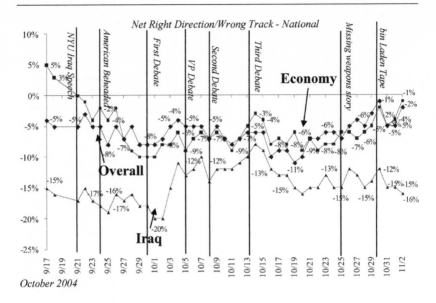

Net Right Direction/Wrong Track - National

October 2004

highest level in nine months. We found out the Friday after the election
that we had the biggest job growth since March in the month of October. In the end, these things mattered.

The Osama tape also mattered to some extent here when you look at
how people looked at this tape. On the one hand, you had a narrow
margin but a margin nonetheless particularly in the battleground states
among Independents of about 3 points of people saying the Osama tape
made it clear that we still face a terrorist threat. We need a president
with the strength and resolve that Bush has shown as opposed to saying
Osama is still there and the Bush policy has been a failure.

So at the end of the day, this was a very close race. Going into the end
we saw Bush going into the lead. But we think there was a late movement
to Bush in the last day or two of the race that put him over the top as we
went to Election Day.

Discussion

TUCKER ESKEW:

Mark [Mellman] and maybe the rest of you, I noticed a couple of times
talking about the convention, you made a compelling case that Vietnam

was not really the dominant thrust of the speech or even the convention. But one thing I think that I'd like to probe on a little bit is the question of Senator Kerry's talking about his own record or not talking about and whether [there was] a dilemma in running a senator who had not put his stamp on one issue or one particular agenda. Just like to probe that a little bit, see if that's something you tested, thought about, how you dealt with it.

MARK MELLMAN:

We thought John Kerry did have a distinguished record in the United States Senate and really accomplished a lot. But we did do some testing on this and found that people were more interested in what he was going to do as president than what he had done as a senator. So we focused on what he was going to do as president. In trying to qualify him as a person, there was a need to discuss who he was as a person and that obviously required some retrospective. It's also true that in his [convention] speech he did talk about things he had done in the Senate. But the major focus was what he was going to do as president and our sense was that's what the public wanted to know.

MARK MCKINNON:

One of the most interesting things I got out of the [Annenberg debriefing] session in 2000 was that there was conventional wisdom that things really turned around in 2000 after the debates. Of course the debates had a big impact. But as we look at the data, the event where the slope turned around was the day that Al Gore came out in support of a strategic oil reserve. While he thought it might be a politically astute decision, it reminded people that Al Gore was very political prior to that specific event. So arguably what happened was that people saw this, thought it was a patently political move and suddenly said, "Oh, that's the old Al Gore" despite the slope previously beginning to turn around. It looks like you're suggesting that Beslan really had a similar impact there and I just want to probe that a little more. I know that there were a lot of children involved. And it occurred to us at least intuitively that this might have an impact on women, on the terrorist component. Could you fill that out a little more?

MARK MELLMAN:

It so happened that you guys had a convention that not surprisingly was going to be focused on the issue of terrorism. And lo and behold there was a major terrorist incident, which captured the attention of the nation at exactly the time you were running this convention to focus on the issue of terrorism. It's a terrible event obviously but propitious timing from your point of view. I think it did focus people's attention on the issue precisely at the point in time when you were coming to a convention to make that the dominant issue. And I think the two worked together. I think it started the day before, the day or two before the convention, and went on.

MATTHEW DOWD:

Electorally, we played in a lot of states. We obviously had lots of grand ideas—Michigan and Minnesota. But we thought this race would come down to Florida and Ohio. That was the election. Now, you could look at our travel. You can look at resource allocation: direct mail, our phone banks, our field operation, all of that. My sense is that you had come to a similar conclusion. You also had what we had, a back door strategy, though you had some other state combination. But in the end it was Florida, Ohio. If we lost one of those two states, it was going to be very difficult for us to win the election. We had to win both. Pennsylvania would have been nice but our election didn't depend on that. And if you look at those two states and the allocation of resources and what was done, if we win Florida by 5 and Ohio by 2.5. And when you add those two together, we won those by 3.6, those two states.

Now understanding the combination of states you have—13 states, I have a different combination that says we won a combination of 9 states that we thought were targeted. I'm trying to present an argument that the national number was not far off the concerted effort we were making in the Electoral College. So the Ohio/Florida strategy I think from both our sides basically mirrored the national number. And in the end, just to remind people, we won; we won Ohio by 3.4 percent in 2000. And we won it this time by 2.5 so we lost .9 in a state that was supposed to be *the* game. So I did actually have a scenario in my mind that if the race was dead even, I thought we would lose the Electoral College. If this race was even or this race was a 1-point race I was fearful that we would lose the Electoral College, but I think in the end the key states mirrored the national numbers.

MARK MELLMAN:

I hear what you're saying. Obviously if you look at the states where we [both] invested effort, put them side by side, slight advantage for us again not optimally distributed. Florida is an interesting case here because Florida really moved down a lot for us from 2000 to 2004. Ohio moved up and Ohio moved in a different direction than did the whole rest of the country. The whole rest of the country moved essentially over 3 points and Ohio moved in a positive direction. So clearly something was going on in Ohio in terms of the very intense competition on both sides. I think in Ohio both sides did a tremendous job in generating turnout. The reality is John Kerry lost Ohio with 400,000 more votes than George Bush won it four years ago. And that's really a testament to both sides' Get Out the Vote activities. The engagement in Ohio produced a result that moved in a different direction from the rest of the country.

MATTHEW DOWD:

I thought you guys ran about as good a race as you could in the environment. Those were the same slides that I was showing to argue that structurally this race was going to be very hard for Kerry to win. I think Ohio was always underperforming for us. I mean I think it was an economic situation in Ohio. It was underperforming before March. We could have a 4-point lead nationally and Ohio was a 2-point lead. I think this was mainly because of the economic situation in Ohio, which drove people's perception. Florida was better for us because the economic situation in Florida was better than 2000.

Question: I'm Lorena Chambers. I'm the Hispanic media consultant for the Kerry-Edwards campaign, so I'm really fascinated by your Hispanic strategy. I'm really curious at what point there was a decision made to go after this electorate and really what was different from what you had done in 2000 or is it really just the genius of Karl Rove all over again?

MATTHEW DOWD:

In 2000 we knew that whatever party begins to capture this vote will become a dominant party. If we now start getting 40, 42 and 44, 45 percent of the Latino vote in this country on a consistent basis, it's very difficult for Democrats to win elections nationally. Can they? Yes, but very difficult if that becomes solid. In the aftermath of 2000, unfortunately a memo got leaked and internally Karl [Rove] wasn't all too happy about it where I said if we got the same percentage of the vote that we got in 2000 among all of the demographics—among whites, among Hispanics, and among Latinos, because of the growth in population, we would lose the 2004 election by 3 million votes and we would lose the Electoral College. We were cognizant of that.

We organized. We recruited folks in states. We, for the first time, had Hispanic fundraisers in states. We knew Florida was key. Two-thirds of the Latino voters in Florida now are non-Cuban. There are more Jewish voters in Florida today than Cuban voters, which is a big change. So we knew it from day one. We knew that's why we'd win New Mexico. We knew that's why we'd win Florida. But the Latino population has grown from 2 percent of the electorate 14 years ago to either 8 or it's 9. If you take 8, that's a 400 percent increase. Twelve years ago Republicans were getting 20, 22, 24, 25 percent of the vote. Now Republicans get 42, 45, and in Florida I think we got 52, 53 percent of the non-Cuban Hispanic vote. It's very difficult for Democrats to sustain a winning majority in this country if that continues to happen.

Question: Richard Johnston (Professor of Political Science, University of British Columbia). Further to the Latino vote. How much of that is a change in the map? I recall four years ago that a number of Republican Hispanic ads were played. Then it was pointed out that some were never aired because the relevant populations were in relatively uncompetitive states. Is there a sense in which Hispanics have also become more important in whatever the current definition of a battleground is, and indeed in a place like Colorado maybe making it a battleground? Is geography a factor in this strategic change?

MATTHEW DOWD:

The answer to that is definitely. Because of the growth of the Latino population, Nevada, which used to be a solid Republican state, is now very competitive nationally, especially in Clark County. Colorado moved more competitively because of the growth in the Latino population. That could be a harbinger of something. Even though the population is growing, the Democrats are now winning it by a smaller and smaller percentage, which they did in those states.

The primary reason we won New Mexico this time was a slight Republican increase in turnout, but we increased our Hispanic vote by 9 percent in New Mexico by itself. So, there is some geography.

There is a reason: Florida is a state that George Bush, the father, carried by 20 points in 1988 and we carried by less than 600 votes in 2000 and by 5 points this time. The state has become more competitive. In Texas, George Bush as governor won a big victory because he got the same percentage [as Democrat Garry Mauro] among the Latino vote. If the Democrats are counting on the growth in Hispanic voters to deliver a state, that opportunity is fast dwindling. If a Latino is voting 42 percent for a Republican, a Latino now is no longer a Democratic constituency. It's now a swing constituency. We showed it in 2000 and we showed it more this time.

MARK MELLMAN:

The good news is they're revising that exit poll number to 40 so it's not 42 percent for the Republican. They got 40 percent. But the reality is I agree with almost everything Matthew [Dowd] said. Some of these states are competitive because of the growth in the Latino population. Some of these states, which are now competitive, have large Latino populations and that makes a huge difference. We did not do as well among Latinos as we could have and should have and will do in the future. I think a lot of attention is going to be paid to that and properly so. We paid a lot of attention to it this year. I think somebody asked when the president started dealing with this. With all due respect, I don't think it was after your memo leaked. I think it was when he was governor of Texas. The one trip he made out of the country was to Mexico. This was an important constituency in the state from which he originates.

It was a constituency he dealt with in that state over and over again. And I think there's a concerted and a long-term effort to try and crack the Democratic hold on Latinos. We are fighting back and have to fight back very hard. When it's still a 20-point split, we're very happy. The Latino population is growing in places such as Nevada, Arizona, Colorado, and New Mexico. That's a good thing for us in the long run.

Question: Brian Rosenwald (University of Pennsylvania undergraduate).

It seemed as if the Republicans pursued a different strategy in going after Hispanic voters than traditionally has been made. I don't know if it was more negative, but it was more targeted to issues. It was more hard-hitting. Is that true?

MATTHEW DOWD:

We made a concerted effort in 2000, spent a lot of money, a lot of time. We spent a lot more money and a lot more time this year. I think Latinos are performing not unlike European immigrants. They're different than African Americans, where regardless of your income level or your education level or your status in the community, you vote 90 to 10, 90 to 10, 90 to 10. Latinos are much like European immigrants of the early 1900s who were Democrat. As they became more part of the democratic mainstream, they owned their house. They earned more money. They entered the middle class. And they became more available for Republicans. That is happening in the Latino community. There's a natural growth of Republicans among this community as Latinos become part of the economic mainstream.

One conclusion that we came to is that you can deliver similar messages. They care about terrorism. They care about the economy. They care about education and they care about [them] in very similar ways. There might be slight differences but very similar imagery. As Alex [Castellanos] said, they predominantly get everything through English media, some Spanish media. The idea that you have to craft a completely different message in a completely different way to this community is no longer true. There's not an issue that the Latino community cares about that is vastly different from the soccer mom in Macomb County, Michigan, who cared about terrorism, who cared about education, and who cared about health care costs.

ALEX CASTELLANOS:

I don't know that there is a lot else to add other than I'm sure that there's a big hunk of that electorate that is not available to us and it's inflexible and it may be stuck at the lower end of the economic scale. But what is in play increasingly is economic mobility and aspirational votes. I think we've got a lot we can say there. America has been very, very good to them.

MARK MELLMAN:

Part of the issue is the economic mobility, upward mobility of the Latino community. There's also a cultural conservative element to the Latino community. And I think if you look at it more deeply, you'll find that a lot of Latinos that moved were people who are frequent church attendees, who went to Catholic churches and heard letters from their bishops talking about the mortal sin of voting for John Kerry the two weeks before the election. . . .

But there's that element to the community as well. The reality is no party should count on any group giving 60, 70, 80, 90 percent of their votes to that party for the long term. You have to earn those votes. We have to go out and earn those votes in the future. I think it would be silly to say Democrats don't still have a very strong base in the Latino community. We've got to build that base back up again and I think there are ways to do it.

The other point I'd make about the Latino community is the war this time. We have a disproportionate number of Latinos serving in the military and there's no question that that had, at least in my judgment, a real impact as well in terms of how they felt about the war and therefore how they felt about both the president's and John Kerry's response to the war.

Student Questions

FOR MARK MELLMAN:

Question: You warned voters to "beware of polls!" What are key things that you think voters should be aware of so as not to be misled? Is there a way to make polls more accurate so that voters can rely on them during future elections? (asked by Michelle Price)

Response: There are bad polls—poorly executed surveys with inappropriate questions or samples. But the point I was trying to make is that in this election cycle normally reputable polls were all over the place. The only remedy I know is modesty. Don't assume that any one poll has a monopoly on truth. Use the law of averages. Averaging together a group of polls done at the same time is more likely to provide an accurate read than any one poll.

Question: According to Matthew Dowd, white women provided two-thirds of the Republican margin of victory. As so-called "security moms" replace pro-choice "soccer moms," and Hispanics vote in increasing numbers for George W. Bush, it would seem that the Democratic party is losing pieces of its core constituency. Is this a temporary effect of 9/11, an effect of George W. Bush, or will this fundamentally disrupt the Democratic bloc created by Franklin Delano Roosevelt? Equally important, are the Democrats making any inroads among groups that traditionally vote Republican? (asked by Andrew Scott Dulberg)

Response: Over the sweep of time Democrats and Republicans are trading some groups. Highly educated voters and Californians, to name but two segments, used to be Republican and are increasingly Democrat. Bush's victory was most importantly a function of September 11, but the fact is Republicans are making inroads in Democratic constituencies and we have come up short at every level, several elections in a row. We need to find more Democrats. Younger voters who are culturally progressive were very strong for Kerry in 2004. The inexorable forces of generational replacement mean they will be an increasingly large share of the electorate and that is good news for us in the long run.

Question: One of your points was that Kerry won (narrowly) where the campaigns were engaged, in the "battleground states." In Thomas

E. Patterson's *Vanishing Voter*, the author describes the Electoral College as an impediment to an effective national electoral process. Does your assessment of Kerry's success in the battleground states translate into a national victory, if the campaigns were engaged nationally? To put it more bluntly, how might the outcome of the election have differed without the Electoral College? (asked by Brendan Darrow)

Response: The whole campaign would have been different without the Electoral College. The target states would not have gotten the level of attention and focus they did. You could argue that more time and money in New York, New Jersey, California, and other base states would have meant bigger Kerry margins there and a popular vote victory. But the truth is, it is very hard to know. The only thing we know for sure is those were not the rules of the game we played. Al Gore won the popular vote but it didn't do him much good.

Question: According to the National Annenberg Election Survey in 2004, the people surveyed thought that Senator Kerry had the same amount of the "right experience to be president" as President Bush throughout the month of July leading up until the Democratic National Convention. However, directly after the DNC (on August 1) Kerry's numbers dropped sharply in that category. Why did so many people lose their trust in John Kerry after the convention? (asked by Reuben Cohen)

Response: It was really a combination of factors. Most important, though, was the combination of the Swift Boat attack, Beslan, and the Republican convention. The major objective of the Republican convention was to communicate that terrorism was the central issue in the race and that Bush, but not Kerry, was qualified to handle it. The terrorist incident at Beslan in which voters were engrossed served to dramatically heighten the impact of the Republican message. They were saying terror was the key issue and at the very same time voters were watching terrorists shoot children on their TV screens. It was a powerful, nightmarish reminder of our vulnerability. Add to that the shameful lies of the Swift Boat Republicans questioning John Kerry's heroism and integrity. Put it all together and serious doubts were created about John Kerry.

Question: You said that "values," when it comes to vote choice, is not fundamentally about gay rights and choice. Instead, it came down to a question of shared values in making decisions. Voters ask themselves, "would this candidate make decisions the same way I would?" My question is: Do you think you can summarize this concept in terms of decision-making heuristics? You suggested that this idea of shared values came from seeing if a candidate has the same set of priorities or principles as the voter. It seems to me that the criteria voters use to make these decisions can be captured through the party heuristic, the endorsement heuristic, and the likeability heuristic. Is this idea of "shared values" actually a new concept, or could it be that you're just combining factors like party identification, endorsements, and likeability under a single umbrella of "shared values?" (asked by Dan Berstein)

Response: I'm not sure it's a new concept. I am sure that endorsements, party, etc. are all part of it, but it is not just that. People want to understand the background, experience, principles, and priorities—the values—a candidate will bring to bear in making decisions. Party and endorsements go some distance in providing that information, but not far enough for many people, especially those small number of swing voters that actually decided the election.

Chapter 4
Debate Strategy and Effects

Bob Shrum

Robert M. Shrum is now Senior Fellow at the Robert F. Wagner School of Public Service at New York University. As a partner in the political consulting firm Shrum, Devine, Donilon he was recently a senior advisor to the Kerry-Edwards Campaign. He began his career in politics as the principal speechwriter to Senator George McGovern in the 1972 Democratic campaign for president. Subsequently, he served as the staff director and chief counsel of the United States Senate Select Committee on Nutrition and Human Needs, and as press secretary and speechwriter to Senator Edward M. Kennedy. Since 1985, Mr. Shrum has provided strategic advice and produced advertising for twenty-six winning U.S. Senate campaigns, for eight governors, and the mayors of New York, Los Angeles, Chicago, Philadelphia, Denver, Dade County, and San Francisco, as well as the Democratic Leader of the United States House of Representatives. In 2000, he was senior advisor to the Gore-Lieberman campaign. As a journalist, Mr. Shrum's work has appeared in New York Magazine, *the* Los Angeles Times, *the* New York Times, *and* The New Republic. *He has been a fellow of the Kennedy Institute of Politics at Harvard University and has taught at Yale University and Boston College.*

The truth is that for us the debates were critical to John Kerry becoming competitive again in the race. If they had been held at a different time, they might have meant that he was president of the United States. There were a lot of happy moments in our campaign, which the press and conventional wisdom foresaw as improbable or impossible, including those debates. They had to serve our strategic imperatives: to get over the national security hurdle, to get to the economy and health care, and the underlying value of fighting for the middle class. But let me focus first on earlier events that influenced our thinking about strategy for the debates.

The Kerry candidacy was all but declared dead in November of 2003 right about the time that Mary Beth Cahill was becoming campaign manager. One commentator said that the principal reason was that the campaign had decided after a fierce internal fight not to run negative television ads against Howard Dean. The report was true. The prediction of the consequence was not. This was also around that time that we made the decision that Mary Beth [Cahill] discussed earlier to go to Iowa. The signs that the strategy was working were clear in the days and I would argue in the two weeks before the caucuses [held on January 19, 2004]. But it was just too hard for the press to believe.

Just before the caucuses, the *Washington Post* ran a front page story about the battle between Dean and Gephardt for first place based on their superior organizations, this even though the *Des Moines Register* had come out with a poll showing that Kerry was in the lead. In reality, Gephardt and Dean, partly by engaging in a conventional and self-destructive television battle, had done great damage to themselves. And in fact the Kerry organization was actually better and the message was right on target. The candidate who was dead in November, who left his presumed natural terrain in New Hampshire, who had to turn down public funding and loan his campaign $6 million even to execute his Iowa strategy, went on to win almost every single primary and caucus. And the debates, especially in Iowa, played a role in that.

I cite this because the primary debates were one of the major influences in the development of our debate strategy for the fall. The primary debates, and I'll cite two of them in Iowa, were obviously a very different breed of cat. You had nine or ten candidates, not much time for any of them to make a coherent case, and an absolute imperative we learned to set a tight strategic goal and execute it. It was clear to us that Democratic voters received an exchange during a debate very different than negative ads on television broadcast against another Democrat. So in two successive debates in Iowa, I think one was on Sunday and the other was either on Monday afternoon or Tuesday afternoon, John Kerry was able to draw critical distinctions first with Howard Dean and then with both Dean and Dick Gephardt.

In the first debate, he asked Dean a question about Osama bin Laden. Governor Dean had recently said that it was not clear to him or he could not conclude that Osama bin Laden was guilty and it wasn't clear that he deserved the death penalty. And Kerry asked a very simple question, "What in the world were you thinking?" to which there was no good answer. This reinforced the view that Dean was too outside the mainstream to win in November at the very time when likely Iowa caucusgoers were focusing on a decisive consideration: Who should, and who could, be elected president? In the second debate, Senator Kerry focused on the issue of middle-class tax increases, which Governor Dean and Congressman Gephardt favored and he opposed. Our candidate prepared for those debates with a very small group and a tight focus.

Bob Shrum

In the case of the first one, the focus had to be tight. The debate preps started at 11:30 at night. The basic approach here mirrored the experience we had had in the preparations for the 1996 Senate campaign debates against Bill Weld.

So as we entered the summer, Mary Beth [Cahill] and I had a long discussion and John Kerry then reviewed a memo outlining recommendations and options for the debate with President Bush. He decided he wanted the core debate team to be small, to begin work immediately and confidentially, and to prepare the debate books early so he could look at them well in advance of any actual prep.

The other influence on this process at least for me, and which I think Senator Kerry and Mary Beth [Cahill] were well aware of, was the large and at times self-defeating nature of the Gore debate preps in 2000, which often involved 30 or 40 people. We heard afterwards that Governor Bush had a rule for 2000—six people in the room; someone new comes in, someone goes out. We weren't quite that tough in 2004. But we were pretty close and Mary Beth [Cahill] made sure it stayed that way. Starting in June, we held a series of meetings outside the campaign to set strategic goals, develop lines, identify potential moments, and prepare a round of preliminary Q & A. I should say that one of the reasons John Kerry was so good in the debates was that the Q & A were discussed and rewritten with him in several sessions in the summer including a long one on the post-convention cross-country train trek.

I have to mention some other people in connection with this process, by the way. The very gifted Ron Klain, Vice President Gore's former chief of staff, was in charge of preparing the materials, along with Jonathan Winer who had worked for Senator Kerry and then as Assistant Secretary of State, and Greg Craig, a former counsel to President Clinton who did an absolutely brilliant job until we banished him to the role of playing George Bush in the mock debates. He was so pitch-perfect at that that in the practices we often heard the exact lines that George Bush used a few days later in the actual debate. In the end, I believe we reviewed with Senator Kerry close to every question that was asked during the four and a half hours of televised debates.

I'll return to process in a moment, but of course there was a fly in the ointment here. We had no debate agreement. Vernon Jordan was our principal debate negotiator. Jim Johnson, who had been the principal debate negotiator in 2000, was working with him. They quickly accepted the topics, formats, and moderators suggested by the Commission on Presidential Debates. And all we heard from the Bush side was the sounds of silence. Then, shortly after the Republican convention, Jim Baker and Vernon Jordan had a telephone conversation and Vernon came back with a proposal from the Bush side that proves the truth of the warning: be careful what you ask for; you might get it. Vernon believed from the start that it was a great deal for us. Three presidential debates—we had expected to get only two; one of them would be a town meeting—we thought the Bush campaign would never agree to that. The candidates would stand at podiums for the non-town meeting debates and could stand and move toward the audience at the town meetings. And the biggest substantive change—the Bush campaign wanted the first debate to be on foreign policy. This was presented as non-negotiable, as was their insistence, inconsistent as it was with their position on the presidential debates on sitting at a table for the Cheney-Edwards debate.

Jim Johnson, Mary Beth [Cahill] and I, and the candidate actually thought that scheduling the foreign policy/national security debate first was probably good for us. If we could hold Bush even there or even beat him, we could redefine the race and set the tone for the rest of the campaign; in any event, apparently "conceding" on this point was certainly worth it to get a third debate. Now there were other elements in the proposal that we didn't like, which proves another adage: "Sometimes it's good not to get your way." We wanted candidate discussion with no set time limits. The Bush campaign not only wouldn't hear of it, they wanted strict and short time limits, which they seemed to assume Senator Kerry couldn't handle. It was as though they were preparing to debate not John Kerry but the caricature they had created of him. They even wanted and got lights on the podium, visible to the television audience, to show if a candidate was exceeding the time limits. This actually helped us since John Kerry proved very good in this format at being direct, succinct, and almost precisely hitting the mark every single time.

Especially in the first debate President Bush stopped so short when the green light was still on that it left the impression that he had run out of things to say, especially when he was repeating over and over the line "It's hard work. It's hard work." The other feature the Bush campaign wanted was a buzzer—and they got it. We hated it; I thought it was like a gong show. If somebody went over twice the buzzer was supposed to go off the next time it happened. We actually were given the option in the first debate of having the buzzer go off on the president because he'd gone over for a third time. We decided not to exercise it. The gong was never heard during the course of the debates.

Finally, there was one dispute about the town meeting, which I think reflected the Bush campaign's concerns about the 2000 debates. There was a line drawn on the floor that the candidates couldn't cross. Now Senator Kerry had no intention of invading President Bush's space. There was some evidence from the Gore-Bush debates, and let me understate it, that this probably wasn't a good tactic. But we had a contentious discussion about it and the whole thing was resolved by demarcating much smaller candidate "sanctuaries."

Now, let me review what we did in our preps. We went to a remote site. I don't know whether the president was prepping at Camp David or at his ranch or wherever, but we went to places where we could have minimum distraction and maximum focus.

We had limited participants. In addition to those on the debate prep team, Mary Beth [Cahill] was there, and at times so were John Sasso, Joe Lockhart, Mike McCurry. On foreign policy, we had Rand Beers, who used to work in the Bush White House, and Susan Rice; in our domestic policy, Gene Sperling and Sarah Bianchi. We did a series of very disciplined practices, first on a set of specific questions that we wanted to hone in on for each debate. Second, in half and full mock debates. We took two and a half days before all three debates to do this, while doing a token event a day so Joe [Lockhart] wouldn't call me up and shoot me saying we had to get it into the papers. I played the moderator and Ron Klain and I ran a critiquing process, in which Mary Beth [Cahill] enforced the rules under which we discussed disagreements among ourselves instead of debating them with the candidate who was very active in rethinking and reformulating answers and strategy. We didn't have free-for-alls; I wanted and, with Ron, led highly disciplined Q & A reviews.

We were also mindful of another lesson from the Gore experience. The spin after the debate matters as much as the debate itself. As Kathleen [Hall Jamieson] will tell you from her [National Annenberg Election Survey] 2000 polling, the people who saw the first Gore-Bush debate on television thought Gore won. People who read about it thought George Bush won. We were determined not to let it happen again.

It didn't. I believe John Kerry won all three debates. I think that is virtually unprecedented. After the first debate, the instant press coverage initially took the usual approach, declaring no winner until the polls started rolling in about 45 minutes afterwards. One of the reasons for this, as someone said earlier, is that in the press room reporters were seeing the Debate Commission feed. Viewers at home were seeing the network split screen, which showed the president, in the words of various newspapers, "agitated," "unhappy," "distracted," "scowling," and "grimacing."

Next let me to outline our strategic objectives for each debate. In the first debate, the foreign policy debate, John Kerry had to be confident, in command, concise. He had to show he could be commander-in-chief. As one reporter said afterwards, he looked more like the commander-in-chief than President Bush. Second, and Matthew Dowd alluded to this, we wanted to de-couple 9/11 and the Iraq war. The Bush campaign wanted to conflate 9/11 and the Iraq war. They weren't paying a price on Iraq because people were seeing it as part of the war on terrorism. Senator Kerry was very direct in saying they were two issues and arguing that Iraq was a distraction from the real war on terrorism—that "it's a colossal error in judgment that the president made. I would not have taken my eye off the goal of Osama bin Laden." And he continued to prosecute the case every time President Bush gave him an opening.

President Bush was asked a question on Iraq and he said, "Well, after all, the enemy attacked us." Senator Kerry, as soon as he got the chance, responded: "Saddam Hussein didn't attack us. Osama bin Laden did." When the president jumped in and said irritably, "Of course I know it was Osama bin Laden who attacked us," I knew we were beginning to move the dial on this. John Kerry kept at it—letting bin Laden escape at Tora Bora, ten times as many American troops in Iraq as in Afghanistan, asking the question: "Does that mean Saddam Hussein was ten times more important than Osama bin Laden? I don't think so."

Third, we thought this debate was our best chance to convey Senator Kerry's own position on Iraq directly to voters. As I said in an earlier Q & A session, he'd answered the hypothetical question—"If you knew there were no weapons of mass destruction, would you have gone to war in Iraq?"—in a speech at NYU weeks before the first debate. Until then, George Bush had been going around saying the two candidates had the same position on Iraq. We knew that when our candidate reiterated this position, he would be attacked for saying he voted for the $87 billion appropriation for U.S. troops already in Iraq before voting against it. John Kerry dealt with this very directly in a single line: "I made a mistake in the way I talked about Iraq. The president made a mistake in invading Iraq. Which is worse?" That, by the way, is the point at which one of the newspapers describes the president as grimacing.

Admitting the mistake was planned. We talked about it before the debate and we hoped that it would lead to Bush being asked about his mistakes because we didn't think he'd acknowledge any, although that didn't happen until the town hall debate.

Finally, we wanted to broaden the terrain, to get to issues like North Korea, to show Kerry as knowledgeable, in command, commander-in-chief. All of the evidence suggests that he achieved these strategic objectives in the first debate.

In the town hall debate, the first and most critical imperative was to retain the quality of strength and to be presidential while connecting with the audience. That was done quite successfully, despite another one of those strange rules that the Bush campaign wanted, no interaction with the audience. So if you asked me a question and you were the person in the town hall and the candidate didn't quite hear your name, he wasn't allowed to say: "Pardon me, I didn't hear your name." Or: "How many children do you have?" We just dealt with that. As the press afterwards noted, Kerry seemed totally confident, totally calm, totally connecting with the audience.

Second, and critically, we had to raise the salience of domestic issues, the question of who will fight for the middle class. It was a dual challenge—to get the economy and health care up and to turn around the Bush charges against Kerry. This is the debate, by the way, where Kerry used the phrase "weapons of mass deception." On raising taxes, it was John Kerry's best opportunity to respond convincingly and directly to most Americans. You saw Mark Mellman's chart on how, in the end, the tax issue was much less of a problem for Kerry than it was for Gore. That's partly because when Kerry was asked "Will you tell me that you won't raise taxes" by a questioner in the town hall, he answered: "Absolutely. I won't raise taxes on working families," right into the camera. "I'm telling you I'm not going to raise taxes."

When attacked for being a liberal, he turned it back on the president. He said: "You know the president is just throwing labels around. I mean compassionate conservative; what does that mean? Cutting 300- or 500,000 kids from after school programs, cutting 365,000 kids from health care, running up the biggest deficit in American history. Compassionate conservative?" He concluded, "Mr. President, you're batting 0 for 2."

We did everything we could in that debate to put the economy and health care at the center of the dialogue. To some extent, we achieved the objective. But there was a warning sign. Much of the press, for example the *Washington Post*'s lead story, focused on terrorism and national security. It was an indication of how hard it was going to be to widen the dimensions of electoral decision. President Bush, by the way, in the town hall did get asked to name three mistakes that he had made. He couldn't do it or wouldn't do it. And it certainly helped cement the sense with the press and I think with voters of how well Senator Kerry had done.

In the final debate, we wanted a relentless focus on the economy, health care, and Social Security—again, on who will stand up and who will fight for the middle-class. President Bush focused on social issues, in particular on gay marriage. One thing was important after the debate: The Bush campaign skillfully deployed the Mary Cheney controversy to blunt John Kerry's victory and to blunt the focus on middle-class issues.

After each debate, the polling showed a Kerry victory. After the first debate in the average of the national polling and ours, Senator Kerry made the single largest gain of the fall campaign and moved into a real lead in the battleground states. Without that debate, I doubt the election would have been so close.

Even after the problems we had in the third debate, we saw a situation in which Senator Kerry continued to move up, and that movement continued until the Osama bin Laden tape on the last weekend, at which point the movement flattened out because in my view, we were moving again relentlessly toward a 9/11 election.

One final note before I offer some conclusions. The Cheney-Edwards debate was also critical to us. It came between the first and second presidential debates. It kept the momentum going when a different outcome would have stalled it. Senator Edwards did a very effective job of defending John Kerry against attacks—and he prepared in much the same way Senator Kerry did. Actually, it was one of the truly funny moments I experienced in the campaign. Or it was fun at least in retrospect. We were at the debate prep and beginning to discuss how Vice President Cheney was going to deal with Kerry and with Edwards. And I looked at John Edwards and I said, "Well he's going to come after you with a machine gun." And Emma Claire, who is about six years old, said, "He's going to bring a machine gun to the debate with my daddy!?" And I said, believe it or not, "Emma, that's a metaphor" (audience laughs). Now she's six years old and I know her and she said, "Bob, what's a metaphor?"

The most important strategic decision that we made during that debate prep with Edwards was that it was more critical to defend Kerry than it was to defend himself. He agreed with that. It was a generous decision and it was clearly the right one. I'd like to offer a few conclusions and then I'll sit down. Liz [Cheney] will refute me and then we'll answer questions. First, I believe John Kerry won the debates because he really knew the issues and he prepared in a focused way. Two, less is more in terms of a debate prep. I've done it two different ways, in 2000 and in 2004. And a tight team and tight discipline are the keys to effective preparation. Three, be careful what you wish for in terms of rules or format. For example, in 2000, Al Gore clearly would have been far better off with the original Bush proposal of three debates on the Sunday talk shows, which then would have been broadcast at night. And in 2004 I believe George Bush would've been better off without the strict time limits and the lights.

Finally, why did Kerry win the debates and lose the election if—only by a switch of as few as 60,000 votes or less in Ohio? One [reason] in my view is unique to this year. As Mary Beth Cahill, Mike Donilon, and others have suggested, this was a 9/11 election. John Kerry used the second and third debates to move as hard as possible on the economy, health care, and domestic issues. But the press and external events like the looted weaponry in Iraq and the Osama bin Laden tape reinforced the 9/11 definition, which the Bush campaign understood and, as Mark

McKinnon suggested earlier, skillfully exploited from the start as the dimension on which they had to win the race. 9/11, by the way, in my view, was bigger even than the identification emotionally that the voters had with the president in the aftermath of that tragedy. I think it also became the reason and rationale that voters could grant the president for his failures or non-performance in other areas. I believe the 9/11 dimension helped insulate him on the domestic issues.

The other reason the debates were less determinative is, in my view, systemic. The incumbent has the advantage of insisting on early debates as removed as possible from Election Day. And the Commission on Presidential Debates has now simply assumed that kind of scheduling. For debates to have maximum impact, they need to be closer to the election itself. When voters could take a measure of the two men on the same stage, John Kerry had a distinct advantage. The stakes were high and the audiences were very high. For example, almost as many people watched the Cheney-Edwards debate as watched the first Bush-Gore debate in 2000. Unfortunately, the Kerry advantage in the debates couldn't quite be carried all the way to November 2. If it had, I think we would have won the election. And now for the refutation, Liz Cheney.

Liz Cheney

Elizabeth L. Cheney *served as a senior advisor and coordinator of vice presidential debate preparation to the Bush-Cheney 2000 and Bush-Cheney 2004 presidential campaigns. She is principal deputy assistant secretary of state for Near Eastern affairs and coordinator for the Broader Middle East and North Africa Initiatives. Prior to joining the 2004 campaign, Ms. Cheney designed the U.S.-Middle East Partnership Initiative, a $150-million program to foster freedom and democracy in the Arab world. From 1996 to 1999, Ms. Cheney was an attorney practicing with White & Case LLP in the area of international project finance. Ms. Cheney also has served as a consultant to the International Republican Institute managing election assistance projects in Kenya and Uganda.*

Thanks, Bob [Shrum]. I have a different take (audience laughs). We looked at these debates really as an overall part of the entire campaign. As we began the process of looking at what the debates were going to look like, how we were going to proceed in the debates, we really knew there were three things that we had to accomplish. We viewed these as three things Senator Kerry had to accomplish as well. They were first of all to demonstrate that we had a forward-leaning agenda; we knew where we were going to take the country on domestic policy and on foreign policy. Secondly, to demonstrate that we had a coherent strategy to win the global war on terror and for us, that included the war on Iraq. And an interesting point here that's been missed in some of the exit polling that we've seen is that in the exit polls, taken at the end of the election, 52 percent of people asked said that the liberation of Iraq was the right thing to do; 55 percent of the people asked said that the liberation of Iraq was connected to the war on terror. What Bob said is absolutely right that throughout, the Kerry campaign was working to unattach these two. We were working to make clear that it was all part of a package and, in fact, as Tucker [Eskew] said earlier, the reasons for liberating Iraq were very much part of the threats that we faced as a result of having been attacked on September 11.

That is not to say that we ever made the case that Saddam Hussein was responsible for September 11. There's been a lot of talk about that. Rather [we made the case] that we lived in a different world and we faced different challenges and that we could no longer wait for a threat like that posed by Saddam Hussein to fully materialize. The president couldn't sit by and allow that to happen.

The third thing that we knew we had to accomplish was basically to pass the living room test and to make clear to the people watching that they would feel comfortable having us in their living rooms for the next four years. This in many ways was a more important test for Senator Kerry obviously than it was for us because President Bush had been in their living rooms for the last four years. When we came out of our convention with what looked to be a 5-point bounce, we went into the season of the debates feeling pretty good and pretty confident. We also went in looking at precedent. I'd say there were two main precedents that we looked at. The first was 2000 and how the debate negotiations had gone then and also how we had performed in 2000. I think there was a sense that the debate negotiations in 2000 had not been handled as effectively for us as they could have been, that we made it too protracted a process, that it was too much part of the public sphere.

There's a very fine line for a candidate, a challenger at that point, between trying to lower expectations basically by not acting too full of hubris and pride about being able to debate. But you don't want to push that too far to look like you're afraid to debate. So we felt strongly that we didn't want to go into this process having a long drawn out negotiation about the debates. Secondly, we felt very good about our performance in 2000. Contrary to what still exists in terms of some of the conventional wisdom, the president did extremely well in those debates. Those debates were a defining moment for us in 2000. We actually like the town hall format. We think that's a good format for us in terms of being able to talk with the audience and to interact with them. We also

Liz Cheney

looked at the Clinton example and knew that there had only been two debates then and thought about two debates and decided at the end that we would go with three debates at the presidential level and one vice presidential debate.

At the same time, as Bob mentioned, you had the Presidential Debate Commission that had put out its own recommendations. In its recommendations for three presidential debates, all [were] seated and a vice presidential debate seated. Now we felt strongly that that didn't make sense in terms of the subject matter of the first debate. We believed, as the Kerry people believed, that we wanted to have foreign policy be our first topic. We believed it because we thought this is clearly the issue that this election is about. This is clearly the issue people are talking about on a daily basis and people are going to make their decision about.

So we went forward with the proposal to have foreign policy be the topic of the first debate. We wanted a town hall setting. We wanted them at podiums and we did want the vice presidential debate seated. At the same time, in a little bit of a different fashion than they had done in 2000, the debate commission came out and announced the moderators for the debates, which we accepted. We didn't have any problem with those moderators.

Bob talked about the issue of timing. I think it is true that if you look at the first debate, Senator Kerry accomplished what he set out to accomplish, what he needed to accomplish. You can attribute this to two things primarily. One is that he went into the debate clearly with lower expectations than we did. And we knew this was going to be the case going in. As an incumbent president, as a wartime president, as somebody who had led the nation through 9/11, we couldn't anticipate that we would be the one with lower expectations.

We had also done a very effective job because of the work of Mark [McKinnon] and Alex [Castellanos] and others at helping to define John Kerry. That helped lower his expectations. Senator Kerry himself also lowered his own expectations. On the day of the first debate, we started getting reports that he had gotten a manicure. We were stunned. We couldn't believe that he would actually do that on the day of the first debate. So he did go in with lower expectations and when we were looking at sort of the structure that would serve us best, we really believed going in that Senator Kerry and Senator Edwards were going to be dangerous for us. Senator Kerry was an extremely talented debater. He'd obviously been in the Senate. He'd prevailed in every debate he'd been in. And Senator Edwards is clearly someone who'd made millions of dollars by convincing audiences of his point of view. So we looked at that and made an assessment about how can we make them less dangerous for us.

And our take on that was if there is a very tight frame, if there's a way for people sitting at home to see that time has expired, then when Senator Kerry goes over time, it will just drive home the point that he is long-winded, that he is used to being in the Senate and he's not able to make concise, clear, and short arguments. I think we have to give credit to Senator Kerry for his preparation and for living within those time limits. I think Bob's right that when we had the lights where people could see the lights at home and when Senator Kerry had clearly practiced to be able to deliver answers within a two-minute time frame, it served him well.

On the issue of sort of the teams negotiating this agreement, I think you saw that there was a difference between the press coverage in 2000 and the press coverage this time. This time from our side anyway, the negotiations were done primarily between Secretary Baker and Vernon Jordan. And having the two of them be able to work the deal out amongst themselves really led to not very much leaking. And I remember at one point being in a meeting with Secretary Baker when Vernon Jordan called and said, "Look, I just read this in the *Washington Post*. It says you guys only wanted two debates. You know what are you doing trying to argue this out in the *Post*?" And Secretary Baker was able to say to him, "Look, if you don't hear it from me, it's not true. And you can just take that to the bank and you can know we're not arguing this out in the press." And I think that did serve us well.

I differ with Bob, though. I would say after the first debate we clearly accomplished what we had to accomplish. And I would say from the vice presidential debate on through the last debate, we prevailed. Looking at the polls after the first debate, we frankly took some comfort because we said this is Kerry at the top of his game. This is Senator Kerry doing the best that he's ever going to do and his best gets him at best even with us. And so we knew that it was too much for him to hope to be at the top of his game for two more debates. And so from our perspective, we knew what we had to do in the following debates and we feel that we, in fact, did accomplish it.

A couple of other points I think it's important to note. In all of the debates, I think President Bush was really doing something that's a little bit counterintuitive for an incumbent. He was not running a feel good campaign. He wasn't saying it's morning in America. He wasn't saying we're going to build a bridge to the twenty-first century. He was being very straight with the American people. He was saying we're a nation at war. We face an historic threat, a threat of historic proportions. We face a challenge that we're probably going to face for our lifetime and he was presenting them his response, how we're going to address that threat, how he's going to keep us safe.

I think that sort of straight talk built his credibility. The American people had come to know him as someone who was very credible, who was going to deal straight with them. And you saw the same thing on domestic issues as well. You saw it with Social Security, for example, where George Bush said this isn't okay. We have to fix it. If we don't fix the current system, you know our kids and our grandkids are going to suffer. And at the same time he had Senator Kerry talking about sort of pushing it off. It's not a problem. It's not an issue. And I think that helped to reduce Senator Kerry's credibility.

I also think throughout that Senator Kerry was never able to lay out a coherent position on the war on terror or on the war in Iraq. You've heard repeatedly how nuanced his position was. You heard him repeatedly throughout the debates talk about and assert that he only had one position and in fact it wasn't the case. If you look just at the second debate, for example, you see Senator Kerry at one point close to the beginning of the debate saying, "I've always believed Saddam was a threat. Saddam was a threat. Saddam was a threat before we took him out. Saddam was a threat in 1998," and then a few pages later, if you look at the transcript, you've got Senator Kerry saying, "the sanctions were working. We should have left them in place. Everything was okay." I think that people felt uncomfortable with the way Senator Kerry tried to align his position on Iraq with whatever he believed was sort of the mood of the country at the moment. I think that had a very negative impact, particularly on women voters.

As I traveled the country, you knew women were listening and they were sort of saying, "Okay, what is George Bush going to do for me and what is John Kerry going to do for me?" The sort of gymnastics that they continued to see with Senator Kerry's position I think raised their discomfort level to the point that they didn't feel comfortable voting for Senator Kerry.

The other thing that I think is a little bit counterintuitive is the conventional wisdom was that we would not do well with domestic issues and the notion that the domestic issues tend to favor Democrats. They tend to be the issues on which Democrats do better with the voters. And I was always surprised to read this in the analysis because in many ways it ignores where George Bush came from. It ignores the fact that he was governor of Texas, that the issues about which he feels very passionately are issues like education, issues like health care, Social Security reform. These are issues that he's been working on for many years, feels very strongly about and in fact has done something about and was able in the debates to talk about the progress that has been made and to offer up a very bold program for the future, to really sort of place himself, place the ticket as the choice for Americans to make if you're looking at sort of how twenty-first-century families are going to live and the kinds of programs we need domestically in order to meet our twenty-first century needs.

I want to say a couple of words about the apparatus around the debates. The first is the instant polls and, as Bob [Shrum] said, this whole structure has built up of instant polls and spin alley where everybody rushes out after the debates to talk about how their candidate does. What happens with instant polls makes them I think especially unpredictive of how somebody is going to vote. Basically someone gets a phone call and the pollster says to them, "Watch the debate and when it's done we're going to call you back and ask you what you thought about it." So a person watching the debate from that perspective is going to be watching it very closely like a debate coach. Who made this stylistic point? Who made that stylistic point? They want to sound informed and have something to say to the pollster when they call back. What we saw repeatedly, and I think this is actually the explanation for why we won the election, was even in the instances where focus groups or people who were being polled were saying that they thought John Kerry was effective on stylistic points, you did not see the same numbers saying that meant they were going to vote for John Kerry.

In fact, Senator Kerry's performance in the debates, at the end of the day, did not do what he had to do to convince people that he was going to be a credible and strong leader, that he had a consistent position, that he could explain his record in the Senate.

If you look back at the debates as a whole and think about the moments that stand out in the debates, in the first debate, which clearly is the one in which Senator Kerry did best, the moment that stood out for us was obviously the global test. I think this fits the pattern that we talked about previously today. What the debates do is either solidify in someone's mind a view that they already hold about a candidate or they change their mind. If a candidate says something, even if it's a slip of the tongue perhaps, you know an unintentional, unpracticed [slip], if it meets a perception that people have had of him before or her, then I think it has an impact. That's what we saw with global test. Senator Kerry was not able to respond about the doctrine of preemption without talking about a global test.

In the days after that debate, I think we saw both campaigns talking about this. The Kerry-Edwards campaign put an ad up trying to explain. One explanation I heard at one point was that global test actually meant American test. That seems to me to be a particularly controverted way to try to explain what Senator Kerry was saying. I would say that was the most lasting moment out of that debate.

In the second debate, I think there was an interesting moment that we haven't talked about, that did not get that much coverage. But again I think it helped reinforce perceptions people had about Senator Kerry. During a question about tax cuts, Senator Kerry was being challenged about whether or not the assertion that he was only going to raise taxes on people who made over $200,000 a year was accurate. He got off his stool, walked around the audience, and he said, "Judging from the way people in this room look, nobody here is going to be affected by having taxes raised if you make more than $200,000 except for me and the president and [moderator] Charlie [Gibson]." And I think people said, "What? Judging from the way we look, we don't make more than

$200,000 a year?" I think [that response] fed into the elitist notion that people had about Senator Kerry.

Finally, I think Senator Kerry's mention of my sister [Mary Cheney] in the third debate[1] was a moment that took a lot of people by surprise. You saw across the country a level of shock at that. And again I think that had an impact because at that point there was a notion out there that Senators Kerry and Edwards would say or do anything to be elected. It was about the same time period [in which] Senator Kerry said if John Kerry were president, Christopher Reeve would be able to walk again. Because it fed into that notion, I think it had an impact. So, just in closing let me say I think the lesson for future campaigns is the debates are always part of the overall structure of the campaign. You're not really trying to accomplish anything different in your debates than in your convention or in the time period after the debates. And you have to look at them in that sense.

It's not accurate to look at the debates and ask, "What did the instant polls say?" "Why did the instant poll say what it said?" You really have to look at whether they had an impact on moving people's choice for president. Against that backdrop, one has to say that President Bush was able to accomplish what we needed to accomplish in those debates. Senator Kerry, although a very skilled debater, according to Matthew the most skilled debater since Cicero, didn't translate that skill into convincing people that he was the better choice of the two candidates.

That's my last point. Voters are very smart. No matter how much you hear the pundits spin what happens, no matter how much you hear talk about instant polls, no matter how much we in the campaigns, frankly, work to come up with great lines that we think people are going to remember, at the end of the day the voters take the measure of the candidate.

They look at the debates against the backdrop of what they already know about these people and they make their decision based on that. In this case, they did a pretty good and accurate job of that.

Questions

BOB SHRUM:

I actually found that a really daring and revisionist interpretation of the debates. I wish the Republicans more such debate victories in the years ahead. And I wish it had been a Social Security election, not a 9/11 election.

I just want to correct the record. Senator Kerry's comment about your sister was meant as a compliment. It was not meant in any other way, shape, or form. He had seen Senator Edwards do it [during the vice presidential debate]. In his mind, saying that someone had a different sexual orientation and the family had dealt well with that was not an attack; it was a compliment. I went into the spin room and everybody was saying, "Third big victory for Kerry." Nobody was talking about the Mary Cheney comment. About 20 minutes later the Bush people began to say this is what ought to be focused on in the debate. Now, that may have been good spin, but it was not what Senator Kerry was doing.

LIZ CHENEY:

I do feel sort of that Bob and I reside on different planets. But I think that at the end of the day I can say that your analysis of that was revisionist or not revisionist. What matters, quite frankly, is 2.7 percent, 2.7 percent on November 2. And you know the point I think of our analysis of the debates is that you can be incredibly skilled, you can go through incredible preparation. You can practice good lines. At the end of the day, the American people are going to make their decision based on what they think is real and what's not real. And I have to say I think the most revisionist part of the analysis was the assertion that somehow Senator Kerry laid out a clear position on Iraq because I think it's just about an impossible [conclusion] to accept and to adopt if you look at the fact that he had eleven different positions. And each time he was sort of pushed or asked about it, it changed a bit.

One thing I'd like to ask you about, and I suspect you'll deny this (audience laughs).

BOB SHRUM:

I will deny that there were weapons of mass destruction in Iraq. Anyway, go ahead.

LIZ CHENEY:

All right, in *New Yorker* magazine, Senator Biden was quoted talking about John Kerry's view on Iraq and his vote on the $87 billion. He attributed the shift in his position from voting for the authorization to use force to voting against the money the troops needed to Senator Kerry coming up with learning about new intelligence. He said that new intelligence was Howard Dean's poll numbers. So this is one of your chief foreign policy advisors talking himself about Senator Kerry changing his vote for political reasons. There were many things you all did very skillfully. But I never saw you climbing out of that hole, being able to say this wasn't for political reasons that he shifted his vote. It was for something else. And I think because it was such an important issue for the country, at the end of the day it really hurt him.

BOB SHRUM:

Well the election is over and you won, actually by 60,000 votes in Ohio. The truth of the matter is Senator Kerry's position on Iraq was perfectly coherent. What you cited actually is incoherent and inconsistent. The fact that Saddam was a threat did not mean that the U.S. had to launch an invasion saying there were weapons of mass destruction that weren't there and doing it without allies, which John Kerry had warned all along was a dangerous and bad thing to do. In terms of your next attack, which was to invoke Senator Biden, he's simply wrong about why John Kerry voted as he did. I spent a lot of time with Senator Kerry when he was making that decision. He thought the policy was completely wrong, that the administration had to be held accountable, that standards had to be set. His position informed by his own experience when he came home from Vietnam and felt that people had to stand up against a policy that was wrong.

But I think one can debate these issues without questioning people's motives. I have not disagreed more with anyone in my life than when I used to debate your mother [Lynne Cheney] on *Crossfire*. But I think she sincerely believes what she says she believes. I have a very different view of the world in terms of what we need to do, for example, in foreign policy. We do live on different planets in that sense. But that doesn't mean that I think that George Bush is badly motivated in the decisions he makes. And I know Senator Kerry's position on Iraq was consistent and sincere. I think he actually successfully de-coupled terrorism and Iraq in the debates. And to cite exit polls on Election Day several weeks after the debate as saying that 52 or 53 percent of the people thought Iraq was part of the war on terror doesn't prove or disprove anything about the debates. At earlier points in 2004, we were dealing with numbers where over 65 or 70 percent of the people thought that Iraq was part of the war on terror.

So I grant the sincerity of George Bush and Dick Cheney's positions. And I think it would probably be fair to grant the sincerity of John Kerry's and John Edwards's positions as well.

LIZ CHENEY:

The issue is coherence, not sincerity. The question is, "To what extent on the most important issue of the race were the two tickets able to lay out a consistent set of views and beliefs?" And whether Senator Kerry changed his vote for political reasons or changed his vote because he had a sincere reason for doing so, being unable to coherently explain—or consistently maintain—a position hurt Senator Kerry. That goes to the heart of the other thing we didn't talk about, the whole issue of alliances, frankly. Consistently throughout the campaign Senator Kerry talked about the need to build alliances while at the same time trashing the allies.

Discussion

BILL KNAPP:

Liz [Cheney], I'm just curious. Was the president surprised by the reaction to the first debate? How did he react to it? Obviously whether you thought he won or lost, the reviews were devastating. You know they were pretty personal about his performance. The other question I have is in the Q & A, did you practice the question "had he made any mistakes?" Is it not something he was willing to admit to? Did you ever have the debate about admitting some mistakes? I'm curious about that.

LIZ CHENEY:

With respect to the first debate, if you read the transcript now, and if you had watched the debate without the cutaways, as Bob [Shrum] pointed out, you had a different view of it. We were all surprised by the impact of the cutaway shots. On the issue of "have you made any mistakes," it's a trick question. No matter what we had said, it's a question that would have immediately opened up a whole range of baseless attack that we didn't need to bring down upon ourselves, frankly. And so I'm not sure there's a good answer to the "have you ever made any mistakes" question. I think the way the president handled it was the right way to handle it. Just as we were pushing Senator Kerry to say would you have voted the same way, I think your campaign was clearly pushing us: "Give us a list of what you think you've done wrong." That would have been a gift to you we didn't want to, we didn't want to give.

NICOLLE DEVENISH:

I'm not doubting what Senator Kerry intended with the comment about Mary. Actually Mary Cheney explained it to me better than anyone else had. It wasn't an attack on Mary Cheney because it was an accurate description. She said, "He didn't attack me." It was the use of Mary to score a political point. I'm certain it was inadvertent [by Mary Beth Cahill] to say that Mary Cheney was fair game [after the debate in which Senator Kerry made mention of Mary Cheney's sexual preference].

We did not say anything in spin alley. It was actually the next day when some of the anecdotal quotes and stories said we were really disturbed by that comment. We did nothing of the sort in spin alley. That was something in the regional coverage the next morning that Senator McCain actually responded to. So I just think the record should reflect the accuracy of that sequencing. It didn't really strike us when Edwards said it. His intention to say something nice was clear. I'm not doubting Senator Kerry's intention. But tied together with your comment about Mary Cheney being fair game, we had a different perception of the three hits on Mary. As Mary educated us, it was not a political attack. It was a true statement. But it was scoring a political point because as you made clear, you were very pleased with the ability to score political points. That's what a debate is. And so it just felt very calculated.

JOE LOCKHART:

I understand that, but you're arguing here that somehow that was a political score pointing. I want to understand since you've all talked about it, what point do you think we scored?

NICOLLE DEVENISH:

I think you lost the point. But I think it was a jump shot that you lost. I think you were trying to score one because, as you made clear, a debate is a contest to score points.

BOB SHRUM:

What was the 3-pointer?

NICOLLE DEVENISH:

I'm not sure.

BOB SHRUM:

There was no 3-pointer here. The fact is . . .

NICOLLE DEVENISH:

Well, Edwards said it. You said it and John Kerry said it so it was obviously a strategic message. So I'm just trying to understand . . .

MARY BETH CAHILL:

On what I said. I went on Chris Wallace after [the third presidential debate] and was asked, "Senator Kerry mentioned Mary Cheney. Is that fair game?" I answered the question and that was stupid. I said she is a loved member of the family. She's a valued member of the Bush campaign staff. She's obviously an important person in the Republican Party. And she's an outwardly gay woman. She's fair game. Repeating the question was stupid. That is completely de-coupled, I think. It became part of the dialogue and part of Kerry's comment. It became something else and it became something else I'm sure with a fair amount of effort because at least it distracted attention from the third debate. That's our point. When Chris Wallace asked me, it was the first question on and I shouldn't have answered it. I repeated what he said.

JOE LOCKHART:

I don't think we need to get into a long debate on the sequencing but I was certainly asked about that in the spin room. It was something that was being pushed. It wasn't something that naturally came out. There's certainly some reservations on our part about perpetuating the story after the debate because it was not a good story for us. We won the debate. We think we won the debate and wanted to continue the momentum. What this did was stifle the momentum. It became a story from Wednesday through Sunday. We all know, stories don't just naturally become stories.

I don't think we were naïve enough to think that this wasn't part of post-debate, that this wasn't part of a strategy that both sides were executing. We were trying to get the story less attention. I think you were trying to get it more attention. Having sat through almost as many of the debate preps as Bob and Mary Beth, I can tell you that to execute a political strategy, you have to have one, which means you have to discuss it in advance. This was never discussed so there was no political strategy. That's not subject to debate. No matter what any of you think, it's not subject to debate. Now, what I'm still trying to get at here is what, given that you have a different set of assumptions, what political point do you think we were making, trying to score?

ALEX CASTELLANOS:

Sometimes there is a perception that Democrats can point out Republican moral hypocrisy. "Aren't they nice to the people who are different?"

So yeah I think there are some obvious political hits that are taken this way.

JOE LOCKHART:

In the context of the historical discussion, I think what would be useful on your part is an admission that this became part of an overt political strategy to change the debate coming out of the first debate.

NICOLLE DEVENISH:

We would have loved to have talked about the answer to that last question for four days because I think George Bush said more about who he was in his answer about love than anyone. I think you have moments that reveal things in campaign cycles. That answer was very revealing. So the notion that there was nothing we would have rather talked about is flat wrong. There are also things, though, that candidates do that reveal things about themselves and we certainly thought this revealed something about John Kerry. Don't take our word for it. It was reflected in the polls. So it was a revealing moment and that was how we talked about it.

BOB SHRUM:

You can't have it both ways with the polls. You can't say "ignore the polls" and then say "don't take our word for it. Take the polls." The truth is that over a period of time, after each debate, the polls showed that people thought that John Kerry won the debates. The data in all of the national polls, aggregated with our polls, showed John Kerry gaining ground after each debate and our data showed us gaining real ground in the battleground states. It was a trend that continued until the Osama bin Laden tape was released. That to me is the bottom line of the debates. Nicolle, you're really good. But I do not believe that you could have spun George Bush's last answer about "love" into a major news story for five days.

NICOLLE DEVENISH:

I didn't say five days. But to think we came out of the debate wanting to talk about nothing other than Mary Cheney is ludicrous and wrong. To think that we didn't want to come out of that debate talking about our performance and . . .

BOB SHRUM:

That we agree on. We are in total agreement. We wanted to come out of that debate talking about your performance and our performance. We should have agreed on that.

NICOLLE DEVENISH:

The day we die that might be it.

LIZ CHENEY:

We felt very good about our performance in that debate. And I think the overall bottom-line lesson in this is it never is useful to bring up an opponent's family. Period. You just don't do it in a debate. Whatever the motive was, whatever the plan was, whatever the strategy was, it doesn't make sense to bring up your opponent's family.

BOB SHRUM:

As I said, there was no motive. There was no plan. There was no strategy. John Kerry was actually trying to pay a compliment to your family.

ALEX CASTELLANOS:

No motive, no plan, no strategy, I've been in that campaign. Your friend, James Carville, on *Meet the Press* the other day said something interesting. He said that he thought the Democratic Party had no narrative. There are lots of words we could substitute for narrative, ideology, a coherent set of beliefs, a North Star. There are some people who think that is the problem with the election and I think it's one reason Republicans get accused of questioning Democrat motives. A certain school of us think we don't know what they are. We really don't see that narrative that Carville was talking about either. There's another school that looks at this election and says, no, no, it was not at all big picture. It was tactical. If it had not rained in Ohio, if we'd had better candidates, if the debates had been later, if the Osama bin Laden tape [had not aired], other things like that.

BOB SHRUM:

First of all I may not give this impression, but I approach all of this with a certain amount of humility and resignation in the sense that if 60,000

votes had changed in Ohio, we would be on different sides of the dialogue than we are today. So in that circumstance where anybody can
attribute any cause to victory and defeat because lots of different factors
could have changed a few votes. I don't think the Democratic Party lacks
a narrative. I think the Democratic Party is fundamentally about fairness,
about standing up and fighting for ordinary middle-class people, about
opening up doors of opportunity. I know you would probably dispute
whether the best way to do that is what I would like to do—for example,
to see to it that 45 million Americans don't go without health care in
this country and that we don't have a prescription drug benefit that gives
$150 billion windfall to drug companies and does dirt to seniors. But I
think the Democratic Party has a narrative.

Look, I was very involved in this campaign. Maybe we didn't get the
narrative out as well as we should have. But I'm also mindful of the fact
that if you change a few votes a whole bunch of Republicans are running
around saying, "Oh my God, what did we do wrong." The truth of the
matter is that this was a close, tough election. I believe it was, in the end,
an exceedingly hard election for us to win. And I did not see how hard,
I will tell you, until after the election. I believe it was fundamentally a
9/11 election. The Bush-Cheney campaign did a brilliant job of creating
the images at the convention and in some of the advertising that connected President Bush with a seminal moment in American history.
Even when John Kerry had passed the threshold on national security,
people were still very reluctant to change the leadership in the post-
9/11 world. You and I have been in 20 campaigns where people call up
in the morning to say: "Turnout is up, turnout is down." Or: "People
are waiting in wheelchairs." You know all the stories that we hear all the
time. I don't think you can attribute this election to any of that.

ALEX CASTELLANOS:

When you look at changes on the Senate, where you look at the changes
in governorships, when you look at partisan decline, decline in Democratic partisan intensity in one of your charts up there, do you think
American people are clear about what the Democratic Party is now?

BOB SHRUM:

I don't think the American people are entirely clear about what the
Republican Party is about. They're very clear about George Bush. And,
as Matthew said earlier, even when they disagree with him, they think he
stands up for what he believes. But I don't believe people—and I think

the president will discover this in the next year—like his Social Security plan at all. I don't think they thought much about it all.

In terms of both parties, people have a set of different impressions. The reason you keep trying to call us "liberal" is because you don't want us to be seen as fighting for ordinary people, fighting for the middle class. You want us to be seen as an ideological fringe. That's what you're trying to do. But it is absolutely true that there is a core set of beliefs in the Democratic Party. If you don't believe that and you believe that it's all sort of incoherent, I invite you to go run in the next set of Democratic primaries for president, say what you think, and see how voters react to you.

Note

1. In the third debate, moderator Bob Schieffer asked, "Both of you are opposed to gay marriage. But to understand how you have come to that conclusion, I want to ask you a more basic question. Do you believe homosexuality is a choice?" Senator Kerry responded (in part), "We're all God's children, Bob. And I think if you were to talk to Dick Cheney's daughter, who is a lesbian, she would tell you that she's being who she was, she's being who she was born as."

Chapter 5

The Press/Campaign Relationship

Joe Lockhart

Joe Lockhart *is a partner with the Glover Park Group, a media relations and political strategy firm. A veteran of political campaigns, he most recently was senior advisor to the Kerry-Edwards 2004 campaign. He served as chief spokesman for President Clinton and the Clinton administration from 1998 to 2000. Before joining the White House in 1997, he was national press secretary for the Clinton-Gore 1996 reelection campaign. He was the deputy press secretary for the Dukakis-Bentsen 1988 presidential campaign, traveling with the nominee. In 1984, he was assistant press secretary for the Mondale-Ferraro campaign and during the 1980 Carter-Mondale campaign he was a regional press coordinator. An award-winning journalist, Lockhart has held key positions at SKY Television News of London, Cable News Network (CNN), and ABC Network News.*

I have a unique job here to talk about the campaign-press relationship in a campaign that I was only in for the last two months. I want to do one thing first which is to acknowledge the work particularly of Stephanie Cutter who was the communications director and was there almost from day one and who slogged through the primaries and many difficult times and many good times. But also a couple other people, Chad Clanton, Phil Singer, David Ginsburg, Joel Johnson, and Deborah DeShong. But because I wasn't there during the primaries I'm really just going to skip over that and try to take a step back and do a slightly more historical perspective. The one nice thing about having gray hair is people believe that you've been doing campaigns for fifty years like I have been. I am also going to take the task here literally of talking about the campaign-press relationship. I wasn't quite sure what that meant so I just decided to take it literally.

I did my first presidential campaign in 1980 for Jimmy Carter—his reelection. That was eight years after the seminal book, *The Boys on the Bus*, which I think a lot of us read and thought, boy, wouldn't that be fun to do. In fact, I don't think it was ever quite as romantic as that, but we certainly live in a world now where it's much less romantic than that 1972 work.

I do remember 1980 and the important moment where, as a young person on the campaign, I was invited over to a bar called the Class Reunion where Jody Powell, the president's press secretary, held court every night. There literally was a small elite group of people who worked all day together and then spent most of the evening together drinking with a certain camaraderie and shared sense of responsibility. I think what struck me having been out of the campaign business or the political journalism for four years, in 2004, is how much that has changed. In 2004 the relationship was best described for me as totally transactional. There is now missing what when I started doing this was a shared sense of responsibility to the system, where both sides felt like there was great value in these campaigns and in government. That has been replaced.

In this transactional relationship, it's now a group of people, and I will include myself in the group, of pretty skilled manipulators, manipulating people who are very well aware of being manipulated. The result of that is campaign coverage that focuses very little on what is happening, what the candidates are saying, what the voters think, and focuses on why we're doing things, what our motivations are, what techniques we're using, and what process we are going through—how we make the sausage. It's a very important point that that is how the coverage is.

The best example I have is what we in the campaign call fake ads. Bill Knapp is looking at me with a very sick look on his face. We had this big war room, and I was on one end of it, and to get to the speechwriters and the bathroom and other things I had to go by this narrow area and walk right by where Bill Knapp sat. Pretty much every time I walked there I ordered up a fake ad. It got to the point where I suggested that he open a take-out counter, where we could just call ahead and say, here's the ad we want (Bill—my solution was to stop drinking water). We did probably two dozen ads in this campaign in the two months I was there that we never had any intention of really putting on the air, never had any intention of really having a voter see, and every reporter who reported on it knew that. There were a few who every once in a while would rattle our cage and talk about the ethics of this. There were times where I forced Bill [Knapp] to find something on Des Moines cable, which cost 12 dollars, to satisfy one of them. So I'm just going to talk for a minute a little bit about where I see the press and then how we reacted to that, at least in the last couple months, and this is my favorite part where I get to critique the press.

The press is very process focused. The best example I have of that is somewhat personal. If you do a Google search on Kerry and you put in key words like North Korea, Iran, terrorism, [you'll find] there are very few subjects that will get more hits than "staff shake-up." Being part of one of these so-called staff shake-ups, this was a story that wouldn't go

Joe Lockhart

away because it involved all of the pure elements of process. Not what the candidate stood for, not who he was, not what he wanted to do, but who was pulling the strings. The only thing that I will give to my colleagues here that's better than a staff shake-up story, is a media staff shake-up story. You did a very nice job with the Rather thing [On September 8, 2004, CBS aired a story questioning George W. Bush's Texas Air National Guard service. When challenged, CBS was unable to confirm the authenticity of the memos] so I give you credit for that. Early retirement is not so bad.

Second. Poll driven. It's clear that the horse race dictates large segments of the coverage. There are a couple problems with that. Most of the public polls were wrong. I think, as Matthew [Dowd] said repeatedly today, this campaign traded in a very narrow band, all the way through. Very little happened in this campaign as far as fluctuations in the public opinion. Almost any day, it was either plus 5 or minus 5. We had polls showing us down 13. We had polls showing us up 8. We had polls showing us up 12 or 11 at one point. They were ridiculous on their face. Why were the polls damaging? Two reasons. One, they dictated how the press looked at the candidacies. There is a winner-loser mentality in the way political journalism works. I'll give you an example that is not about this campaign so it doesn't look like I'm whining here. I think it goes back to the first year of the Bush presidency.

Most people look back at the first year of the Bush presidency and say he had a very good and popular year. But if you look a little closer, that's not true. He had a trajectory that was upward and then hit a very significant bump. Then September 11 happened and changed the dynamic. If you go back and look at what was involved with that bump, a lot of it was the coverage. So what changed the coverage? It's my belief that what was the tipping point was Jim Jeffords moving from being a Republican to being an Independent [on May 24, 2001]. And again, this is oversimplification, but I think a group of reporters came to the White House every day before that saying, "We think they're geniuses, we think they know what we're doing, so we better say good things about them." But every day they were getting a little less sure. Jeffords's move obviously changed that.

In campaigns these public polls had a negative impact in the last two months on our ability to make the case that we knew what we were doing, which is important. Two months in a campaign is long-term planning. You need to be able to, in a strategic way, lay brick on brick on brick to build a strong structure. It's like a business that wants to make long-term investments. The same thing with business on Wall Street we have with the press. Businesses are constantly forced to do quarterly earnings and meet a number, and that often shortchanges long term strategic goals. We were forced on a day-to-day basis at times to do things which didn't necessarily make sense in a long term, as far as building brick on brick a strong structure, because we had to show that we were in this race. It precipitated a very healthy and interesting debate within the campaign about when we spend our money. I think we had a core belief from 2000 that we didn't want to get outspent at the end, but September first, second, third, and fourth, I had a pretty core belief that if we lost touch with the president we might never be in this campaign. We ended up kind of splitting the difference. But it was something worth looking at academically in the future.

The third thing is, and some of this is fairly obvious, is conflict-driven. Nothing has importance unless there's a she-said to go with the he-said. And we saw that throughout the campaign.

Fourth is what I call the gotcha journalism. Just consider these two examples. The president of the United States sat on a bus with Matt Lauer and in the course of what I guess was a 30-minute interview at one point said, "Well I'm not sure you can win the war on terror." Put that aside. The *New York Times* worked for six months on a Sunday story that was about 10,000 words which was a comprehensive indictment of the intelligence abilities of this country post-9/11. The Matt Lauer story reverberated for the rest of the campaign. It was a big story for two or three days, and it didn't mean anything. It was a nuanced argument and I think we understood what [the president] meant by that. But politics is politics—we exploited it. And the press went crazy for three or four days. It came up in the debates. It just never seemed to go away. The 7,000 (sic) word story died an immediate death. It was dead on arrival on people's doorsteps on Sunday morning because it was complicated. Because there was no great moment in there where Condi turned to Ridge, saying, "We don't know what we're doing, do we?" There was no real significant gotcha in it and that I think makes the point.

The last is that reporters are human beings and they're informed and their priorities are formed by their own experiences. We look at campaigns within the broader context of what's gone on in the last few decades but these reporters did not live through the recession and high interest rates and high inflation of the '70s, Watergate, the civil rights movement, even Operation Desert Storm. 9/11 was the seminal moment in their reporting career and probably their lives as far as news coverage. It was very difficult to get past that and get reporters as a group to think there were other issues in this campaign that were important. There was no energy talking about health care in this campaign. There was no sense either of this is important and I believe it's important and my editor will put me on the front page and my career will go somewhat better if I do an exposé on the manufacturing crisis, which was something very real to a lot of people, but not necessarily the people covering this campaign.

Impact on the campaign. I joined the campaign in late August and I think August was a very difficult month for the campaign as articulated by all of the people who have come up here for a lot of reasons. But I think the fundamental decision we made immediately was what I call, "let's stop banging our head against the wall. Let's stop worrying about the press covering process and then let's give them process that helps us get our message out." There were a couple immediate ramifications of that. One of the things the Swift Boat attacks did, in addition to whatever it might have done to the public, was change the press's impression of John Kerry. I can't overstate the importance of how they judge winners and losers. There's nothing more boring than covering a candidate who's not going to win, who isn't fighting back. As a reporter, you are going to penalize that person. I think Kerry paid a price, whether it was the right decision or not, for waiting, or not counter-attacking when counter-attacked. It got into reporters' psyches about John Kerry. So we knew that we had to change that. One of the ways we did was we went looking for a fight wherever we could find it. Sending Max Cleland down to Texas [August 25, 2004] had the beginnings of a significant impact on the reporters covering us because at least they saw that if they were going to be on the wrong side covering the wrong campaign they were going to have a little fun doing it. We were going to push back.

The second example I have of that is the midnight rally in Ohio after the Republican convention. . . . We knew that weekend was important to blunt the surge coming out of the convention, and we, for whatever reason, were not [planning on] starting until about 11:30 in the morning. That concerned me a lot, but he had been on vacation and the scheduling worked that. Someone came in and said there was a rumor the president was going to Scranton to do an event that night. I just went crazy and said we can't wait 'til noon the next day. We've got to do something. We've got to schedule a counter event. They were looking at the morning. Ten minutes later someone came in and said it's a bad rumor. It's not happening. So I went back to what I was doing and it struck me. Well, we started looking at doing a midnight rally in Ohio. And we did it. Again it played into the idea that we needed to prove that we were aggressive, not passive, and we were viable. This had nothing to do with affecting the poll numbers and impacting the ultimate effect on the election.

In the 2000 election debriefing my partner, [Gore adviser] Carter Eskew, said that he had totally underestimated how different presidential campaigns are from governors' races and senate races and how important the free press is, the earned media, whatever you want to call it. In senatorial and gubernatorial races, by and large, until the very end, the local press doesn't cover the races. People don't see a lot of that on television and in the newspapers. I can't explain the reason for that. It just is. The primary way you get information about candidates is through ads. In presidential campaigns, the way you get information is a blend, and very often the free media pushes the paid media and sometimes it works back and forth, but they always work in concert. Campaigns that are successful are able to couple those. In campaigns that are not successful, the public gets mixed signals and that was certainly the case here. One of the main things we tried to do was couple up what we were doing with our paid media with the things we were trying to do with the free media.

Because we needed the free media to get our message out, because at this point in time we were behind, we changed the way we looked at the events. Our message had to meet three different criteria for getting on the schedule. They go very much to the process of the press. One, there had to be some fundamental indictment of some policy of the president. It could be Iraq. It could be foreign policy in general. It could be the economy. It could be outsourcing. But it had to be there. But that wasn't enough when it came to Bush. Secondly, it had to go to motivation. "Okay, so why would he pursue a policy that results in lost jobs?" There had to be a piece of that in there. And finally, the third piece had to be a Kerry solution. It's a formula that worked because it wasn't such a bad formula in and of itself. We did lose, but the strategy did work for us as far as getting our message out because the press understood it and it was exactly what they wanted. It was mirroring what they were looking for in this game of manipulation that goes on back and forth. That is a broad point.

The ultimate point was to try to unleash John Kerry's message in the most effective way. We've come at this from a bunch of different ways today. I'll do it my way very quickly, which is Iraq, and the war on terror, and John Kerry's position on Iraq, which was central and essential to being able to get his message out. As Bob [Shrum] mentioned, there was a fight going on all year between how you looked at Iraq, whether you looked at it from one end, which was as part of the war on terror, or from the other end, which we wanted people to look on it as having nothing to do with the war on terror, and, in fact, taking it one step further, undermining the war on terror.

Where we were on September first made it impossible for us to prosecute that case. There was a Gordian knot that needed to be cut. It needed to be cut in a way where John Kerry could get out and speak more forcefully on his opposition to what was going on to Iraq. Now it was not the easiest thing in the world to do. One, I think the campaign was rightfully concerned about how you answer this next question which is "Okay, you're fully into the trap that was laid for us, if that's your position, Saddam Hussein would still be in power in Iraq." That was a very serious strategic hurdle which took some time for us to get over. We came to the conclusions that it was essential to get over it in order to prosecute the case we wanted to prosecute, both on Iraq and on other issues, domestic issues as well.

The second thing was the press believed that they had us in a box that they wanted to see if we could get out of. It wasn't as if we could stand up one day and say, "Okay, well on Iraq, forget yesterday. This is what we're saying today." So we did this pretty methodically. We did a series of four speeches, culminating with the NYU speech, which I think did open up the ability for John Kerry to press his case. He did it most effectively in the debates, but I think relatively effectively at various moments through campaign events, and I think it did allow us to more effectively make domestic issues part of this campaign because it fell into a pattern we were trying to sell that the president had made wrong choices on both foreign policy and domestic issues. So, from the campaign message and press operation, that was the most important thing that happened. Those speeches gave Kerry a lot of running room; obviously, not enough at the end.

There's a lot of talk in our campaign about reaching a threshold and I agree. I think we reached it. I think what was needed beyond that was to take Iraq and show that it brought in to question the president's ability to prosecute the war on terror. I think that's where we fell short for a number of reasons. I think the bin Laden tape is important. Beslan is important. I think we got one thing done well, the second thing not so well.

I wrote down a note on the way up here about the biggest miss of the press. I think it's that the press covered this campaign in a manner that didn't reflect what was going on in the campaign; the press covered it primarily by taking a poll once a week and saying who was ahead and who was behind and they were polling in the wrong places. They were doing a national poll which didn't have a lot of relevance in any given time. It ended up at the end of the election sort of falling in line. That might have been an accident. While they were saying all the right things about how important Ohio and Florida were, they weren't spending a lot of time polling in Ohio and Florida, and Wisconsin and Iowa, and in all of the other places that were important to this campaign. I remember complaining to someone who's in the news business at a senior level and getting this gentleman to admit that, yes, their polls drive their coverage and that, no, they're not polling in the states that are important. He allowed to me that that reason was financial. They couldn't afford to do it like we could. It struck me as a major lapse in the coverage. The ones who were self-aware and smart enough knew that they didn't have the tools to cover this campaign properly but still covered it using inadequate tools. I think that hurt us a lot.

It is hard to measure looking back on a campaign empirically how it hurt, but it is my instinct and feeling that spending so much time making the case that, yes, we could win this campaign hurt our ability to actually go out and talk to voters about why we should win this campaign.

Battleground strategy. This was a different campaign than I have participated in before in a couple ways. Campaigns are generally about making a national case using national media. I think in the two months I was there we sat maybe half a dozen times at most with network anchors or major newspapers to do interviews. We did satellite interviews in local markets almost every day of the campaign with John Kerry and with the other three principals. There were local anchors on a first name basis with our principals because they were talking with them so often. I know the Bush-Cheney campaign did also. Editorial boards. I had always started campaigns thinking you had to go in and talk to the big newspapers. We talked to none of them in this campaign. We did sit down with the *Des Moines Register,* the *Milwaukee Journal,* the *Columbus Dispatch,* the *Orlando Sentinel,* half a dozen others, and we actually did pretty well in those. You can argue the effectiveness of them.

Transformed media. There has been a lot of discussion about how transformational this election was on the electorate. I don't tend to believe that we know enough [to know whether] the electorate in this country has changed. I do think, though, that we're going to look back at this election as a transformational election on the media and how people get information. I think this is the last gasp of the network news dominance and prominence, of the major newspapers. Nothing ever dies cleanly but I think we are seeing a dying medium. In struggling to figure out what happened in this campaign, it's one of the things that I focused on. If I look back as objectively as I can and say, Okay, do you look at two months of a campaign, which is 45 nights of network news? Did we win or lose the 45 nights? I think we won more than we lost. If you look at the major newspapers, was their coverage better for us or better for them? I think we did Okay. I think we probably did a little bit better. We still lost.

What I take from it is there is a transformation going on. People don't trust their normal filters and they're now building their own because they now have the tools to build them. That's only going to increase. The Internet is not well understood. We focused on fundraising, using the Internet not as much on organizing as I think our counterparts did.

I'll give you two examples of how powerful a medium it can be as far as dealing with getting information out. First with Swift Boats. I don't think we—and I wasn't there, but, I'm pretty sure the Internet was not used primarily as a defense. [The campaign mounted] a more conventional defense; John Kerry got up and gave a speech saying you're all crazy, you're lying about my record. There were some ads, and the result was not such a pretty picture for us.

The second example is an attack on us by Sinclair Broadcasting. They wanted to put up this hourlong documentary that was not complimentary of Senator Kerry's Vietnam record. John Kerry never gave a speech about Sinclair Broadcasting. Some very determined people using the Internet and alternative sources literally brought a major corporation to its knees. They were in our office with their lawyers begging us to back off. We could honestly say, we didn't control it anymore. It had taken on a life of its own. We certainly seeded it and fed it but it had taken on a life of its own.

To the extent that anybody here is sitting here in 2008, I predict that we're going to be looking at a much different media world. It is impossible to predict at this point who it helps and who it hurts. The smart people will figure it out. The manipulators will figure out how they can get into that manipulation business.

Nicolle Devenish

Nicolle Devenish *was appointed assistant to the president and director of communications for the White House in January 2005. She served as communications director for Bush-Cheney 2004 from May 2003 through November 2004. Prior to joining the campaign, Devenish was special assistant to the president and director of media affairs at the White House where she oversaw regional press strategy and outreach. Devenish was Florida Governor Jeb Bush's press secretary in 1999 and communications director for the Florida State Technology Office in 2000. She also served California's Assembly Republican Caucus from 1997 to 1998 and worked for the California Republican Party in 1998.*

There were cases in which the two campaigns would describe themselves as being on "different planets" as Liz Cheney and Mr. Shrum just did. I don't think the press staffs from the two campaigns felt that way. We shared a lot [of experiences]. We were on a lot of the same [cable] shows together. We shared reporters—some were kind and some were crazy. We were all in the same stories. People are surprised to hear that the two campaigns, at least in communications, weren't nearly as harshly divided as maybe the country seemed to be.

I think it's also significant that the Democratic candidate for president

Nicolle Devenish

and the Republican candidate for president both had women in charge of their communications operations. That was a first in the history of presidential campaigns.

The last general thing I'd say about communications is if you're interested in communications, if you're here or interested in politics, message is a lifeline for campaigns. Message development and strategy, which is what I was going to focus on, are central to everything that happens in a campaign. Much of the discussion about advertising has [focused on] its intersection with earned media, and so much of your travel is to deliver a strategic message in a market where maybe your polls were doing something. And so much of your event planning and [deployment of] your surrogates is determined by the message that you need to convey on that day in that market.

I think the most important words we uttered in the campaign were 14 words: you may not always agree with me but you'll always know where I stand. They captured George Bush's strengths and they really pinged Kerry's weaknesses for a large duration of the campaign. Women especially were uncomfortable with a man who couldn't seem to commit to a single position. I don't need to debate it. This was the message that we delivered to the press on Kerry's position on Iraq. As a Republican campaign, you don't tell the press anything [and expect] that they [will] take your word for it. You must show it. So this is what we laid out:

John Kerry voted for the war on Iraq. His brother was referenced in a New Hampshire paper saying there were some political considerations there because he was going to run for president. John Kerry said to Doyle McManus on *Face the Nation* that a vote against the 87 billion dollars with troops in the field in combat would be, quote, irresponsible. Two weeks later John Kerry voted against the troops in the field in combat. John Kerry then said that he voted for it before he voted against it, famous words uttered in West Virginia. He said a few weeks later that it was, quote, a complicated matter, and then he said to Diane Sawyer before the first debate that he's, quote, proud of that vote and that it was, quote, a protest vote.

As a Republican communicator there's very little persuasion you do with the press. You rely on research. You rely on your opponent's record. And you rely on facts and our response operation. [In these areas] I think [we] broke a lot of new ground. In December of '03 I hired a director of response, Steve Schmidt, who was one of the real stars of this campaign. [Steve currently serves as deputy assistant to the president and counselor to the vice president]. He had a staff of 10 people on the campaign. We had a screening of [the film about the response team developed by the Clinton 1992 campaign] *The War Room.* In December of '03 when the Kerry team and my counterpart Stephanie Cutter were fighting for their political lives over there and getting out messages to defeat the other Democratic candidates, we were already conjuring up messages targeting at whoever emerged from the Democratic primary. So in December, our quotes in the papers were, "whoever emerges will be someone who was against the ban on partial birth abortions, against the Bush tax cuts aimed at working families, by and large against funding for our troops, and by and large looking at nine of them, they mostly had weak positions on intelligence and defense." We introduced values in December of '03 and we used a values argument to describe the field of nine candidates.

The message creation for the president came from the president. I can't overstate the gift we had in him. Someone who knew exactly what he wanted to do, exactly where he wanted to lead this country, and exactly what made him different from his opponent. Crafting messages for the president is really just a matter of capturing policies he believes in, places he wants to lead the country, and messages he wants to communicate. With our Kerry message, a lot of what we did was to rely entirely on his votes and on his record and there was very careful attention paid to accuracy and our credibility.

I think if you study Republican campaigns, one thing you have to work hard at is getting a fair shot with the press. If Joe felt like he swam uphill sometimes with the press, we were vertical sometimes. We did feel that we got a lot of fair coverage from a lot of individual reporters and I'll leave the bashing of media institutions to others. I didn't have time to think too much about it.

The message creation was really central in our campaign. I'd describe it as live wire between the vice president's communications folks, the White House, and the campaign. 24/7 it was really buzzing. The group created [and adjusted] the message around the clock and [responded to] whatever happened in that day. We were faster, more nimble, and more agile than certainly any incumbent campaign had ever been in responding and driving the message. And much of that was because of this response operation that was given a mandate of being on offense. Response operations of previous presidential campaigns were rapid response—responding to the attacks. The message that was delivered, and these stories are often the stories written by the reporters traveling with your opponent, so this would be the Kerry press corps, was often responding to whatever issue Kerry had attacked us on. We tried to turn that around and shove every response through the prism of what we were offensively try[ing] to convey about Kerry. So if he attacked on Iraq, we got in our points about these positions, "well, that's an interesting comment from Kerry today, somebody who's had 11 positions, voted for the war, against [the war, etc]." Our response got back to our offensive messages about Kerry.

Something else that we paid a lot of attention to obviously was local media. Tucker [Eskew] and I actually ran the local media operation at the White House. I remember being out on the road, very early bus trip with the president in mid-May. He was doing a regional roundtable, the first one of the campaign. Somebody asked whether we were doing these on all of the trips. About four of us nodded and said yes. There was a real investment in the regional media. We talked to regional print reporters on just about every trip from March or April of '04 through July. We didn't really start doing a lot of national interviews until August, leading into and coming out of our convention. Then we relied on those relationships, the reporters that the president had a rapport with, to help shape Kerry's coverage when he went into those states. I think both sides really made the same investment in these local reporters. Frankly I think there were actually some reporters in Wisconsin and Ohio [to whom] we'd offer the president and they said, "Oh, God, I've got to take my kid to the doctor, can I skip this one? Will you guys be back?" We'd say sure, sure you can do it next time.

Turning response into offense is epitomized by two things Kerry said that we then turned into very offensive statements. The president had given a speech in Tennessee [on July 12, 2004] where he said knowing now what I know the removal of Saddam Hussein was still the right decision and America is safer because of it. Maybe four weeks later, he had a statement in his speech that said, "There are some things a commander-in-chief must answer with a clear yes or no. John Kerry has not answered whether the removal of Saddam Hussein was the right thing or the wrong thing knowing now what we know." We, as Matthew [Dowd] said, were prepared for him to go one way or the other but were frankly surprised with his response on the lip of the Grand Canyon [on August 9, 2004], where he said that he would have voted the same way. We immediately used it with our press and with his to undermine his credibility on the attacks. How can he attack us for something he just said he would have done the exact same way?

I don't think press people [like Joe Lockhart and me] are the best people to go back and forth on the policy [debate, to rehash things after the fact, in a setting like this]. But the press did not buy that John Kerry had a consistent position on Iraq. They never did and they still don't. They view that as one of the hurdles that he was never able to overcome in communicating a credible alternative on Iraq and the war on terror.

The other gift that stretched his credibility and that we milked for weeks was, he did a lot of shooting guns, and he said "I actually share the conservative values they feel in places like this." He uttered those words in Wisconsin.[1] [He could have said:] "I share the mainstream values," maybe. "I am more in sync with the things people really care about." He could say that "I share their priorities." But I don't know what conservative values he was talking about. He repeatedly stretched his credibility while we, 100 percent of the time, guarded ours as a campaign.

These guys [our ad team] hated showing me their ads because sometimes I would ruin all the fun and say, we can't [say that], but there were no examples of us trying to test our credibility with the press. We knew we needed it and you, as I said, have to work harder at keeping it as a Republican campaign and as an incumbent.

Some other contrasts that got us on offense at times when Kerry [should have been able to] pummel us in the press were the [times we made an optimism-pessimism contrast]. He would attack us, and we [responded by pointing to the inherent pessimism in his attacks]. Ours [ended up being a more powerful message because] it fueled what people were already a little uncomfortable with about the way he sounded and looked and it really blunted a lot of his attacks. For a long time in the spring he was attacking on the economy and when [the economy] didn't look quite as strong he [unveiled] something called a "misery index." I think ultimately they dropped it because it backfired. Talking about a misery index as the economy was growing stronger was a message that didn't work for someone who seemed to step on his own message by having this pessimistic message about the economy when people had generally accepted that it was getting better.

Another kind of broad construct, and we always tried to shove our responses in these broader themes, was talking about the past [versus] talking about the future. I think what stayed with people about the Swift Boats was it was a discussion about the past. It happened at a time when we were about to unveil our plan and vision and message about a second term. We'd waited and waited. We never could have imagined that our message about our vision and plan for a second term could have come at a time when Kerry was so mired in a discussion about the past. And we certainly never could have imagined that a discussion about his service would become a negative for him. So again [we offered] the larger contrast in a discussion about the past with a discussion about the future. Message-wise, we were very disciplined about keeping all of messaging around the convention with this detailed discussion about the president's [vision for a] second term.

We tied paid and earned media together nationally and regionally every day. Every story and every ad and every speech, whether it was Rudy Giuliani in Iowa or Bernie Kerik in New Hampshire or Senator Frist doing something for us, was tied to a paid media release. Every story was reinforced by both of them. We did this because neither was enough to drive a network story alone. You can't just release an ad and not talk about the issue and make it a new package. But if you put together a top notch guest like Rudy who'll go on the *Today* show, you release an ad on terrorism and the vice president gives a speech about it, you can bundle together enough pieces to increase your chances of having network coverage. Certainly when you do that in a local market with an ad targeted to that state you increase your changes significantly of having coverage in that state.

I think our best success was the "winning weapons" [ad that featured disappearing weapons]. That ad was given to the *New York Times* for a national earned media hit. There was an ad created for national cable and then about 25 or 30 events around the country at weapons facilities that earned media in those markets and in those states. There were about 12 state-specific ads that included weapons created in those states that obviously affected the local economies. Again, time was on our side since we were able to plan a lot of this activity in December, in January, and February; what we rolled out in March was a coordinated offensive of paid and earned media.

Tucker Eskew

Tucker Eskew, *president of Eskew Strategy Group, LLC, and senior advisor to Bush-Cheney 2004, began his political career in the national press office of President Ronald Reagan's 1984 reelection campaign. Recently, he led communications campaigns during the Afghanistan and Iraq wars, the Bush-Cheney transition, the Florida recount, and the 2000 South Carolina Republican presidential primary. As deputy assistant to the president and director of the White House Office of Global Communications until December 2003, Mr. Eskew headed the development of strategic communications to promote administration policies and American values around the world. Previously, as director of the White House Office of Media Affairs in 2001, he oversaw strategy and tactics for "outside-the-beltway" news organizations, talk radio, specialty media, and the president's official website.*

I'm reminded of my old South Carolina political days, when I learned that if you're the last dog pulling the sleigh the view never changes. I'm the last speaker in the last session at the end of a good but long day, so I'll try to be brief. You know the view never changes when you're in politics and you think the media focus on process too much. I'm in total agreement with Joe [Lockhart]. They do. Of course they do. In my first national campaign, 1984, the Reagan-Bush campaign, I was quoted in the *New York Times* about Walter Mondale's visuals on Labor Day—how he was walking down a street and the cameras panned to the audience and there was no one there. It was a metaphor; it fit the narrative as we call it. If he couldn't get a crowd in New York, things were really bad. And so the press were focusing on process twenty years ago, and together we still are, but I think some things were different this year. I thought I would touch just a little bit on one or two of those, focusing on the way the White House and the campaign dealt with the press and the way the press dealt with us.

If you examine the narratives through the whole campaign and even some of the analysis leading up to it, you see a press corps seeing the White House as having tried to learn lessons from 1992 and the father's campaign. There's not much talk about that, now that we have the real substance of the campaign to chew on, but we did most things differently from '92 but maybe they were the same in one respect.

A friend who worked on that campaign and this one told me around March, "It feels awful out there. The press, they just hate us." Now I don't necessarily share that exact perspective but I know what this person was getting at. We had a lot of rough patches, not the least of which over the course of the Bush presidency and even in the 2000 Bush campaign is the fact that we're boring sometimes. We're so consistent, so devoted to message discipline and consistency and loyalty to our candidate, our president, and so leak averse, that the media don't have much use for us at times.

Now, is the press biased? Well certainly they're biased for conflict. That's something that goes back a long ways in academic circles, the bias in favor of conflict. There is also bias against institutions, and incumbency, particularly within the presidency, is an institution like no other. We faced the ill effects of an anti-incumbency bias. And I think yes there was ideological bias. Early on in the campaign, Evan Thomas said there was a 15-point advantage to Kerry from media bias. He later revised that downward to 5 points and we could argue that all day and spend another whole seminar, not to mention a number of best-selling books, on the issue of media bias. But going back to that first campaign of mine, I think we learned from Ronald Reagan that you overcome it. It is what it is. You deal with it and you either beat it or it's part of what beats you. You get what you deserve, in a manner of speaking.

You overcome it by being a really strong leader who, as Nicolle points out, said you may not always agree with me but you know where I'm coming from. You also overcome it with a more aggressive effort to respond within the news cycle, and we actually did that this time. It was one thing I think we did differently from 2000 and I think even differently from the first term. Nicolle and I had both been at the White House and been part of an operation that somewhat deliberately pulled back from the

Tucker Eskew

style of rapid response that Joe and Mike McCurry and others at the Clinton White House put on display to a degree that maybe no one will match in our political careers. Yet we sort of backed away from that. [Our decision reflected] the style of an incumbent who thought long and hard about what he believed and stated those principles and put his stake in the ground and tended to stand by things for a little longer period of time if not a lot longer.

Responding more aggressively within the news cycles with our principals—with the president and the vice president, and with others—was something that we did differently that actually helped us some with the press. It goes without saying that, if anything, the press have a bias for news. We were more likely to make news within the news cycle when we usually had previously.

There were a couple of other minor things we did differently. We were much more aggressive with the surrogate operation than we had been in 2000 and in the White House. And Nicolle understood the need very early on to build that up. One of the first conversations we ever had after she went to the campaign was about surrogates and Taylor Griffin in that shop did a masterful job for us. I think the Kerry campaign did very well and was very aggressive with that as well. I did a good bit of that stuff myself, and Brooks [Jackson, director of Annenberg FactCheck.org], forgive me if you've heard me say this before because I've said it a lot. That TV stuff does feel a little like a cheap date. There's no true love. There's no true love, just a little bit of mutual gratification and then you go home. (laughter)

Some of that television stuff we just participated in a lot more heavily than we had in the past. I think Joe's right, media are changing and we're going to all have to adapt to that. On cable, it's like this: You get a soundbite, they get a bite. You get a bite, they get a bite. Get out of here. It's not very gratifying to viewers or participants, but it fills the bucket.

There were a few other novel things. Dr. Jamieson mentioned when we talked before this, the CNN approach to town hall meetings, where Paula Zahn did hour-long debates. I did a couple of those with Tad Divine. Liz Cheney did one. Ralph Reed did one for us. It was longer form programming and as such maybe a little more thoughtful. To echo the message of the president, since we're so good at that, I'll tell you: those debates are hard work.

I sweat through my shirt doing those two hours. It's not easy in preparation or being out there on camera for an hour. An hour of questions coming at you from every direction. It got even harder the second time. The first one, we're told, "You get a minute and a half to respond." The second time, Paula Zahn said to me as we walked out onto the stage, "Oh, by the way, we're just going to let you have 45 seconds." Forty-five seconds to answer a question about whatever, immigration policy, homeland security, you name it. I complained to them later, so I'm not telling you anything I didn't tell them. I think that gave short shrift to what was a pretty good idea, notwithstanding my participation in it.

So that's one thing the press did. I'll give examples of a couple of others. Going into those debates in that spin room. It is surreal and it never gets more surreal than when you're standing there talking and all of a sudden, Triumph the Insult Comic Dog comes up and you're talking and he's opening and shutting his mouth in time to everything you say. Then it gets worse. You get told by the puppetmaster and writer Robert Smigel, who's really a funny guy, very talented *Saturday Night Live* guy, "Oh come on, do a one-on-one with Triumph, because the chief of staff to the president Andy Card has just talked to Triumph." At that moment, every defense I had put up crumbled and I stood there and talked to this damn dog. Joe, you did it. You did it.

NICOLLE DEVENISH:

Ralph Reed might have got[ten] the best interview with the dog.

TUCKER ESKEW:

Ralph Reed had a good one.

JOE LOCKHART:

I'm bitter about this because they didn't use my best stuff. The insult dog asked me, did John Kerry talk too much about Vietnam and I, of course, looked at him and said, no, you can never talk too much about Vietnam. Matter of fact I've been there and I think I had your brother for lunch. (laughter) And he didn't use it, so I'm bitter. I don't like the insult dog. I thought you were supposed to insult the dog. Insult dog.

TUCKER ESKEW:

I'm not going to repeat what I said. I used a word I have never used in a campaign before. Ever.

NICOLLE DEVENISH:

On TV.

TUCKER ESKEW:

On TV.

JOE LOCKHART:

Important point.

TUCKER ESKEW:

Also at one of these debates, CNN, a network I've just complimented, sets up one of their shows and literally the show takes place in the middle of a mosh pit of students. It was a shout-fest. I guess it was entertaining for people at home, but it led to another moment I'm just completely ashamed of. I'm not going to repeat it, but I was on there with [Paul] Begala and you know that's gonna go low (Joe—into the mosh pit) so I think some things were done well in this campaign and some thing[s] were done differently.

I started a blog. Since I wasn't internal to the campaign, I had a little more freedom to do things differently and I learned a little bit from that. I felt that if I'm going to be a communicator and advise others, I should participate in and understand the blogosphere. Mike McCurry, Joe's old friend and partner in this campaign, has said blogs may be to the Democrats what talk radio has been to the Republicans. We'll have to see how that plays out over time, maybe there are some similarities there, maybe some differences, but I'll be right there with you watching it all.

MARK MCKINNON:

There are so many interesting observations about the media that Joe touched on. There are several books being written that are going to examine this cycle. There are many fascinating media stories about this election and the coverage. The Rather story. The blogs and the role of blogs.

Joe talked about conflict. There's a great example that happened during the campaign that testifies that only when there is conflict is there a story. As you probably know, during the course of the campaign there were a number of critical books written about the president. They kept coming out and they'd just keep banging us. There'd be a week's worth of news and we'd put up all our people arguing about the book. There was [Joseph] Wilson's book. There was [Paul] O'Neill's book. There was Anonymous's book. Over and over again a book would come out saying something critical about the administration. We'd put up Condi Rice or Colin Powell or Dan [Bartlett] or Nicolle to argue about the content of these books and [the story] would overwhelm us for two or three days or a bunch of cycles. And finally, I think it was Nicolle, at least I give her credit for it, who said, "You know what, let's try something different. The next one that comes out, and it happened to be Woodward's book, right, let's try an alternative strategy. Let's love it to death. Let's love the book we're with." (Nicolle—we figured no one would do it if it was on our website.) And she said "Let's put it on our website." So the book came out and we put it on our website and let people know that it was on our website so therefore we liked the book, or we must have thought enough of it that we put it on our website. Conflict gone. There's no conflict. We thought the book should be on our website. Everybody should read it. No story.

NICOLLE DEVENISH:

We should have done it with Dick [Richard] Clarke [former George W. Bush adviser who wrote the book *Against All Enemies*, which criticized how the Bush Administration handled terrorist threats. The book was published March 22, 2004].

TUCKER ESKEW:

That might qualify as manipulation. I don't know. I didn't agree with you much about manipulation.

NICOLLE DEVENISH:

If media bias is going to come up it's like resisting dessert when you see someone with the crème brulée. It's stunning to me that the network's [CBS's] position on the story and on the documents is that they were forged but accurate. I can't wait to see what happens when the report comes out, if the network will change its official position but if you go to the website or look at their last comment on that story that's it. I don't even know what that means, forged but accurate.

TUCKER ESKEW:

I told Dottie Lynch the other night at CBS it's always the crime not the cover-up, which they often remind those of us in government. I mean they were responsible for making it worse by the way they explained it, defended it, and attacked those who questioned their original story. And that was their big error. The press, which spends so much time thinking about process and strategy and how we do it, does a terrible job themselves of strategy (Nicolle Devenish: crisis management) and explaining themselves and crisis management, and politics when it comes to their own story.

JOE LOCKHART:

As I was just telling the CBS internal review board in my meeting with them. . . . This goes to one of the things that happens, and again this is obvious but talking about the obvious sometimes is worthwhile. There may or may not have been any news in the president's National Guard

service. I think that's one of those things we won't know. It could be
no story. There could be some story that hasn't been told. But it's very
interesting to see how that all developed. The CBS process drove a lot
of other news organizations to print stories, perhaps before they were
ripe. And the controversy over the CBS story killed some stories that may
have ripened. We just will never know but there is something wrong with
the process where you have what I always call situational ethics in media,
which is you apply one set of rules unless you're under pressure, and
then you apply a different set of rules. And then there's some push back
and you have a new set of rules. You never saw a bunch of investigative
reporters who invested a lot of time and effort in a story run from it
quicker than in the aftermath of the CBS story. That's not what journalism is supposed to be about. It's supposed to be about getting to the
bottom of something, and unfortunately this is just one story we're never
going to know. And again, I will point out, there could be something
there, there could not be. It can be unknowable but I don't think this
particular episode, even if you take CBS out of it, is a particularly good
one as far as looking at how journalists cover campaigns.

MARK MELLMAN:

It seemed to me you guys did a great job on selling the press on the
conflation of the vote to authorize use of force and support for a particular war and invasion at a particular time. I think most people would say
those are two different things, but my question really is, was that an easy
sell? Was it a hard sell?

NICOLLE DEVENISH:

John Kerry's quotes about the first Gulf War made it easy. We have his
quotes. He described it as a vote to authorize war. We held John Kerry's
statements to the Kerry standard in a lot of cases and that was one of
them. I can email you the quotes (no, no, different vote on different
resolution—interrupting comments continue).

TUCKER ESKEW:

We didn't have many things outside of that construct where we were
pushing on an open door with the press, but Nicolle is right: The
absence of talking about the Kerry record gave us more traction when
we really talked about it substantively with just the facts. The more we
did that in the absence of a Kerry defense or even better a promotion of
his record, the more effective our message was. I told people back dur-

ing the spring I don't ever remember working with or for or alongside a campaign where the candidate did not, in speech after speech after speech, say something about something he'd done in a previous job or a previous office or as a civic leader. John Kerry never did talk about his record.

JOE LOCKHART:

I think it was an easy sell but I don't think that's why it was. And I don't think it was just the quotes. I think in looking at this objectively and honestly and looking at it in the way the press keeps score and views this as a game, it was an easy sell because John Kerry seemed tied up by this. I remember a conversation that I had with him where he went through and very logically could tie each and every statement and each and every action and it made sense. My point to him was, great, if we can sit every voter down and take the ten minutes that just took, we're gonna be fine. Absent that, it was too easy to distort. And again, I don't want to devolve back into substance and much of campaigns is about distortion and it goes both ways, but I believe Kerry's views were distorted and his statements were distorted. But, it didn't matter what I thought. The voters weren't clear, and that's why we had to go through the process, which was painful, that late in the campaign, to clear it up and to clear out this sort of political underbrush to get people clear on where he was so he could prosecute his case against the president. That's what the early part of September was about. And if you look at the numbers that were behind us before, we weren't sitting in very good shape. And I think a big part of moving back into a competitive position was his ability to make a clearer connection with the American public on where he stood on Iraq and to make a very strong indictment of the president's prosecution of the war. He couldn't do that earlier. I don't think it was just because of some statements here or there. I think your guy's campaign did a very effective job in tying him [John Kerry] up in knots on this. But he had to do the untying himself and he did that and I think, who knows, if that was done at a different time in the campaign, what the result would be, but again, I think Iraq was an important voting issue for us. It just wasn't enough to get us over the hump by however many votes we lost by in Ohio or in anyplace else.

KATHLEEN HALL JAMIESON:

Let me exercise moderator's privilege and ask three questions and then we'll close. First, what's the biggest deception you think the other side perpetrated about your candidate that the public believed?

JOE LOCKHART:

Can I answer something in the neighborhood of that question and not the question?

KATHLEEN HALL JAMIESON:

No.

JOE LOCKHART:

Then I will dress it up but I have no intention of answering that question, and that's an answerer's prerogative (Kathleen Hall Jamieson—yes, then you can dress it up. Call it distortion if you're more comfortable). No, deception—it's not so much about John Kerry but it was in, and it was central to their campaign and it's just my belief—I know they'll disagree—was in conflating the war in Iraq with Osama bin Laden and the attack of 9/11. You're right, I cannot go and find an explicit quote, but there was a sense created that these things were part of the same thing and directly related when I don't think they were, and I think it was central to the campaign strategy. I know what the answer coming back's gonna be because I've heard it before, but I do think if you're looking for a central deception in this campaign that was it, in my view.

TUCKER ESKEW:

This is one of the different points of view, because when we talked about it, we talked about the way it affected our commander-in-chief. I'm talking about it meaning 9/11. And you can go all the way through all of his discussion of that and that's what it's about. It said something real about him and that's why your efforts to sort of undermine that didn't work. I'm not answering your question, but that didn't work because the majority of voters got it about him. They hadn't just bonded with him personally, which they had over his handling post-9/11. They understood he was going to do whatever it takes, and that going into Iraq was about that.

NICOLLE DEVENISH:

I would say the attacks on Tora Bora were a pretty gross—I mean gross in every way—kind of attack in that Kerry himself had embraced the military strategy in Tora Bora [to use Afghan warlords to try to capture Osama bin Laden at Tora Bora in December 2001]. And his political attack was disputed by [General] Tommy Franks. That doesn't get exactly all the aspects of your question, but the attack that I thought was the greatest distortion of his own past statements. I don't know if everyone remembers this. Kerry, and I think this is what hurt, you talk about the bin Laden tape having an impact. The impact was that in the news cycle where the bin Laden tape came out, Kerry attacked Bush for letting bin Laden go, and said that if he'd been president he would have caught him at Tora Bora. And I think that was so distasteful. Bush's statement that he did, not at a campaign event but he went and stood in front of Air Force One and said John Kerry and I can agree today that no terrorist is going to influence a United States election. In the same cycle Kerry took a whack at him for letting bin Laden go at Tora Bora. On *Larry King Live* in January of '04, Kerry had embraced the military strategy and said, we're probably doing the right thing to protect the lives of the U.S. military and the right thing being . . .

JOE LOCKHART:

Can I just take a . . .

NICOLLE DEVENISH:

But I'm just answering the question about distortion.

KATHLEEN HALL JAMIESON:

One follow-up so I understand what your position is. Do you think the public believed the Kerry position then?

NICOLLE DEVENISH:

Yes.

KATHLEEN HALL JAMIESON:

. . . because the question was two parts . . . what the public believed

NICOLLE DEVENISH:

It was probably, and I don't imagine this team did anything that didn't have a political impact that benefited them, so I've got to assume that attacking Bush for incompetence in tracking down bin Laden had a benefit to them.

JOE LOCKHART:

Well, I think this goes to distortion and sometimes you start believing your own talking points. And on both of these things, the facts do matter here and again. I'm not doing this to devolve into rehashing the campaign, but it does go to taking a step back. Both of those things have an element of truth to them and an element of distortion. So let's look at them. Unfortunately before the tape came out and was made public, we did not have a CIA briefing [about] what was on the tape. John Kerry was doing an interview. Should he have repeated the line he used a hundred times in thirty days about Tora Bora? Probably not. But he had no idea what was on that tape and when he was given the briefing and I was sitting there when he was given the briefing, his first instinct was, I've got to go out and make a statement that says we're all together as Americans, which is exactly what he did. So sure, it was in the news cycle, but didn't know what was on the tape, hadn't seen it—hold on, hold on, let me finish. From a tactical point of view, if we can roll this back and say you shouldn't have said that, sure because it gave you an opening. But it didn't go to John Kerry's character, which is where you took it, and which is a legitimate way to run a campaign.

The second thing you talked about was Larry King. Again this goes to people starting to believe the half-truth in there. The reality of that interview with Larry King, because I went back and looked at it, was he was being asked by a caller, "Why don't you go in and napalm those mountains and caves?" What he was trying to do in that interview was say, "You know what, overall I think our strategy is right." But John Kerry was the first public and most frequent critic of the operation in Tora Bora and there are military commanders who were there who were quoted in the papers as saying that it [the strategy in Tora Bora] was wrong. I don't question Tommy Franks. I'm just questioning that this was something done contemporaneously. You can take a piece of anything and make it mean something it doesn't. That's what politics has become and that's what a lot of this campaign was. So, again, you can conflate a lot of things and add it up to something, but it doesn't necessarily go to where the candidate is.

NICOLLE DEVENISH:

If I could just respond to the response. And so went my life the last eighteen months. Bin Laden doesn't change it up too much, folks. He's got a stump speech and he sticks to it. So if you knew there was a new tape you had a pretty good sense of what bin Laden had to say, so I don't really buy that he hadn't seen the tape. I hadn't seen the tape.

JOE LOCKHART:

In fact there had been two tapes in three years so I don't know that's a stump speech, although we didn't give a stump speech twice in three years. We gave a new speech every time so given that . . .

NICOLLE DEVENISH:

The notion that this defense about attacking Bush on the day the bin Laden tape came out is that they hadn't seen the reel is ludicrous.

JOE LOCKHART:

Here's my point.

NICOLLE DEVENISH:

But it doesn't matter that I thought it was ludicrous, people thought it was ludicrous.

JOE LOCKHART:

I'm not sure that people did think it was ludicrous. I think that the reality is you can focus on anything you want. And if politics was a 100 percent pure, honest business, which it's not, you would have looked at the fact that once the tape had been seen, both of them gave statements that were strikingly similar. I mean that really was the story that day. If we weren't in a competitive environment trying to get every last vote and we were both doing it, and I don't deny [it] on our side. But, I mean somehow the idea that a negative character trait manifested itself in John Kerry that day is just not true, but it's all legitimate as far as the back and forth in a campaign.

KATHLEEN HALL JAMIESON:

Second question. We spent a lot of time trying to get at what the public learned this year and it's important for us to know from the perspective of the campaigns, what was the most important thing you thought the public should have learned from you. So when we're assessing knowledge, we're making all these inferences about what you're putting out there. But it would be helpful for us for you to say, at the end of the day, we wanted this thing known. Not these 75 things but this thing. Was there something central that we should look to our knowledge inventory and say, if the public knew "X," that campaign thinks it succeeded at something important.

TUCKER ESKEW:

Strong leader.

NICOLLE DEVENISH:

I think you saw what we wanted people to have received information on was when the president did his first press conference after he won, what he communicated back were the three or four big policy issues we'd run on and that he was going to follow through and do what he said, so those would be success in the war on terror, growing the economy, strengthening Social Security. . . .

KATHLEEN HALL JAMIESON:

So if we get those in the survey, you've been successful?

NICOLLE DEVENISH:

Yes.

KATHLEEN HALL JAMIESON:

What about Democrats?

MARK MELLMAN:

I guess from our point of view there are probably two things. One was that John Kerry—I guess I'll make it three . . . —that John Kerry was strong and decisive, that he cared about opportunity for the middle class, and that George Bush's policies in Iraq and on the economy had failed.

KATHLEEN HALL JAMIESON:

So the John Kerry position on health care isn't one of them.

MARK MELLMAN:

In so far as it goes to two and three it is, underpinning to two and three.

KATHLEEN HALL JAMIESON:

And the last, this is one for each side so it's cheating. Is there anything you'd redo on Swift Boat attacks? If you could go back and rerun the campaign?

JOE LOCKHART:

You know I wasn't there so I can't answer that.

KATHLEEN HALL JAMIESON:

Anybody?

MARK MELLMAN:

We would have won that one exchange. (laughter)

KATHLEEN HALL JAMIESON:

Okay. Is there a way you would have won the exchange?

MARK MELLMAN:

Honestly I think it's hard to know whether there was a way to win it. I mean, obviously what we did was not successful. That's clear. Was there some other set of things that could be done? It's hard to know. Not to belabor the point but I said many times, first of all you had a set of accusations that were completely ridiculous. You have people on TV saying that John Kerry has rice in his rear end from blowing himself up and yet X-rays saying there's shrapnel in his leg. It's absurd. So you had those things that were clearly false and distortions, and completely taken seriously. However, people stood by their water coolers in the office talking about, "Did you hear what John Kerry did in Vietnam, did you hear what was going on there?" People did talk about that. I would wager that nobody sat by their water cooler and said, "you know we save a thousand bucks under John Kerry's health care plan." There was a story implicit in the Swift Boat ads. It's a false, inaccurate, distorted, absurd story, but it's a story that people can talk about and tell each other. In most of the other stuff that happens in this campaign there isn't such a story so I'm not sure honestly if there's anything specifically anyone could have done differently. There's a lot of things could have been done differently. Would it have changed the outcome? There's no way of knowing.

KATHLEEN HALL JAMIESON:

Last question. We've spent more than 10 years studying political talk radio. We have now captured political consultants for the Republicans and we would like to ask this question. What does it do for you? What do you do with it? Particularly [Rush] Limbaugh and [Sean] Hannity?

TUCKER ESKEW:

It's reinforcing. People go to their own corners in politics. They go back to their own framework and look for a medium or message that is reinforcing. Certainly talk radio helps us. As Matt [Dowd] said, Democrats may go to CBS news or the *New York Times*. "Echo chamber" isn't the right name. Megaphone. Unlike the blogs, it reaches mass, has big scale. And what do we do with them? Sure, we get information to them. Some of them are more prone to using talking points than others. We respect that. Some of them use guests, other don't. Those who use guests, we book very aggressively. So, we work very closely with them.

NICOLLE DEVENISH:

Hannity and Rush are to us what CBS is to the Democrats. It is a place that is entirely friendly and receptive to the Republican message. You don't get that in any mainstream media. It's all at best skeptical and that's all that we can expect. I don't think you can expect the mainstream media to be friendly or embrace your policies, it's not their job. But talk radio is a place that is friendly, receptive and welcoming to [the] Republican message. And let me tell you, I've been on both sides. I was a communications major. I have a master's in journalism from Medill. And I don't have any hostility or anger. I don't rage against the media bias machine. I think it's a waste of time. I wouldn't spend a minute after this campaign doing any of that. But I don't think you can fail to take advantage of the mediums that are friendly to you. You're crazy if you don't. What [did] we do for them? Anything they wanted [in terms of booking guests, allowing them access to events].

JOE LOCKHART:

I want to acknowledge for the record how helpful the Democratic organs—the *New York Times* and CBS—were for me during impeachment. Thank you. We never would have gotten out of it without you.

TUCKER ESKEW:

I'll go back to anti-institutional, anti-incumbent, pro-conflict. Those are all other big factors that also worked against Joe [Lockhart].

Bob Shrum and Tucker Eskew with Mark McKinnon (in background)

MARK MCKINNON:

The media is evolving. The elite media is gone. It is dead. It is turning into fossil fuel. But there's a proliferation and expansion of media across the spectrum. I take myself as an example. I customize my news now. I go to realclearpolitics.com to get all my reading for the day or to Drudge as a home page. The news that I'm getting, and I know it, is a brand of news. I know that it's news that appeals to me; it appeals to my ideology. But as people get more customized in their media, we're going to have customized consumers getting customized news just as they do on talk radio or as they do on CBS or with the *New York Times*. That's going to have an interesting impact on the electorate. So that will be something that will be interesting for you all to watch as it evolves.

Student Questions

FOR JOE LOCKHART:

Question: You mention in the context of the Swift Boat controversy that there are few things more boring for the press than to cover a losing candidate who won't fight back, and that, consequently, the Democrats went looking for a fight wherever possible. With regard to Swift Boats, did you ever consider picking a fight with the press? (asked by Eli Kaplan)

Response: The worst of the Swift Boat controversy was over by the time I joined the campaign in the late summer. Instead of engaging further on those attacks, my strategy was to divert attention from the issue and to refocus the debate by trying to draw blood from the other side.

Question: The Republicans were very successful at downplaying the accusations about Bush's National Guard record by arguing there was a liberal bias in the media, and that received a lot of exposure. Do you think more forceful attacks arguing that the press coverage was journalistically irresponsible could have affected agenda-setting? (asked by Eli Kaplan)

Response: As far as I know, there is no deep-seated bias in the press corps. But there's an important point here: rather than an issue of bias, people should look at the press as the third player in the Republican and Democrat ping-pong game. Journalists will deny an active role in that game, even though they love playing it. In this campaign, Republicans played the game better than us and got better press coverage as a result. But the biggest mistake you can make on a campaign is to assume that your case will be judged on truth and facts alone—it very rarely is.

For Nicolle Devenish and Tucker Eskew:

Question: Mr. Eskew mentioned the surreality of the mix of humor and politics in the post-debate spin room; in that same vein, I want to know if you have any opinions on political information/commentary/meta-communication delivered through comedy. I'm thinking specifically of *The Daily Show* on Comedy Central as well as Leno and Letterman. How important do you think this avenue was in terms of increasing political knowledge and/or influencing voter perceptions? Do you think this could be the Democratic answer to talk radio or is it too even-handed to be effective in that capacity? (asked by Jennifer Reiss)

Nicolle Devenish's response: I'd like to think late night comedy is too "even-handed" to be the Democratic answer to talk radio.

Tucker Eskew's response: I believe humor can be very effective, but I wouldn't be looking to the comedy industry to be an effective echo chamber for any particular point of view. Another way of asking your question used to come from my Republican friends, especially just before and just after the 2000 election: "What can we do about Letterman/Leno/Stewart? They're making George W. Bush out to be a dummy!" I reminded them that similar things had been said about Reagan and look where that got the Democrats. The fact that you can't control the comics' message proves, it seems to me, the point that they're not effective team members. They can help—when their slings and arrows have the wind of public opinion behind them—but the parties would do well to echo the jokes they like, ignore the rest, and work ever harder to have a positive message and to win elections and news cycles. And maybe to be a little boring: that's the worst thing to the comics!

Question: This question regards the Dan Rather/Ben Barnes interview. After the Rather interview with Ben Barnes aired, and the issue was framed and reframed, what were the potential effects for the Bush campaign? Initially, the interview framed Bush negatively and questioned his military service. How did you respond to this initial charge and reframe the issue? In the end, after Rather apologized, do you think there were any effects at all on Bush or was the issue of his military service completely forgotten and overshadowed by the Rather-bias controversy? (asked by Sara Levine)

Nicolle Devenish's response: The American people considered the questions about the president's guard service "asked and answered" so the entire discussion turned quickly to the CBS-Rather-bias debacle.

Tucker Eskew's response: We believed (and stated often) that Sen. Kerry had served honorably and that so had the president. The fact that we'd been saying that since February or March 2004 was evidence to us that (a) the story wasn't going away unless some intervening news shook up the narrative, and (b) our consistency was working—most Americans thought this general topic was irrelevant to their lives. The White House's response is widely reported: we didn't know about the documents, the White House was only shown them just before broadcast, and their illegitimacy speaks volumes—loud enough to drown out this non-story.

Question: In dealing with the press, did you find one particular issue on your agenda that was especially difficult to convince the media to put on its agenda? If so, which and why? (asked by Nathaniel Hake)

Nicolle Devenish's response: It was very difficult to get the press to scrutinize Kerry's proposals in the context of the amount of spending they'd require. We had a very tough time getting the press to focus on the cost of Kerry's health care plan and other proposals and we could shout until we were blue in the face that his numbers didn't add up without getting much traction in the press.

Question: How important was the current administration's relationship with the press in connecting the war in Iraq with the overall war on terror? What methods did you use to ensure that the two became part of the same coherent narrative? (asked by Dominique De Armond)

Tucker Eskew's response: I think our relationship with the press was bruised by the non-discovery of WMD in Iraq and that therefore we had an uphill fight to convince them that Iraq was part of the larger war on terror. Americans at-large (a majority of them, at least), however, shared the president's sincere belief that getting rid of Saddam makes America safer.

Note

1. In a July 3, 2004 *New York Times* article, Robin Toner wrote, "In a local interview in Cloquet, Mr. Kerry was critical of the administration's economic performance. The net job growth this month, he said, was 'very weak,' adding that American workers were being hurt 'every day' by the loss of well-paying jobs overseas. . . . In general, though, Mr. Kerry was not relying only on economics to make his connection here. When asked how he hoped to connect to rural voters, the Massachusetts Democrat replied, 'I actually represent the conservative values that they feel'" ("Kerry, in Midwest Tour, Laments Lost Jobs," C1).

In a July 15 Associated Press story, Melissa Trujillo wrote, "[Bush] started the day at the Waukesha County Expo Center in suburban Milwaukee, telling the crowd of more than 5,000 supporters that his approaches to national security and the economy are working so well that Democratic rival John Kerry is trying to embrace conservatism. 'He said he was the candidate of conservative values,' Bush said of Kerry's comments on a recent trip to the Midwest" ("Bush Brings Message to Wisconsin in One-Day Tour").

Chapter 6
Republican Spenders

Brian McCabe

Brian McCabe *is a partner at DCI Group, LLC, a full-service public and govern-ment affairs firm based in Washington, D.C. McCabe is one of the founding part-ners and CEO of CustomScoop, an electronic news clipping service specializing in corporate public policy news tracking, and he also serves as president of Prog-ress for America Voter Fund and Progress for America, Inc. Prior to founding the McCabe Consulting Group in 1996, he served as executive director for Bob Dole's NH primary campaign. Before joining Sen. Dole, McCabe worked for Representa-tive Bill Zeliff, serving on his congressional staff and managing his 1994 and 1996 campaigns.*

I think everyone knows that the Conservative 527s really got a late start. All of us, especially Swift Boat Veterans and [Progress for America] PFA Voter Fund, waited until the FEC non-ruling in May.[1] PFA did not get started until May 27. When we started we were 100 million dollars behind the fundraising success of all the liberal 527s. We saw our man-date as helping level the playing field, to be the equalizers with what the liberal 527s were doing. We had some challenges on our side because a lot of the Republican time had been spent talking about how we didn't need 527s and that they were wrong. Once the FEC decided not to rule, we had to make the decision—either we continue with just our 501(c)(4) [501(c)(4) groups are social welfare organizations that primarily con-duct charitable, educational, and recreational activities, rather than political activities], or we also enter the game as a 527. We obviously made that decision to enter the ballgame with a 527 organization.

This chart (Chart 26) gives you an overview of where we spent our money.

We ended up spending $28.2 million on TV alone. We focused on five key states. We spent $44.5 million in Iowa alone. Wisconsin [was] $5.5 million. In Ohio, we spent $2.8 million and that was in the last two weeks alone. The same holds true for Pennsylvania and Florida. We did not start advertising in those states until October 19.

CHART 26.

PAID MEDIA
National $28.2 million

New Hampshire
Wisconsin $1,063,650
$5,575,337 (861 GRPs)
(51,260 GRPs)

Minnesota
$844,242
(4,218 GRPs)

Nevada
$1,356,406
(6,506 GRPs)

Iowa
$4,507,165
(45,893 GRPs)

New Mexico
$955,416
(4,102 GRPs)

Missouri
$1,972,549
(10,826 GRPs)

Ohio
$2,867,920
(13,093 GRPs)

Pennsylvania
$2,540,970
(7,857 GRPs)

Florida
$3,046,773
(8,731 GRPs)

Arkansas
$253,205
(1,171 GRPs)

We got our start advertising in June with two ads, "What If?" and "Why Do We Fight?" They went up in Nevada and New Mexico. The first ad, "What If?" was right before July 4 and the second ad, "Why Do We Fight?" was just after July 4. We obviously took July 4 off. We spent one million dollars in both states combined, running two weeks at 1,000 points a week in each state. As we saw it at that point, we had some early fundraising success, but we needed to get up on the air someplace. So while we also set the tone that our issue and message would be about the war on terror, we knew we had to let our donors, the conservative donors who we were reaching out to, see what we would do with it.

The first ad was "What If?" and it set the tone for the theme we ran the whole campaign.

TV Advertisement—"What If?"

ANNOUNCER: 9/11 . . . A leader showed strength and compassion—President Bush. He held us together and began to hunt down terrorist killers. But what if Bush wasn't there? Could John Kerry have shown this leadership? The Kerry who

Brian McCabe

voted against billions for America's intelligence even after the first World Trade Center bombing? The Kerry who voted against 13 weapons systems our troops depend on? President Bush will win this war on terror. Progress for America Voter Fund is responsible for the content of this ad.

"What If?" and "Why Do We Fight?" are designed to go together. Every place we ran them, they always ran in tandem.

TV Advertisement—"Why Do We Fight?"

ANNOUNCER: Why do we fight? Years of defense and intelligence cuts left us vulnerable. We fight now because America is under attack. Positions are clear. A president who fights to defeat terrorists before they can attack again. Or the nation's most liberal senator with a thirty-year record of supporting defense and intelligence cuts. The war is against terror and President Bush has the strength and courage to lead us to victory. Progress for America Voter Fund is responsible for the content of this ad.

The elements in these ads ran through everything we did: President Bush's leadership on the war on terror and what we saw as John Kerry's thirty-year track record of defense and intelligence cuts. One of the other themes, as you'll see, was Senator Kerry's statement that "I voted for the 87 billion before I voted against it." We ended up using that in four different ads.

So June was really about marketing. We actually did not go back up on the air until August. Then we expanded our media buy to Iowa and Wisconsin. When we set up that buy, we went with "What If?" and "Why Do We Fight?" again. With Iowa and Wisconsin, we wanted to pick two states in which we would stay on the air through the rest of the cycle. We ended up running nine ads in Wisconsin and Iowa starting about August 23 and we stayed on the air in those states to the end.

In September, we expanded the states [in which] we advertised. In the Midwestern cluster, we added Minnesota and Missouri. At this point we went with four ads. The first was "Veterans." This ad features four veterans talking about the war in Iraq.

TV Advertisement—"Veterans"

ANNOUNCER: Four veterans from the front lines of Iraq and Afghanistan.

VETERAN #1: If we don't win the war on terror, then 9/11 is going to be a stepping stone.

VETERAN #2: President Bush will be the best man to lead us in the war against terror.

VETERAN #3: President Bush sticks to his policies. I'd ask Senator Kerry, 'Why would you vote to go to war or vote not to support our troops over there?'

VETERAN #4: I don't think Senator Kerry has what it takes. He doesn't have the resolve.

ANNOUNCER: Progress for America Voter Fund is responsible for the content of this message.

We had run three serious ads at this point. The next ad we went with was "Surfer Dude." We figured we had been pretty heavy on the war on terror. We wanted to find a different way to introduce our message. "Surfer Dude" also happened to be our first ad on national cable. We spent $250,000 on the national cable portion and we also ran the ad in Iowa, Wisconsin, Minnesota, and Missouri. We only ran it for five days for 500 points in each market. It got a ton of earned media publicity.

Since John Kerry windsurfing is a little out of the normal presidential context, people paid attention to it.

Once we had done this ad to kind of catch some attention, we went back to a focus on the war on terror. This was probably one of our most poignant ads of the entire campaign.

TV Advertisement—"Finish It"

ANNOUNCER: These people want to kill us. They killed hundreds of innocent children in Russia, two hundred innocent commuters in Spain, and 3,000 innocent Americans. John Kerry has a thirty-year record of supporting cuts in defense and intelligence, and endlessly changing positions on Iraq. Would you trust Kerry up against these fanatic killers? President Bush didn't start this war, but he will finish it. Progress for America Voter Fund is responsible for the content of this message.

The next ad that we went with was "Absolutely Incorrect." Like "Surfer Dude," that ad was about changing positions on Iraq. This is the one in which we focused most heavily on the $87 billion. We used a quote from Senator Kerry where he says, "I've never wavered in my life," and then we played the $87 billion quote.

Since we always knew the ad we wanted to end with, we were actually working backwards with our advertising. We kept focusing on that Midwestern cluster but we knew we were fundraising to go across a broad spectrum of states at the end.

In October we added Florida, Ohio, Pennsylvania, Arkansas, and New Hampshire. On October 12, we ran "Tougher Hand" in just four of those states. That ad was really an effort to tee up "Ashley's Story."

Sixty-five percent of our total spending was behind "Ashley's Story." Ashley Faulkner is a young girl who lives in Ohio. She went to a campaign event with her next-door neighbor Linda Prince. She had attended a similar rally four years before. On 9/11 Wendy Faulkner, Ashley's mother, was killed in the World Trade Center. Ashley had totally gone into her shell since then. It was at this campaign event in just one moment with the president that she really came to open up again. We cut this ad in July and we held on to it until the end. We used it to fundraise.

The first time we talked with the Faulkner family, the father, Lynn Faulkner, was telling me about Ashley and about his other daughter Loren and what they had been through. You cannot help but well up when you hear the story and the emotion behind what the family had been through. Then you meet the family and just see what a great family they are. When the film crew was done, they called afterwards. They said there was not a dry eye anywhere on the team.

TV Advertisement—"Ashley's Story"

LYNN FAULKNER: My wife Wendy was murdered by terrorists on September 11th.

ANNOUNCER: The Faulkner's daughter, Ashley, closed up emotionally. But when President George W. Bush came to Lebanon, Ohio, she went to see him, as she had with her mother four years before.

LINDA PRINCE (family friend): He walked toward me and I said, 'Mr. President, this young lady lost her mother in the World Trade Center.'

ASHLEY FAULKNER: And he turned around and he came back and he said, "I know that's hard. Are you all right?"

LINDA PRINCE: Our president took Ashley in his arms and just embraced her. And it was at that moment that we saw Ashley's eyes fill up with tears.

ASHLEY FAULKNER: He's the most powerful man in the world and all he wants to do is make sure I'm safe. That I'm okay.

LYNN FAULKNER: What I saw was what I want to see in the heart and the soul of the man who sits in the highest elected office in our country.

ANNOUNCER: Progress for America Voter Fund is responsible for the content of this message.

We knew as soon as we saw the final product that this ad spoke better than anything to President's Bush's character, compassion, and leadership. We thought it was essential to get it out to as wide a group as possible. So we were actually back end buying [started buying time for the end of October then moving to earlier weeks in October] all the TV time we possibly could.

We did a post-election survey looking at ads. Public Opinion Strategies' survey using open-ended questions revealed that "Ashley's Story" was the most successful ad of the year on open-ended questions. On an aided ballot, 68 percent of voters in battleground states recalled seeing "Ashley's Story." The highest recall was among independents and female voters. What's most interesting in the POS survey is the top three ads on recall of the cycle were "Ashley's Story," "Swift Boat Veterans," and "Wolves." Tony Fabrizio did a separate poll that had the same conclusions as to the top three, and Bob Moore of Moore Information, who was our pollster, also did a survey and came up with the same conclusion. These three ads were the top three recalled ads of the cycle.

We think "Ashley's Story" created a favorable impression of the president. It was most effective in Ohio and Wisconsin. The Ohio part shouldn't surprise anyone since Ashley Faulkner is from Ohio.

We ran an $18.8 million comprehensive surround campaign. It's the largest television buy behind a single message. How we did it? Television—we spent $16.7 million on this TV ad. We had a sixty-second spot and a thirty-second version. We ran them at about 1-to-1 ratio across the 11 states. All in all, the ad ran 29,875 times which is obviously pretty phenomenal. To make sure that we wouldn't get blocked out, we actually started making our buys in August. We didn't reserve the time, we pre-bought all our time at the top of the rate card so we couldn't be blocked out at the end. We actually had all our time bought by the end of September—the first $14.2 million of time had been bought by the end of September.

It wasn't until the end of September that newspapers starting asking us about the buy. The weekend before the ad was to go up, everyone in the press started to call to say, "We're hearing that this is a negative ad." The word out on the street was that this ad is incredibly negative. We knew the whole time that it was going to be a positive spot. There was a high risk in going with something positive at the end. We were trying to continue to get the message out about the war on terror. We needed an ad to cut through the clutter and we obviously thought this would. Once we launched on October 19, we were still able to buy another $2.5 million of TV time.

The second thing we did is direct mail. We spent $1.5 million to mail out 2.3 million pieces of direct mail. There were 937,000 copies mailed in Ohio. Again Ashley and Lynn were from Ohio. It just made sense that if you wanted to get your message and your issue out, you should go to the place where it's going to resonate the most and we thought obviously it would cut through [the clutter] there more than any place else.

We also borrowed a page from some other groups' books and really put a lot of focus on the Internet. Instead of just putting this ad up on the PFA Voter Fund's website, we started a whole new site, AshleysStory .com. The whole messaging around this ad was about Ashley's story. It wasn't about a TV ad, it was about getting Ashley's story out there.

The home page had the appearance of a scrapbook. You have a picture of the hug, "Ashley's Story," and then also a link to Ashley's mom's foundation. From there we gave everyone the opportunity to send it on to five friends. We really wanted to create some viral marketing. What

CHART 27.

we saw was that people not only went to the site, saw the ad, but also sent it on to a lot of friends.

We launched the ad on Tuesday, October 19. By Thursday of that week, we had made it to rank #2 on Blogdex. I didn't know what Blogdex was before. It originates at MIT and tracks blog traffic on the Internet. So we went from zero to two in two days. We did that by being very aggressive with a banner ad campaign when the ad launched. We paid for 62 million impressions, 35 million of which were on Drudge alone. We also ended up sending out 20 million emails. The first day I think 4 or 5 million went out; the other 15 came in over time. We raised $6.2 million from the launch of Ashley's Story [ad and website]. We had actually stopped fundraising at that point. Money was just coming in over the Internet. It came from people calling us who just wanted to be a part of it. We were able to take $2.5 million of that, and that's how we went up in Arkansas and Massachusetts and New Hampshire. We were also able to add onto our national cable buy, as well as buying additional time in Ohio, Florida, and Pennsylvania, with Ohio getting the most spots. In Ohio alone, the spot ran 7003 times.

The other component was earned media. Seven hundred and sixty-two articles were written that talked about "Ashley's Story". . . . We thought for Progress for America Voter Fund, "Ashley's Story" was the key to our success of getting the message out about the war on terror.

Obviously we got a late start but we think in some ways we helped counter liberal 527s. We raised $50 million in five months. We actually raised it in 48 states, so if there's anyone in Hawaii or North Dakota who'd still like to contribute, we'd like to get it up to 50 for 50. We ran 9 ads altogether in 11 states. PFA Voter Fund focused resources on public policy issues during key times. We spent our money when we thought people would be paying attention to our issues the most, and then we were able to spend it in states where there was already a lot of attention on the issues. We think we helped define the public policy debate on the war on terror. We created a favorable image of President Bush's public policy agenda, while at the same time raising doubt about Senator Kerry's ability to lead the war on terror.

Where do we go from here? PFA Inc, which is a 501(c)(4), has been around since 2001. We did file the 527 on May 27. However, we have a long history and we have every expectation that we will continue with our 527 and our 501(c)(4). There's absolutely no reason any of these issues will go away and other issues will come along. There's every opportunity for us to continue talking about the war on terror, but we also look to expand onto issues such as tort reform, judicial nominations, as well as tax reform.

Chris LaCivita

Chris LaCivita is an independent political consultant specializing in general campaign strategy, media planning, and voter contact mail. Recently, he served as chief strategist for Swift Boat Veterans for Truth and co-producer of their TV ads. LaCivita was also responsible for production and management of their entire paid media contact plan. In the 2002 election cycle, LaCivita was national political director and director of issue advocacy for the National Republican Senatorial Committee under the leadership of Sen. Bill Frist. He served as political director for former Governor George Allen as well as assistant secretary of administration, and in 2000 LaCivita was campaign manager of Allen's successful bid for the U.S. Senate.

In May of 2004, the Swift Boat Veterans for Truth put together a press conference here at the National Press Club. They didn't get the coverage that they felt they deserved to get their message out. So they came to me in June, along with some other folks, asking, how do we get our message out? It's been reported in the press that the main reason why these guys came together was because of John Kerry's anti-war activities. The real reason they came together was they started reading Douglas Brinkley's book, *Tour of Duty*, which really started repeating a lot of the things that these men found offensive. It started talking about things that these men had never seen happen while they were in country in Vietnam in '68 and '69. That was the real reason. So if anybody wants to direct any anger at what we did, they can go thank Douglas Brinkley. And we thank him every day.

Who are the Swift Boat Veterans? It's over 250 Swift Boat officers and enlisted men who served in Coastal Division 11, which was Kerry's unit. Sixty of these guys actually served alongside John Kerry, including his entire chain of command. I spent ten years in the Marine Corps so I can tell you what the chain of command actually is. These are the guys who are responsible for the day-to-day supervision and operations of their men in Vietnam. Over 50 prisoners of war, men who were held captive by the North Vietnamese at varying times. The group's founder is retired Rear Admiral Roy Hoffman, who was the Commanding Officer of Coastal Division 11.

With this 527, the Swift Boat officers actually ran the group. They were active in every aspect of the organization from the beginning to its current place. This was a true grassroots organization. This was what 527 organizations were actually established to do. They were citizens who came together, who then sought out professional help to help them get their message out. This was a group established by these men, American citizens who obviously have the right and earned the right to have their

Chris LaCivita

message told. Bill Franke ran the day-to-day operations, John O'Neill obviously is the author of the *New York Times* bestseller *Unfit for Command* and he served as our chief spokesman. The book actually sold over 450,000 copies.

Fundraising: the total raised since August 5 was $27.2 million, over $7.5 million from the Internet alone, $2 million from direct mail and over 100,000 individual owners from all 50 states. It didn't start out that way in early August. Our first ad obviously generated an enormous amount of controversy. The ad, "Any Questions," was aired in markets in Wisconsin, Ohio, and West Virginia. Small markets, somewhat rural in nature, so that the costs per gross rating point would not exceed our budget, which was 500,000 dollars. That's what we spent on the first ad.

Obviously the goal was to generate attention, drive earned media right around the time when we released the book. That's what we wanted to do. We wanted to generate controversy. The result—according to a survey conducted by the Annenberg Public Policy Center: from August 9 through 16, 60 percent of those surveyed knew or heard about the ad. We only spent 500,000 dollars. I can't even quantify for you the amount of times the ad was actually run on cable talk shows and on broadcast

TV that the organization didn't pay for. It was truly a phenomenal experience. The ad was circulating on the Internet like wildfire. Our website crashed three times and we had thirty, forty servers patched together throughout the country to maintain the sheer volume. We had anticipated what we were going to do was going to have an impact, we just didn't figure it would actually last as long as it did. Our original budget was actually only four million dollars. Obviously we ended up raising quite more than that.

The plan basically was an aggressive paid and earned media plan which was assembled to tell these guys' story—quite frankly, the story the press didn't want to hear and still probably doesn't want to hear about it because they're still getting it wrong. The story that these men were committed to telling, they're going to continue to tell it and they're not going away. There were two, really two focuses.

One, John Kerry, according to these men, wasn't the war hero he portrayed himself to be. We focused on several different issues related to that. One was that a lot of his actions and a lot of his self-proclaimed heroism was rebutted by personal accounts of men who were actually with him. That includes his first Purple Heart, which was actually self-inflicted. The Bai Hop River incident, which I'm sure everybody knows about—Kerry was on a boat, [James] Rassmann, a Green Beret, falls off. Christmas in Cambodia, which turned out never happened. His entire chain of command basically said none of this stuff happened. So that was the focus of our shot.

Quite frankly, people speculate why the Kerry campaign didn't respond. As someone who's been involved in campaigns, I can tell you that they actually did respond but they used surrogates. When you're advising a campaign and a third party attacks a principal, you never have the principal respond, because then you're just elevating the charges. So we just had him wedged. But the bottom line was the campaign was not briefed on the incidents that occurred in Vietnam. They knew we were going to hit them on April '71, his testimony before the Senate Foreign Relations Committee. They knew we were going to hit him on his meetings with the Viet Cong. They knew we were going to hit him on his anti-war activities. But they never imagined that we would actually go after him for specific actions he claimed he did while he was in Vietnam. So I think that really was one of the reasons they didn't respond as they should have.

Then of course Kerry's actions when he returned home from Vietnam actually hurt the war effort and caused prolonged suffering for POWs. That was essentially the second goal. To advance it we used the following: the testimony of 1971 in front of the Senate Foreign Relations Committee, his meeting with the Viet Cong in Paris, [and] throwing his medals away. All of these issues were used to reinforce the main points that we were getting at and the main point really was you could not trust John Kerry. We use John Edwards's famous line, and I thank him to this day for giving it, "If you want to know what John Kerry is made of, ask the men who served with him in Vietnam." [We responded] "okay." And basically used that statement by Senator Edwards to tee up everything that we were going to do.

This is the first ad that we ran.

TV Advertisement—"Any Questions"

JOHN EDWARDS: If you have any questions about what John Kerry is made of, just spend 3 minutes with the men who served with him.

AL FRENCH: I served with John Kerry.

BOB ELDER: I served with John Kerry.

GEORGE ELLIOT: John Kerry has not been honest about what happened in Vietnam.

AL FRENCH: He is lying about his record.

LOUIS LETSON: I know John Kerry is lying about his first Purple Heart because I treated him for that injury.

VAN ODELL: John Kerry lied to get his bronze star . . . I know, I was there, I saw what happened.

JACK CHENOWETH: His account of what happened and what actually happened are the difference between night and day.

ADMIRAL HOFFMAN: John Kerry has not been honest.

ADRIAN LONSDALE: And he lacks the capacity to lead.

LARRY THURLOW: When the chips were down, you could not count on John Kerry.

BOB ELDER: John Kerry is no war hero.

GRANT HIBBARD: He betrayed all his shipmates . . . he lied before the Senate.

SHELTON WHITE: John Kerry betrayed the men and women he served with in Vietnam.

JOE PONDER: He dishonored his country . . . he most certainly did.

BOB HILDRETH: I served with John Kerry . . . John Kerry cannot be trusted.

ANNOUNCER: Swift Boat Veterans for Truth is responsible for the content of the advertisement.

There was only a half million dollars put behind it. That ad really teed up and gave us the opportunity to start focusing on the next sort of messages. This is probably the most, in my opinion, this was the most effective ad, which was the most fun to produce. It was the one we spent the most money behind. I can't tell you actually how much money we put behind this specific ad but it was an enormous, enormous amount of money.

The second ad, "Ravaged," was run during the Republican National Convention. . . . There was a lot of talk in the press corps about whether [the] Swift Boat [ad] was going to go down during the Republican National Convention. Our position was that it would really have no impact with the Bush campaign; we're not working with him, we don't care about the Republican National Convention. Our goal is simply to get the message out about John Kerry. What better way to do it than during the Republican National Convention when everyone is watching. So we placed approximately 1.3 million dollars on national cable, most of it on Fox, during the week of the convention. We had an instinct that Fox was going to have very, very high viewership during the Republican National Convention.

TV Advertisement—"Ravaged"

JOHN KERRY (from Senate Testimony in 1971): They had personally raped, cut off ears, cut off heads . . .

JOE PONDER: The accusations that John Kerry made against the veterans who served in Vietnam was just devastating.

JOHN KERRY: . . . randomly shot at civilians . . .

JOE PONDER: . . . and it hurt me more than any physical wounds I had.

JOHN KERRY: . . . cut off limbs, blown up bodies . . .

KEN CORDIER: That was part of the torture, to sign a statement that you had committed war crimes.

JOHN KERRY: . . . razed villages in a fashion reminiscent of Genghis Khan . . .

PAUL GALANTI: John Kerry gave the enemy for free, what I and many of my comrades, in the North Vietnamese prison camps, took torture to avoid saying. It demoralized us.

JOHN KERRY: . . . crimes committed on a day to day basis . . .

KEN CORDIER: He betrayed us in the past, how could we be loyal to him now?

JOHN KERRY: . . . ravaged the countryside of South Vietnam . . .

PAUL GALANTI: He dishonored his country, and more importantly, the people he served with. He just sold them out.

ANNOUNCER: Swift Boat Veterans for Truth is responsible for the content of the advertisement.

The *Newsweek* article that was published said that we used a voiceover. That's no voiceover. That's John Kerry's voice. Of course that was just one of many instances in which reporters never bothered to call us and ask us actually what happened and how we put it together. But that's actually John Kerry's voice, it is not an actor.

These ads are all sixties. These are not thirty-second ads, these are one minute long. By running [at] 1.3 million dollars on Fox, we actually raised on the Internet that week $2.2 million, basically driven from this ad, which enabled us really to squirrel it away and put it up on broadcast in some of the battleground states as we got closer to the end of the debate.

We ran "Medals" at the end of August. It was our first thirty-second ad. We actually produced "Medals," and then we produced the second ad, "Dazed and Confused." We ran them in tandem. And I'll start with this one.

TV Advertisement—"Medals"

ANNOUNCER: Symbols. They represent the best things about America: freedom, valor, sacrifice. Symbols, like the heroes they represent, are meant to be respected. Some didn't share that respect, and turned their backs on their brothers.

JOHN KERRY: . . . renounce the symbols that this country gives . . . and that was the medals themselves—I gave back, I can't remember, 6, 7, 8, 9.

ANNOUNCER: How can the man who renounced his country's symbols now be trusted? Swift Boat Veterans for Truth is responsible for the content of this advertisement.

Of course, that's not an actor either. And then this is "Dazed and Confused." We got a nice letter from ABC when we ran this one.

TV Advertisement—"Dazed and Confused"

JOHN KERRY '04: I've been accurate precisely about what had took place . . .

JOHN KERRY '71: . . . renounced the symbols . . .

JOHN KERRY '04: . . . I threw my ribbons over . . .

JOHN KERRY '71: . . . I gave back, I can't remember, six . . .

JOHN KERRY '04: . . . ribbons . . .

JOHN KERRY '71: . . . seven, eight . . .

JOHN KERRY '04: . . . and took the ribbons . . .

JOHN KERRY '71: . . . nine . . .

JOHN KERRY '04: . . . I didn't have my medals . . .

JOHN KERRY '71: . . . and that was the medals themselves . . .

JOHN KERRY '04: . . . that is absolutely incorrect . . . medals, ribbons . . . we threw away the symbols of what our country gave us . . . and I'm proud of that.

ANNOUNCER: John Kerry. Can you trust anything he says? Swift Boat Veterans for Truth is responsible for the content of this advertisement.

We actually ran a couple of ads in September. We ran one with the wives of POWs. We decided to shift to make the message pertinent to the women and how it affected the wives of POWs. I don't have that ad here, but this is an ad that we ran, we introduced a new piece of information. In 1970 John Kerry actually went and met with the Viet Cong in Paris. Now we still don't quite know what he was negotiating, but he did it while he was a U.S. Naval Reserve officer. We ran this ad in Pennsylvania. Basically, with this ad we focused in the Rust Belt. We ran it in southern and eastern Ohio, we ran it in Pittsburgh, in Altoona and a lot of different areas in Pennsylvania, and in West Virginia. And it of course has a familiar face in the end.

TV Advertisement—"Friends"

ANNOUNCER: Even before Jane Fonda went to Hanoi to meet with the enemy and mock America, John Kerry secretly met with enemy leaders in Paris, though we were still at war and Americans were being held in North Vietnamese prison camps. Then he returned and accused American troops of committing war crimes on a daily basis. Eventually, Jane

Fonda apologized for her activities. But John Kerry refuses to. In a time of war, can America trust a man who betrayed his country? Swift Boat Veterans for Truth is responsible for the content of this advertisement.

Obviously, the goal there was to position Kerry to the left of Jane Fonda.

The final two ads were more like a summary of everything that had been done up to that point. They're both sixties, both of these ads ran in a 60-40, 50-50 rotation in battleground states; Ohio, Florida. [One of] the gentlemen [in the ad] . . . with the Medal of Honor around his neck, his name's Bud Day. This was a guy who was a POW in Vietnam at the Hanoi Hilton for five years. He escaped once a year for the five years he was there. He also was shot once every time that he tried to escape. He's also John McCain's best friend.

TV Advertisement—"They Served"

ANNOUNCER: They served their country with courage and distinction. They're the men who served with John Kerry in Vietnam. They're his entire chain of command; most of the officers in Kerry's unit, even the gunner from his own boat. And they're the men who spent years in North Vietnamese prison camps, tortured for refusing to confess what John Kerry accused them of—of being war criminals. They were also decorated, many very highly. But they kept their medals. Today they are teachers, farmers, businessmen, ministers, and community leaders. And of course, fathers and grandfathers, with nothing to gain for themselves, except the satisfaction that comes with telling the truth. They have come forward to talk about the John Kerry they know, because to them, honesty and character still matter, especially in a time of war. Swift Vets and POWs for Truth are responsible for the content of this advertisement.

And the final ad . . .

TV Advertisement—"Why?"

JOHN EDWARDS: If you have any question about what John Kerry's made of . . .

VAN ODELL: Why do so many of us have serious questions?

LOUIS LETSON: How did you get your Purple Heart when your commanding officer didn't approve it?

STEVE GARDNER: Why have you repeatedly claimed you were illegally sent into Cambodia?

BOB ELDER: When it's been proven that you were not.

JIM WERNER: How could you accuse us of being war criminals?

KEN CORDIER: And secretly meet with the enemy in Paris?

MIKE SOLHAUG: And promote the enemy's position back home . . .

PAUL GALANTI: When I was a POW and Americans were being killed in combat?

BUD DAY: How can you expect our sons and daughters to follow you when you condemned their fathers and grandfathers?

JOE PONDER: Why is this relevant?

TOM HANTON: Because character and honesty matter, especially in time of war.

REAR ADMIRAL ROY HOFFMAN: John Kerry cannot be trusted.

ANNOUNCER: Swift Vets and POWs for Truth are responsible for the content of this advertisement.

Now as I said, I know they're rough, but there's no way of sugar coating the message. The media that we actually placed, Nevada 1.2 million dollars (see Chart 29). For those of you that are wondering what "GRPs" are, that means "gross rating points." For every 100 gross rating points, the average person in your targeted demographic sees the ad one time. The demographic that I know that we bought and I think that Steve [Moore] buys and that Brian [McCabe] bought at PFA was the 35-plus demographic. Most of our TV was prime time because groups like PFA and MoveOn and a lot of the presidential campaigns were buying the news adjacencies and the typical programming. We were spending much more per gross rating point because we were buying a higher rating of the program. [We were doing that], quite frankly, because we didn't have the luxury of laying down the money ahead of time because so much more money was coming in late. So we had to adjust our media buys every day.

Colorado, we dropped 700,000 dollars there. It wasn't a huge buy but it was enough. New Mexico, that's a lot of money in New Mexico when you're buying one media market, which is Albuquerque, which covers

CHART 28. SWIFT VETS PAID MEDIA IN BATTLEGROUND STATES

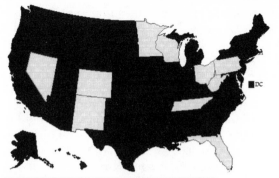

Swift Vets Paid Media in Battleground States

Battleground State	Paid Media	% of State Expenditures	Gross Rating Points (GRPs)
Colorado	$705,390	4.3%	1,201
Florida	$3,583,870	22.0%	9,345
Minnesota	$498,315	3.1%	609
Nevada	$1,204,790	7.4%	4,787
New Mexico	$967,780	5.9%	3,420
Ohio	$5,137,730	31.6%	13,495
Pennsylvania	$3,594,090	22.1%	9,701
Tennessee	$35,000	0.2%	244
West Virginia	$351,220	2.2%	2,300
Wisconsin	$204,330	1.3%	1,479
National Cable	$2,992,342		257,777,800 Impressions

Swift Vets and POWs for Truth

about 80 percent of the state. Minnesota, 609 gross rating points wasn't a lot but it was a lot for the Saturday, Sunday, and Monday before the election. That was spent in three days. We did not play in Wisconsin at all other than with our first ad. Tennessee, we put that on one day on one TV station and that was the day that Kerry showed up to speak at the American Legion, so we ran the "Medals" ad. Anywhere that John Kerry was making an issue of his military service, that's where we went and that's where we ran the majority of our ads. Florida 3.5 million dollars, West Virginia 351,000, Ohio 5.1 (million), Pennsylvania 3.5 (million). National cable, total spent 2.9 million, 257 million impressions.

In terms of the overall message, how we managed it and the tactics that were used, it wasn't just TV. We had a great PR shop and creative response concepts led by Greg Mueller and Mike Russell. Truly phenomenal street fighters who dealt with national media on a day-to-day basis trying to push the message out. If any of you followed what was going on this cycle, you never saw me on TV, you never saw our spokesman on TV, the men that you saw on TV, the people that you saw on TV were the Swift Boat officers. I mean we put Larry Thurlow, a farmer from Kansas who's never been on TV, we had him on *Hardball*. It was like, what are you crazy putting this, this very sincere, honest man on *Hardball* because we knew Chris Matthews was going to overreact. We knew he was going to try and pummel this very simple guy who's led an honorable life and had a message to tell, and that's exactly the response that the people who were getting back to us got. You know, "It's horrible what they did to him." So we were very aggressive in terms of who we had on, but you never saw the paid guys. It was always the Swift Boat Veterans themselves or the POWs that carried the message because it was their message, and that I think that increased our credibility with a lot of folks.

We started with a half million in paid TV, but we ended up putting 19.3 total. We did over 3 million pieces of direct mail to battleground states, basically any household that had a veteran in it. That was two pieces of mail. The first one was twelve pages long, the second one was eight pages long. Just like our TV ads, you couldn't tell the whole story in thirty seconds, and in a piece of mail you couldn't tell the story in two pages. It takes time and you have to be able to lay out a story, which is essentially what we were doing.

The Swift Boat sailors and POWs did over 1,000 radio appearances, talk shows all across the country. We were constantly on the radio getting the message out. I can't even tell you how many TV appearances that the guys did, not only on a national level but on a local level as well. We did these satellite TV tours which basically targeted—this was in the middle of the summer, toward the end of the summer—where we would rent satellite time and call TV affiliates in states where we were buying, we were buying time on their TV stations to air the ads. And we called them up and said, "Hey, we're doing a press conference via satellite, and some of the guys we have available to do interviews are from your viewing area. The local media was more than willing to tell the story with a local angle. So it was quite effective. We did twelve press conference tours in the last few weeks where we actually had POWs and Swift Boat officers go around to all the battleground states and actually held press conferences in these targeted states.

In post-election surveys the ads run by Swift Boat Veterans for Truth were either the first or second most memorable ads run during the entire issue debate. A survey conducted by POS showed that the Swift Boat ads in Florida were the most remembered by all demographics. So obviously we had an impact, we had an effect. Our goal was driving home the point that Kerry wasn't to be trusted. That's how we ended every single advertisement—Kerry could not be trusted. That was the major focus of the entire effort.

Stephen Moore

Stephen Moore *is president of the Club for Growth and a contributing editor of the* National Review. *He previously was the Cato Institute's director of fiscal* *policy studies, and continues to serve as a Cato senior fellow. He is the co-author of* It's Getting Better All the Time: 100 Greatest Trends of the Past 100 Years *and author of* Government: America's #1 Growth Industry. *Mr. Moore served as a senior economist at the Joint Economic Committee under Chairman Dick Armey of Texas. There, he advised Rep. Armey on budget, tax, and competitiveness issues. He was also an architect of the Armey flat tax proposal.*

Chris, those were fabulous ads, tremendous job you all did. When you were showing the ads it reminded me that one of the ads that we had run at the Club for Growth was an ad, if you look at that 1971 testimony that Kerry gave, it's just a gold mine of information about the real John Kerry. One of the things that you may recall that John Kerry said in that testimony was that we cannot win the war against terrorism, I mean win the war against communism, so we shouldn't try. We took just a little excerpt from that testimony where Kerry says we should stop trying to win the war against communism. And two weeks after President Reagan's death we ran an ad juxtaposing Kerry saying we can't win the war against communism and then showing Ronald Reagan famously before the Berlin Wall saying, "Mr. Gorbachev, tear down this wall." So that testimony that Kerry gave was extremely damaging to his presidential prospects.

The ads that we've run and all our 527 groups run are not meant to elect or de-elect any politicians. They're meant to inject issues into campaigns. So for example, in all the ads that you've seen today and you'll see later, you don't see the terms "Vote for John Kerry" or "Vote for George Bush" or anything about elections. We ran something in the neighborhood of 10 to 15 million dollars worth of ads in this cycle. So I hope you'll all keep that in mind as you think about the activities of the 527s.

One thing that makes us a little bit different from many of the other 527s that you've already heard from and that you'll hear from later today is that we were very much involved in not just the presidential race, but actually more so the Congressional and Senate races, which we felt were equally important to the presidential outcome. The other thing that's a bit unique about the Club for Growth is that our main mission is not to run TV ads and radio ads but to actually raise hard dollar contributions for the candidates who are running for the House [and] Senate. I don't think we raised any hard dollars for President Bush; he had enough hard dollars himself. But we probably raised about 12 million dollars in hard dollars for Senate candidates and House candidates around the country, which made us the largest giver to Republican candidates around the country. That will continue to be our main mission. We have 30,000 members around the country. This year we chose about 24 candi-

Stephen Moore

dates who we thought were quite outstanding on the economic growth issues that we care about. On average we raised about a half million dollars for each one of them.

It was a spectacular election, if you were a Republican. Out of the 28 candidates that we backed, 19 won and 9 lost. And those 28 were all highly competitive races so we were extremely pleased with the outcome in those elections. I think it still hasn't quite sunk in to a lot of Democrats how devastating this election was. It wasn't just that President Bush won; almost up and down the ticket, almost every competitive race went Republican. In some cases, I might add, George Bush clearly had coattail effects in this election, which might seem surprising because it was only 51 1/2 to 48 percent in terms of the margin of difference. But if you look at, for example, what happened in Louisiana, where maybe my biggest surprise outcome of the election was that David Vitter won the senate race without a runoff. I talked to David Vitter the day before the election and he said he didn't think there was any chance he would get to 50.1 percent, which you need to do in Louisiana to avoid a runoff.

The Club for Growth also actually intervenes quite heavily in primary races. We think that's where our money can be best spent. In the presidential race and some of these battleground Senate races, millions and millions and millions of dollars were being spent. So coming in with say an extra half million dollars in a race where 25 million dollars is being spent will produce minimal impact. But in the primaries where the amount of money that's being spent tends to be a quarter to a fifth, in some cases a tenth of what's spent in the general election races, we can make a difference. Our most important impact in 2004 was that in virtually every primary that we intervened in, and these were Republican primaries and our idea is to try to elect the most free market, conservative person in every Republican primary around the country, we were able to have great success, partly because if you put half a million dollars of direct campaign contributions into a primary race, you could have a very dramatic impact in the outcome of that election.

Washington is really the place of unintended consequences. And if you look back at when McCain-Feingold was passed and you listen to the things that John McCain was saying, in fact there was a very famous interview John McCain gave right before the Senate vote when he was asked why are you passing this legislation, why do you think this is so important? And he said, well we have to pass this legislation to put groups like the so-called Club for Growth out of business. And I think that John McCain and many of the people who voted on the McCain-Feingold bill actually thought that this legislation would put groups like ours out of business, that is to say that 527s would go out of business if you pass this law. And in fact exactly the opposite happened. It's precisely because of the McCain-Feingold bill that you saw the sprouting up of groups like Swift Boats and Progress for America and MoveOn.org. What essentially happened is that most of the ads that you've seen this morning are the types of ads in past elections that would have been run by the parties themselves because that's where all the donors gave their money to. Now the main change of the McCain-Feingold bill was to substantially reduce the amount of money that the parties could raise. Well, there was a demand out there for those donors to give money for issue ads. Essentially what happened is the money that used to go to the parties went to 527 organizations.

I'm very worried about what's going to happen with the future of 527s. We felt very strongly that the McCain-Feingold bill was unconstitutional. I think it was one of the darkest days of President Bush when he signed that legislation into law. If you look at the origins of the First Amendment, it's very, very clear that our founding fathers had in mind when they talked about free speech, what they were talking about was precisely political speech. If we had the McCain-Feingold bill in law during the colonial times, many of our founding fathers would have been put in jail for criticizing King George, especially if they did it 30 or 60 days before an election.

We think that this is, by the way, what you saw in the outpouring of money to all these organizations on the left and the right, in my opinion was exactly what a lot of the liberal groups say they want, which is more civic participation. Contributing a thousand dollars to Swift Boat Veterans was a form of civic participation by these donors. The types of ads that all these organizations were running heightened the interest in the policy issues that were debated in the election. All of the spending that took place in this election season, by the left and the right, was a good thing, not a bad thing.

One critical mistake that I think Bush and the Republican National Committee made was challenging the ads that MoveOn.org was running. In retrospect the Republicans made a very large strategic error that almost cost them the election. . . . The challenge by the RNC had a chilling effect on conservative donors. They said, well, gee, we can't give to 527s because of this court challenge against it. We had a strong feeling the RNC was going to lose that challenge, as they did, quite correctly. I've always said I don't agree with one word that George Soros says, but I defend his right to say the things that he's said. And by the way, I love the *National Review* cover, I don't know if you saw it last week, which had a picture of George Soros with a George Bush [picture] and a line through it, and it said, "I spent 26 million dollars and all I got was this lousy T-shirt," which was I think a wonderful summary of the election. In any case, I think that was a critical error and that some result of it was that the liberal groups had about a hundred-million-dollar lead in fundraising by the end of the summer, and they had about a five-month lead in terms of raising the money. Luckily, we were able to catch up.

Well let me with that show you some of the ads that we ran. We probably ran about 15 to 20 ads throughout the election season and I thought I'd just show you some of the ones that we ran, and this is the first one.

Television Advertisement—"Dean and Taxes"

ANNOUNCER: What do you think of Howard Dean's plan to raise taxes on families by 1900 dollars a year?

ACTOR #1: What do I think? Well I think Howard Dean should take his tax hiking, government expanding, latte drinking, sushi eating, Volvo driving, *New York Times* reading . . .

ACTOR #2: Body piercing, Hollywood loving, left wing freak show back to Vermont, where it belongs.

ACTOR #1: Got it?

ANNOUNCER: Club for Growth PAC is responsible for the content of this advertising.

This was an ad that we ran in the first two weeks in January, the week or so before the Iowa caucus. After the Iowa primary was over, there was a political roundtable of reporters who were in Iowa. One of the questions they asked was what do you think was the most effective and memorable ad of the political season there. This was the ad that almost everyone remembered, which was remarkable because it ran probably one-tenth as many times as many of the ads that Kerry and Dean ran.

TV Advertisement—"Blowing in the Wind"

ANNOUNCER: John Kerry has a little problem making up his mind. OK, a big problem. In 1996 he opposed the death penalty for terrorists. Now he claims to support it. Sometimes he's for welfare reform, sometimes he's against it. For a 50-cent gas tax hike, then maybe not. Kerry voted for higher taxes 350 times but now says he'd cut taxes. So, in the middle of a war on terror can we trust John Kerry? The answer is blowing in the wind.

This was the first or second issue ad we ran about John Kerry's policy positions. We feel it had a big impact. It ran before the Republican Convention and Bush and a lot of the other Republicans started echoing this theme about blowing in the wind.

TV Advertisement—"Foxhall Road"

ANNOUNCER: It's a long way from Aberdeen to Foxhall Road. This is Tom Daschle's new two-million-dollar house on Washington's ritzy Foxhall Road. It's a great place to entertain Hollywood liberals, politicians, and lobbyists. In Washington, Daschle opposes cutting taxes for South Dakota families. Maybe they don't want tax reliefs on Foxhall Road.

RESIDENT: But we sure could use it here in Aberdeen.

This was a highly effective issue ad in South Dakota. Daschle did everything he could to get the ad taken off the air. People were saying there's two Tom Daschles. There's the Daschle in Washington who's a liberal and there's the Daschle in South Dakota who portrays himself as a Prairie State populist.

TV Advertisement—"Specter and Taxes"

ANNOUNCER: He fought to slash the Bush job-creating tax cut. He voted for eight huge tax hikes. He supports greedy trial lawyers instead of Pennsylvania doctors on legal reform. He's blocked school choice education programs. And he's rated one of the Senate's most wasteful spenders. John Kerry? No. Arlen Specter. Fact is, nearly 70 percent of the time Specter and Kerry voted the same way and that makes Arlen Specter 100 percent too liberal.

This issue ad was designed to show how liberal Arlen Specter's policy positions were on economic issues.

TV Advertisement—"Flu Shot"

ANNOUNCER: Waiting in line for flu shots . . . Why? A shortage of vaccines across the nation . . . Why? There used to be seven flu vaccine makers in the U.S. Attacks by trial lawyers helped close all but one. So now we rely on undependable foreign labs. When Congress had the chance to protect our vaccine supply from lawsuit abuse, John Kerry opposed it. Kerry failed to put your health ahead of his friendship with the trial lawyers. It's enough to make you sick. ClubForGrowth.net is responsible for the content of this advertising.

This issue ad ran in states where Democrats opposed litigation reform in Congress.

I think you're going to see 527s flourishing in the future. The stakes are huge in these elections. We know that John McCain already has legislation to try to muzzle 527 organizations. We will very much oppose that. As I said earlier, we think this is a very important area of free speech that needs to be protected. And so my prediction is that we're going to continue to see an escalation in activity by 527s both in political and policy campaigns in the future.

BROOKS JACKSON, DIRECTOR, FACTCHECK.ORG:

A question briefly for all of you. There were restrictions in the McCain-Feingold, what you could say within 30 or 60 days prior to the election, did these have any effect on what you did?

BRIAN McCABE:

Absolutely. I think every one of us hit on the key point that our focus is on issues. You didn't see any 527 talk about elect for or against a candidate. There was no express advocacy, it was all about the issues. There was confusion especially in the donor community, about the 30- and 60-day window rules. They just assumed once we got inside the windows we would never be able to run any ads. Part of the donor education was explaining the rules. One of the things we did, as I bet everyone did, is we segregated our dollars. Anything we raised from individuals we kept separate from corporate donations to our 527; we have two separate checking accounts. We have one for just individual donors and one for any corporate contributions. Having said that, about 99 percent of our money turned out to come from individual donations. We always thought that we would raise 60 percent from corporations and 40 percent from individuals and that was one of the things we were very wrong about.

STEPHEN MOORE:

We used exactly the same strategy. We had been a 527 since 1999, and the law basically said if you raised even a dollar of corporate money your whole 527 is essentially contaminated and wouldn't be able to run issue ads within 60 days of the election. So what we were forced to do is create a new 527 that took no corporate funds.

One last thing I would add is that the ban on doing activities within 60 days only applies to radio and TV, so we were running a lot of print ads. I've come to the conclusion, though, that print ads aren't particularly effective, especially newspaper ads. People don't really read newspapers anymore, for the most part. But you can do Internet. You can produce a good ad and with a zap of the button, you can get that thing, through viral marketing, out to a million computers. So I think one of the things you're going to see in the future is people finding ways that they can spend money other than TV.

CHRIS LaCIVITA:

Every time we're nearing a 30- or 60-day window and you come up with a new television advertisement, you have to produce for the Federal Election Commission a report called Form 9 which basically lays out all the donors and how much money they've given. We had so many individual contributors that it was driving our accountants completely crazy because the sheer volume of the report that they had to file every time we went up with a new TV ad. We raised over seven and a half million dollars over the Internet. The average contribution from that seven and a half million dollars was $78. So we had thousands and thousands of people that we had to file a report [on] every time we went up with a new TV ad.

BROOKS JACKSON:

Question for Brian [McCabe], I observed over the years covering independent spending that it's overwhelmingly almost exclusively negative and in fact I was almost to the point where I thought there was a law that it had to be negative. You're telling me your Ashley ad, which was clearly a positive ad, was the most memorable ad you ran; you ran the most money behind it. To say more about why you did that and why you think that ad was effective.

BRIAN McCABE:

Well, let me back up and say how we got to Ashley Faulkner. Many people may remember that there was the picture of the hug was spreading across the Internet. The story behind it is interesting. Lynn Faulkner actually took that picture and he sent it to seven family members. It was one of those family members who sent it to a local press outlet in Ohio. From there it got spread across the Internet. Well, we saw it like a lot of people and so we called up the Faulkners to see if they wanted to do the ad. Once we had cut the ad, Brooks, it was June as I said, we just knew that we had an ad that was so emotional that we thought, even at the end when there is a lot of clutter and it's difficult to get people to pay attention to it, that the emotion of this ad would really highlight the issue we wanted to. It was a risk. As we were sitting on that ad there were many times where we wanted to just say okay, let's run the ad now, because we had it.

We were very careful, we wouldn't email it to anyone, we wouldn't give anyone a copy, we only had three copies on DVDs. And I controlled two copies of that because we just didn't want it to leak out. So it was a risk. We think it worked out pretty well.

BROOKS JACKSON:

Was there any controversy within the organization on running a positive ad?

BRIAN MCCABE:

Oh, I think so, but when you looked at the ad, how could you not agree with Ashley Faulkner? If it was something else, I don't think it would have worked, but the emotion in that ad just carried the ad.

BROOKS JACKSON:

Okay. I noticed that your ad's images included Ground Zero, September 11. President Bush ran an ad showing 3 seconds of those images and there was a firestorm of criticism in the press. Chris, your ads accuse John Kerry of selling out his country, something that I can't remember any presidential campaign saying about any opponent ever. My question to all of you, do independent groups have freedom to say things that are, that the candidates themselves could not say about their opponent?

STEPHEN MOORE:

Is that a trick question? No, that's obviously a yes.

CHRIS LACIVITA:

Depending on what view you have, that's the good part of a 527, and for others, that's what makes 527s so worrisome. But you know the bottom line is that if you have a message, whether it's negative or not, that you believe has to be out there because it affects or has an impact on what people need to know about a certain individual, it's your constitutional right to do it. I'm sorry it's negative, it's the truth. It's not pretty. There's no other way of doing it. This isn't comedy, what we did. It's nothing that you can laugh about, it's nothing that you can really sugarcoat, so yeah, it's pretty rough. I don't have much more to say other than that.

STEPHEN MOORE:

First of all, the answer to your question is clearly yes. It's much better to allow the candidates themselves to do positive ads about themselves and an outside group to do issue ads that attack the congressman's voting record. The main reason people do negative ads is because negative ads get noticed and effect policy outcomes.

[Brad] Carson [a Democratic Congressman in Oklahoma who ran for the U.S. Senate against Tom Coburn in 2004] made one critical error that cost him potentially the election. There was a completely contrived, dirty allegation made against Tom Coburn, that he had sterilized this woman against her will. Every piece of evidence said that this woman, this girl, had made up this story. In any case, when Carson ran an ad attacking Coburn for sterilizing this woman, Carson's numbers tumbled after that because the ad was so over the top. So negative ads can backfire in a very significant way. It has to be done in a way that's credible to voters or else it's going to hurt the attacker more than the one who's being attacked.

KATHLEEN HALL JAMIESON:

Stations have a right to reject your ads. Were any of your ads rejected, if so, by which station, which ads, how, when, and why?

STEPHEN MOORE:

Well can I start? In the race between Chet Edwards and Arlene Wohlgemuth [for the 17th Congressional District in Texas]. Edwards, who's been in Congress for twenty years, had a vice grip hold over the media in Waco, Texas. We tried to run three issue ads attacking Edwards for not voting with Bush. In every single case, the networks took down that ad. We were running the same type ad, by the way, in other Texas districts. I'm still fuming about that. There was no false allegation that was being made in these ads; it was just that these stations are in the hip pocket of the candidate. So we got that ad pulled off the air.

BRIAN McCABE:

We didn't have any rejected, but I will tell you that one of the things we did was basically over-prepare when we shipped all our ads. We sent down an unbelievable amount of documentation. One station asked for more documentation, once I think on "Finish It" or "Absolutely Incorrect," and I don't remember which, and it was in New Mexico.

CHRIS LaCIVITA:

Extensive exhaustive research is your best friend, whether you're working for a campaign or whether you're working for a 527. When I was at the Senate Committee in 2002 under Bill Frist we ran 57 million dollars worth of issue ads in 17 different states. We had them all backed up methodically, line by line. We always had two sources for every line in the ad. We basically took that and applied it to the Swift Boat ads. Every single line in every ad that we produced had to be backed up by something. One TV station refused to run the first ad. It was a Fox affiliate in

Wisconsin. We only bought one spot on Sunday morning. It was 389 dollars. It would have cost them 400 dollars to get a legal opinion whether or not they could run it. So for them, from a monetary perspective, it just wasn't worth it.

We had one station in Toledo that threatened not to run, but then Rush Limbaugh was on the radio trashing them and their phones lit up and they called and begged us to tell them to stop, and it went up. We didn't have any of them rejected with the exception of Fox News national. Cable networks are notoriously much more difficult to get ads placed on because you need a greater lead time, especially if you're buying national. You can't buy national ABC News, I mean you can't buy a national broadcaster. You can buy national cable, and it takes a 3- to 5-day lead-time. Fox News refused to run our ads, not because of what they claim to be an inaccuracy. They just thought the ads were too negative. What you may or may not know is that broadcast, cable TV, TV stations in general are under no legal obligation to run anything that we produce. They can just tell us no and they don't have to give us a reason.

STEPHEN MOORE:

We had the same problem with Fox News. I bet this would surprise everyone in this room because everyone thinks, oh, Fox News, they're a big conservative megaphone. The only network that we actually had problems getting our ads on was Fox News. They have by far the most stringent fact checkers.

PETER OVERBEE (NATIONAL PUBLIC RADIO):

Aside from John McCain, someone else who had very strong opinions about 527s during the campaign was President Bush, who attacked the content, essentially, and I'm wondering if his stand has anything to do with what you guys are going to do going forward or if that's all history now.

STEPHEN MOORE:

I'm not sure exactly what you mean in terms of "his stand."

PETER OVERBEE:

He came out very strongly against 527s.

STEPHEN MOORE:

Oh right, right, right.

PETER OVERBEE:

So do you all expect that that's going to have any impact on Capitol Hill? For instance, does it have any impact within the party, within the conservative movement, or is it just a bygone?

STEPHEN MOORE:

Well, we just think he's wrong on this. You know, as I said, Peter, we think this is the right of organized groups, to express their right to political free speech, and you know we agree with George Bush on a lot of things, but we think he's just dead wrong on this. And as I said earlier in my comments, they made an almost critically damaging move earlier in the year by attacking 527s and silencing groups. His actions only served to muzzle groups on the right, not on the left. And you'll hear from the groups on the left [later]; I'm sure they'll tell you that they weren't dissuaded one bit by what George Bush was saying about 527s.

CHRIS LaCIVITA:

And when the president of the United States attacked the content, let's be specific. Up to the point where we became involved, he was under attack by MoveOn by over 60 million dollars worth of negative attack ads. So let's make that distinction.

ADAM CLYMER:

Hi, I'm Adam Clymer from the Annenberg Public Policy Center. We've found in some of our polling, particularly with respect to Swift Boat ads, that a lot of people thought the Bush campaign was behind them regardless, not that they're having any evidence of improper connections, but that's what they thought. Have any of you folks ever heard at a point after a campaign, when you're not consulting, that some candidates thought your ads hurt them because of their negativity and because, regardless of what you said about who was sponsoring them, people thought the candidate was behind them?

CHRIS LaCIVITA:

When I ran Senator George Allen's campaign in Virginia in 2000, an organization came in and wanted to run ads. They [ran] an ad talking about the incumbent Chuck Robb's bad prescription drug plan. [I wondered] why in the world are they talking about this issue, it's the last thing we want to talk about, why bring it to the forefront? I think it happens quite frequently. I know when I was at the Senate Committee in '02, we produced 158 individual TV ads for 17 different states. On some occasions, some of the ads that we produced [caused] some of the candidates to wince. But great care is taken to ensure that you don't overreach. Now with the Swift Boats, as I said earlier, there was no way to sugarcoat, there was no way to say he was dishonest. These men said that he lied, so there really wasn't any, there wasn't really any effort quite frankly, on our part about worrying about what backlash. I mean, we did think about it, but our goal was to get the truth out about John Kerry and everything else be damned.

BRIAN McCABE:

I agree with Chris. We had set for ourselves the issue of the war on terror. In a way you can't worry about what others are going to think. Once you pick your path you just have to go with it. . . . One of the things about 527s is that they really are wild in that regard and could turn out to actually hurt as opposed to, you know, help the issues you're trying to support.

CHRIS LaCIVITA:

Yeah, we don't like 527s that we can't control.

STEPHEN MOORE:

527s by law, as I think everyone in this room knows, have to be totally independent. There can be no coordination with the campaign. . . . We've been involved in campaigns where the campaigns said, "We really protest that ad that the Club for Growth is running." But the truth is we think it's sort of a wink and a nod. . . . A perfect example of that was an issue-oriented campaign we ran a year and a half ago when we were trying to get Bush's capital gains and dividends tax cut passed. And we did some really, really devastating ads against [George] Voinovich and Olympia Snow that you may recall. The White House of course immediately said, "We protest these ads, we think they're terrible." We think that they did have a big impact in turning around Voinovich's vote in Ohio, which was the critical vote needed to get the tax cut passed. So, sometimes they may say they protest the ad when in fact they're kind of winking and nodding.

Note

1. In its May 13, 2004 ruling, the Federal Election Commission "refused, for now, to put limits on independent political groups spending millions in unrestricted contributions, clearing the way for these organizations to exert considerable influence over this year's presidential race. . . . The six-member commission, which is split evenly between Republicans and Democrats, rejected in divided votes three attempts to impose new rules. It then unanimously voted to delay any new regulations on the political groups for 90 days" (Glen Justice, "F.E.C. Declines to Curb Independent Fund-Raisers," *New York Times*, May 14, 2004, A18).

At its August 19 meeting, the FEC "passed a series of complicated campaign finance rules . . . in an effort to make it harder for some independent political groups to spend millions in unrestricted contributions in future elections. Backing away from tougher restrictions that it had considered earlier, the commission voted, 4 to 2, to approve a compromise that will require some of the groups known as 527 committees, for the section of the tax code that applies to them, to raise far more money in small contributions and rely less on larger unlimited donations known as soft money. The rules, to take effect early next year, will have large effects on some organizations but not on others, depending on how the groups are legally organized, how they raise and spend money and what activities they undertake. . . . This year, the commission declined to restrict the 527 committees for this year's election" (Glen Justice, "Panel Compromises on Soft Money Rules," *New York Times*, August 20, 2004, A16).

Chapter 7

Democrat Spenders

Erik Smith

Erik Smith *is a veteran of national, statewide, and congressional campaigns. For fourteen years, Smith has acted as a lead strategist and counsel to senators, congressmen, and party committees developing communications strategies with a specialty in crisis management. Smith was the senior communications advisor to Representative Dick Gephardt in both the House Minority Leader's office and his presidential campaign. Most recently, Smith led a $60-million national Democratic issue advertising campaign as president and treasurer of The Media Fund.*

The Media Fund was created to make sure a Democratic message was on the airwaves at competitive levels. In 2003, people in our party were looking at a situation where the opposition had two tremendous assets. One is the Republicans consistently and historically have out-raised and outspent Democrats. Second, an incumbent president also traditionally has dramatically outspent any challengers. You combine those two things and we're looking at a really daunting challenge. The Media Fund was created to try and respond to that.

In particular, our mission was to try and fill some holes, to look for places where the Democratic message wasn't being communicated. On a more tactical note, when the group was founded and organized, one of the things we tried to do was go beyond traditional political creative ad campaigns. We wanted to combine both the best of the private sector and of the political arena. In doing so we did a lot of outreach to Madison Avenue. Private sector firms located around the country did a lot of work for us, and a lot of consulting. We tried to bring the best practices of both the political arena and the private sector together, trying to cherry-pick different techniques that we thought would be most effective.

We did a lot of focus grouping, dial testing, and market testing. Bill Zimmerman, campaign manager for MoveOn.org Voter Fund, was really a pioneer in that. As someone who is a veteran of not just political cam-

Erik Smith

paigns but party committees, testing was always one of those luxuries that we never really had time or money to indulge in. Early, we agreed that we weren't going to put anything on the air unless we knew it worked, unless we knew it to be effective, and unless it was proven to be effective. So that was the benchmark with which we approached everything.

We had a 60-million-dollar budget and spent more than 50 million dollars on the air in 82 media markets in 21 states and D.C. We were on D.C. cable for a period of time. That 50 million dollars on the air is just the media buying. It doesn't include production and research and all the other expenses. In other words, 85 cents of every dollar we raised went on the air in the form of media buying.

We didn't just do TV ads and radio ads; we did print ads, Internet ads, and direct mail as well. So we tried to be as well-rounded as we could be.

The first major accomplishment of our organization occurred in the early spring. Everyone was focused on this period when a Democratic nominee would emerge, probably beaten up after a tough primary, and very, very likely broke. Everyone just accepted the fact that it would be

CHART 29. TOTAL GROSS MEDIA EXPENDITURES BETWEEN MARCH 3 AND MAY 4

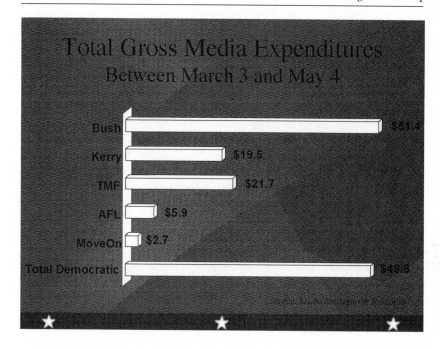

some time before a Democratic nominee could get up to speed. Further-more, the Republicans were out there saying, according to the *New York Times*, that they had a 90-day strategy to beat the Democratic nominee. They wanted to put this thing away early. They wanted to use their financial advantages to try and end the race really before it started. So we saw that as our first big opportunity. Specifically, this was a time, clearly, when a Democratic message was not going to be on the airwaves at competitive levels. So, we organized early to get up and do that.

This chart (Chart 29) looks at the spending during the first eight weeks.

As you can see, if Kerry and Bush were advertising alone, there would have been a tremendous disparity and the Bush campaign might very well have achieved what they had set out to do in that first 90 days. Instead, other organizations communicating a Democratic message including ourselves, AFL-CIO, and MoveOn, did a lot to make up the difference. As you can see, at the end of that period, spending had reached relative parity.

An aside. I'll mention an achievement that is probably not noteworthy unless you're active in Democratic politics. There was a great partnership and cooperation and coordination on the 527 side. Clearly we could not coordinate with the campaign or with the DNC. But 527s can coordinate with each other. We did that and I think we did it very effectively.

The chart doesn't do justice to what AFL and MoveOn did because it's one snapshot in time but it is important here to mention the fact that we were talking regularly. We had weekly conference calls with a larger group of 527s to make sure that no one was duplicating efforts, to make sure that no one was doing something that someone else was more better suited to do. In particular during this 8-week period, The Media Fund, AFL, and MoveOn talked regularly to make sure that we were spreading our resources effectively to cover the 18 battleground states. We were focusing in different places, and making sure we were complementing each other. I'm particularly proud of our ability to do that. As anyone who has been involved in Democratic politics knows, it's not always that easy.

The quote from the *LA Times* (see Chart 30) talks about our success in leveling the playing field during that period along with our partners. Another from the *New York Times* talks a little bit about how our ability to put a Democratic message on the airwaves helped fend off that Republican barrage in early spring. Without our ads on the air, the Republican strategy probably could have put that race away before it began.

Pew and CBS polls in February (see Chart 31) provide a sense of where the race was before that Bush 90-day campaign to define Kerry and end the race, and where it was after. So we feel we were effective in that regard, and I think the numbers prove it.

I want to show a couple of the commercials that we ran during that period.

TV Advertisement—"Prescription Drugs"

ELDERLY MAN: There's 14 drugs I take. If I—if I don't take it, I would not be here. It's as simple as that.

ANNOUNCER: Prescription costs are climbing, yet President Bush sided with the drug companies, blocking Medicare from negotiating lower prices and banning Americans from importing low-cost drugs from Canada. For Bush, drug company profits come first.

ELDERLY MAN: If they ever stop me from going to Canada, my feeling is, let the government arrest me, let them pay for my drugs; put me in jail. (*On screen: Paid for by The Media Fund* www.seethefactsforyourself.com)

Chart 30.

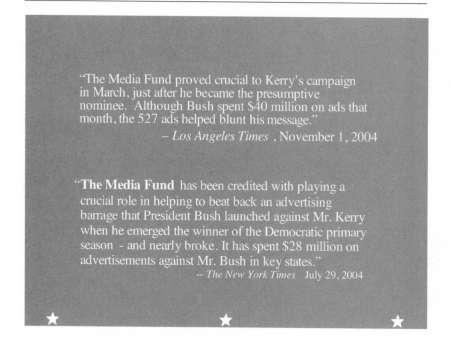

"The Media Fund proved crucial to Kerry's campaign
in March, just after he became the presumptive
nominee. Although Bush spent $40 million on ads that
month, the 527 ads helped blunt his message."
— *Los Angeles Times* , November 1, 2004

"**The Media Fund** has been credited with playing a
crucial role in helping to beat back an advertising
barrage that President Bush launched against Mr. Kerry
when he emerged the winner of the Democratic primary
season - and nearly broke. It has spent $28 million on
advertisements against Mr. Bush in key states."
— *The New York Times*   July 29, 2004

This, and Chart 31, the next one I'm going to show you, are good examples of the type of advertising we were doing in the spring. Of the ads
we ran between March and June, these two tested the best.

TV Advertisement—"Scary"

WOMAN: When I think about getting older, it's not dying I
worry about; it's living and being buried under a pile of medi-
cal bills I can't pay for.

ANNOUNCER: Health care costs are soaring. Millions more
Americans are uninsured, and those who have coverage are
paying more out of pocket, yet President Bush offers no plan
to curb costs and his new Medicare law would actually ban
the government from negotiating lower prices from drug
companies.

WOMAN: The cost of these drugs, it's very scary. (*On screen:
Paid for by The Media Fund* www.seethefactsforyourself.com)

CHART 31. NATIONAL POLLS: FEBRUARY 2004

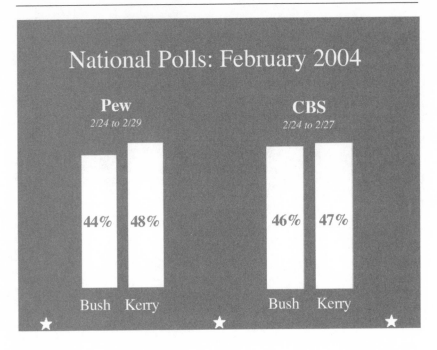

Both of those, by the way, were produced by Axelrod & Associates in Chicago. We had a lot of different projects going, a lot of different campaigns. The other one I wanted to highlight today was our African American initiative. Our party has traditionally focused on African American advertising late in the campaign, in the closing weeks, as essentially a get-out-the-vote message. One of the things that popped up in our research early in 2004 and something we also learned in 2003 was, particularly with African Americans between the ages of eighteen and thirty-five, it was no longer simply a turnout question. We needed to have a prolonged communication with people in that demographic. Democrats were going to have to fight for the support of those individuals. So, Cornell Belcher, who is an excellent pollster here in town, did a lot of work on this to get us started.

When we decided to launch this effort, we planned on a 5-million-dollar initiative eventually growing to 6 million dollars. We employed an advertising agency from St. Louis called FUSE, which is the fifth largest African American advertising agency in the country. FUSE has done a lot of work talking to that specific demographic for Sprite and other clients.

We also employed the Walker Marchant Group with Jamal Simmons here in Washington, D.C. We're really proud of some of the results.

We started with ads that talked about the Bush administration.

TV Advertisement—"2.7 Million Jobs"

ANNOUNCER: Bush is encouraging factory jobs overseas.

GRAPHIC: 2.7 million factory jobs have disappeared under George Bush.

ANNOUNCER: Fifteen percent of the factory jobs held by African Americans have disappeared.

GRAPHIC: Black youth unemployment is over 30 percent.

ANNOUNCER: Don't keep getting played.

GRAPHIC: The Media Fund is responsible for the content of this advertisement. www.breakbushoff.com

BreakBushOff.com was a website created solely for this campaign. We found it to be very successful. We ran this ad on BET and national African American cable networks. We also used a little local TV and a lot of radio, with an interesting 15-second format which is really quick and fast.

The earlier panel was talking about the electioneering period. One of the things you have to do during an electioneering period is a longer disclaimer. On radio it's about an 8-second disclaimer. If you're doing a 15-second radio ad, that's not always economical.

We have found this specific advertising campaign to be very effective. Anecdotally, whenever we were doing additional research groups, people volunteered they had seen them, heard them, and they were effective. BreakBushOff.com actually got more than 10,000 hits a day, which we found very encouraging.

TV Advertisement—"Stand Up"

ANNOUNCER: Only a man who stands up to his government can truly lead. John Kerry fought and bled in the Vietnam War. He fought side by side with brothers who could not get out of the draft because they didn't have a rich father like George W. Bush. John Kerry understands war and who was disproportionately affected by it. The way this war is going, our 14-year-olds will be fighting in Iraq in four years. You better wake up before you get taken out. The Media Fund is responsible for the content of this advertisement. www.break bushoff.com

Admittedly very hard-hitting, very tough stuff, but again this was a project that was created by a group that knows this audience very well.

As I said, we did 50 million dollars in time buying and probably ran four dozen television commercials and additional radio ads, Internet ads, print ads. In the fall, we put a little more than 10 million dollars behind a "Saudi campaign" talking about the close ties between President Bush and the Saudi royal family. This set up another mini-campaign of the sort that Brian alluded to earlier. We set up a BushandSaudis.com site and we were driving traffic there. The reason I bring these up is that research told us they proved to be the most powerful spots we created in the entire cycle. That's why at the end of the campaign we threw so much money behind them. It's not something we anticipated or planned; it's something we discovered. Once we believed it, we invested in it and committed to it. These are very controversial ads, and probably rightfully so.

There was a lot of debate internally about whether or not this was something we wanted to do. So we borrowed a market testing technique from MoveOn, which I think took the technique from the private sector. I had never before heard of a political campaign doing market testing. In short, you run the ad in a television market for a week, and poll before and after. I think MoveOn usually does two weeks. We didn't have that much time. We decided to run it in St. Louis because the Kerry campaign was no longer advertising there, the DNC was not advertising there, but the Bush campaign was. We wanted to go somewhere we would be going head to head with the Bush campaign so that we could compare the power of the messages.

Also, one of the rules in our eyes of 527s is, "Do no harm." Our job was to get a Democratic message out while not hurting any Democratic candidates anywhere up or down the ticket. So we ran 1,000 gross ratings points in St. Louis. Incidentally we did a national cable buy. To answer Dr. Jamieson's question, these two were the only ads turned down by anyone this cycle. Fox News turned it down, citing their refusal to air one of the Swift Boats as a precedent. Our ad that was turned down by Fox was one of two Saudi ads that ran together; each is 30 seconds.

The email traffic back and forth with Fox News was interesting. They said at first that the reason for the turn down was that the content of the ad was "heresy." I realized later they meant, "hearsay." It was just a typo.

After the week that the ads ran in St. Louis, a survey of voters who recalled the ads found a 17-point shift toward the Democratic ticket, which was stunning. Independents shifted by 26 points. One of the things that you always balance is: does your ad work with your base or your swing voters. In this campaign we found ads that worked with both. Bush's job numbers plummeted by 16 points; the belief that he was tied to oil companies that influence his decisions increased by 5 points; there was a 9-point increase in "putting his own needs ahead of the needs of the country." Finally, there was an 18-point leap in describing Bush as "too close to the Saudi family."

TV Advertisement—"All In The Family"

ANNOUNCER: The Saudi royal family . . . wealthy . . . powerful . . . corrupt. And close Bush family friends. The Saudis have invested tens of millions in Bush business ventures. Rich Saudis bailed out George W. when his oil company went bust. And even though 15 of the 19 hijackers were Saudis, top Bush advisor James Baker's law firm is defending Saudi Arabia against the victims' families. Kind of makes you wonder . . . Are Bush and the Saudis too close for comfort? The Media Fund is responsible for the content of this ad.

And these two ads, we ran them together in a 50/50 rotation.

TV Advertisement—"Missing Pages"

ANNOUNCER: When congressional investigators issued their report on 9/11 . . . there were 28 pages missing. Twenty-eight pages of evidence that the Saudi government funded the terrorists who killed nearly 3000 Americans. Evidence kept secret under orders from George Bush. Was it to protect his Saudi friends? Or was Bush helping Jim Baker—a top advisor whose law firm is defending the Saudis in a lawsuit brought by the victims' families. Either way, Bush and the Saudis are too close for comfort. The Media Fund is responsible for the content of this ad.

These were produced by McMahon, Squire & Associates. We retested them a couple of times to make sure they worked and we tested them in places as different as Green Bay, Wisconsin and Jacksonville, Florida. We found that they worked everywhere. They worked across demographics, across party identification, and across geographics.

The earlier panel talked a little bit about clutter on the airwaves. The one thing we heard when we were trying to listen to people talk about these commercials was that this was new information to a lot of people. They didn't accept all of it at first, even though it was all factually based and everything had multiple sources. They listened because it was new information and it was something that they were interested to hear more about. We found that reflected in our website also.

Bill Zimmerman

Bill Zimmerman *is a partner in Zimmerman & Markman, a political consulting firm based in Santa Monica, CA. The firm specializes in campaign management and in television, radio, and print advertising for Democratic candidates, ballot initiatives, foundations, and public interest groups. Since 1975, Zimmerman has served as the campaign manager or lead media consultant in over 200 elections for ballot initiatives and for offices from city council to president of the United States. From mid-2003 to November 2004, Zimmerman served as campaign manager for MoveOn.org Voter Fund.*

Before I begin, I feel compelled to say something about Vietnam. This isn't the place to debate the merits of the Vietnam War. But, as someone who spent eleven years of his life working in the antiwar movement, I want to tell you that, especially since most of you in the audience here are students whose primary knowledge of the war in Vietnam comes out of history classes rather than personal experience, if you had lived through the years of that war, a majority of you would have stood with John Kerry in opposition to it, just as a majority of the students in my generation did when we lived through it.

You have all heard a great deal about this election in terms of red states and blue states, about how the United States is divided between a coastal and Great Lakes zone on the one hand and the rest of the country on the other. The former being blue and the latter being red. I looked at some numbers last week and discovered a more interesting division. If you divide the country into those states that were part of the old Confederacy, and those who were not, in the 13 states in the old Confederacy, Bush won by 5 1/2 million votes. In the 37 states that were not part of the old Confederacy, Kerry won by 2 1/2 million votes. So that too is a meaningful way of looking at the [political] geography of the United States today.

MoveOn.org began its commitment to the presidential campaign in June of 2003, long before the other groups that are presenting today. We based our strategy on several assumptions. One, that a few states would swing the election, as was true in 2000. We didn't see a great deal

Bill Zimmerman

of change in the country between 2000 and 2003. So we made the assumption that if we focused our efforts in a few states rather than in the entire country we could be more likely to influence the outcome of the election.

Second, we assumed that the electorate [would] engage earlier in this campaign than in most presidential campaigns. We made that assumption for two reasons. One, the closeness of the election in 2000 in which the incumbent president had actually lost the popular vote; and two, the fact that we had an ongoing and controversial war in Iraq, which forced the citizenry to pay closer attention to politics, especially at the presidential level, than they usually do.

We also assumed, third, that Bush was vulnerable on a number of bedrock economic issues, principally jobs, health care costs, and the costs of prescription drugs. We assumed that his administration thus far had been a failure in those areas and that those bedrock economic issues were generally the issues that undecided voters and independent voters made their decisions around.

Fourth, we assumed that nobody else would be going after Bush before the Democratic nominee was chosen. Usually in presidential elections, if there is a Republican incumbent the Democrats spend all their time going after each other and finally emerge with a nominee who's broke and bruised and ill-prepared to begin a general election campaign. So, we launched a campaign with the intent of trying to reduce any lead that Bush would have at the point at which a Democratic nominee would be selected. Given the front loading of the primary campaigns in 2004, we assumed that that nominee would emerge on March 2, so-called Super Tuesday.

We also made the assumption, which was a bit of a guess and a risk on the part of the organization, that we could raise 10 million dollars from MoveOn members in this early stage of the campaign. We knew they were motivated; we weren't sure they were motivated to that extent. Ten million dollars would have been an unprecedented amount of money to raise. Remember, this was at a point long before Dean demonstrated that substantial dollars could be raised over the Internet.

We began by focusing on five states: Florida, Missouri, Pennsylvania, West Virginia, and Nevada.[1] Our theory was that any of the three large states that we selected (Florida, Ohio, Missouri) had enough Electoral College votes to swing the election if we could move one of them from the Bush column where they had been in 2000 to the Democratic column in 2004. Alternatively we could swing the election by moving both of the smaller states (West Virginia and Nevada). Combined they had enough Electoral College votes to swing the election. These were five of the six states that Bush had won by the smallest margins in the 2000 election. The sixth was New Hampshire, which is a very difficult state to campaign in because most of the television viewing in New Hampshire comes out of Boston. So you have to buy the Boston media market and pay for everybody in Massachusetts in order to reach the people in New Hampshire, not a very cost-effective buy. After removing New Hampshire, we focused on five of the six states Bush had won by the smallest margins.

During the course of the campaign, we used a lot of advertising on national cable and on cable in Washington, D.C. and New York. The primary purpose of that advertising was to drive news coverage. We were trying to influence reporters and editors who reside in Washington and New York to cover something to a greater extent than they otherwise would have. Today I'm just going to focus on advertising that we made that was designed to reach voters directly in the states that we were targeting.

We began in June of 2003 with a spot that was based on what was newsworthy at the time; the weapons of mass destruction that the Bush administration had assured us were present in Iraq and [whose presence] was used as a justification for the invasion. It was becoming clear in June of 2003 that those weapons didn't exist, had never existed, and that the administration knew that they didn't exist when they first started prosecuting the war. So we made a spot on that subject. We also made the spot with the intent of using it as a brand. We were going to brand our campaign with a theme that was developed in this spot and repeated in all of the spots that the MoveOn Voter Fund eventually aired.

TV Advertisement—"Misleader"

ANNOUNCER: George Bush told us Iraq was a nuclear threat. He said they were trying to purchase uranium, that they were rebuilding their nuclear facilities. So we went to war. Now there's evidence we were misled and almost every day, Americans are dying in Iraq. We need the truth, not a cover up. Log on to Misleader.org today. MoveOn PAC is responsible for the content of this advertisement.

We ran that spot in combination with a full-page ad in the *New York Times*, which had across its top the headline "Misleader" with "Mis" and "Leader" in slightly different color tones. At that point, we began to see numerous news articles, editorials, and columnists picking up the word misleader. Obviously at that point we wanted to call George Bush a liar, because that's what he was doing, lying to the American people about the war in Iraq. But the word liar was too strong. People wouldn't accept it; it would encounter too much resistance had we called an incumbent president a liar.

So we came up with "misleader" as a more acceptable alternative and found that once we started using it, the press began to use it as well. Misleader was a word that this advertising campaign put into the political dialogue, and did it very effectively. We did not run any more advertising until December.

Between June and December, we began to lay the groundwork for the coming campaign. To do so, first, we raised money; we had to test the assumption that we could raise 10 million dollars from MoveOn members. Secondly, we secured a commitment to provide matching funds from billionaire currency trader George Soros and Peter Lewis, founder of Progressive Insurance. They agreed to give us a 50 percent match on any money that we raised from the members. By January of '04 we had raised 10 million dollars. With the 50 percent match, we had a total fund of 15 million, which we spent between December and March.

In that period we also began to poll and do focus groups in the five states that we had targeted. We had made a very serious commitment to research. We were determined never to run advertising that wasn't tested. We also developed testing techniques that had never been used in politics before. To begin with, we started doing market tests. Erik [Smith] alluded to that; let me explain it a little more thoroughly. We would put a spot on the air in a small media market, for example Charleston, West Virginia, and run it for two weeks at fairly high levels. We would do a full-blown political poll before and after that two-week advertising period. We then would go to a demographically similar media market, for example, Erie, Pennsylvania, and do the same polling there at the same time that we were polling in the test market, Charleston. But we ran no advertising in Erie. So we used Erie as a control market and Charleston as a test market. As a result of use of this method, we were able to tease out national trends that were moving opinion in the control market and look at differences between those trends in the control market and the test market making the assumption that in the test market it was the advertising that was altering the national trends.

Political campaigns don't usually engage in market testing, not because you have to be a genius to figure it out, it's an obvious thing to do, but rather because we lack the time and money to carry out that kind of research in political campaigns. It's usually too rushed. You don't have two weeks to test the spot before you have to get it on the air. Because we were starting a year in advance, we had an enormous advantage in terms of designing a more effective testing program than is usually used with political spots.

Most political spots are tested in focus groups. We think that's a terrible way to test political advertising. Focus groups and dial groups, which is a newer phenomenon, are the dominant means of testing political ads. But we think it is far too artificial a way of testing television advertising.

When you watch television advertising, spots come at you in streams of seven to nine. There is no time to discuss the content or veracity of the ads with the people you're sitting next to. The ad makes an impression, and then it's gone. If you're going to test the effectiveness of spots, they have to be tested in some kind of environment that comes close to actual viewing, not in a focus group where you watch a spot, ten people talk about it, and each has a reaction. In a focus group, everybody thinks they're a producer. They say, "I would have used color over there," or "I would've changed the soundtrack over here."

Market testing is a far more valid way of measuring the effectiveness of spots. However, we knew that we'd get to a point closer to the election where we didn't have two weeks to test spots. So, we developed a way to test them over the Web. To do this, we would convene focus groups of a thousand people on the Web. They were polled before and after watching one or several spots. We began to do this in conjunction with market tests in November of '03 as a validity check. We were sure the market testing was the right way to test spots but were less sure about the Web testing. So every time we market tested, we web tested to see what the correlation was between the Web test and the market test. Since we found a 65 percent correlation between the results of the market tests and the Web tests, by April and May of 2004, we were relying exclusively on the Web testing. Let me show you an example of some of the surprises you get when you test spots. Here are two spots called "87 Billion" and "Hoover."

TV Advertisements—"87 Billion"

ANNOUNCER: We could build 10,000 new schools or hire almost 2 million new teachers. We could rebuild our electric grid. We could insure more of our children. George Bush is going to spend $87 billion more in Iraq. But after almost three years, where is his plan for taking care of America? The truth is we're not being led; we're being misled. MoveOn PAC is responsible for the content of this advertisement.

"Hoover"

ANNOUNCER: George Bush is doing something Bill Clinton didn't do, his father didn't do—not Reagan or Carter, or Ford, or Nixon—not L.B.J. or J.F.K—not Eisenhower or Harry Truman—not in any of F.D.R.'s four terms. No, George Bush is going to be the first president since Herbert Hoover to lead an economy that loses jobs—over 2 million so far. Didn't George Bush say his tax cuts would create jobs? MoveOn PAC is responsible for the content of this advertisement.

What we learned was that one works and one doesn't. The first spot moved the presidential vote in Charleston, West Virginia, by 8 points. The second spot didn't move it at all. That was a little surprising to me. I thought the second spot was more effective than the first. But that's not what voters felt. When we saw that 8-point shift in our market test in Charleston, West Virginia, we put the first two million dollars that we had into two weeks of advertising in the five targeted states that we had selected beginning on December 1.

That was the start of what became a continual advertising campaign from then until March 2. For three months, we were on the air at 600 gross rating points a week in those five states continually. We were not in a couple of markets in Florida where the Democratic vote had been very high, such as Miami and Fort Lauderdale. But other than those exceptions and some of the very conservative markets in the Florida panhandle, we were up for three months with the first spots you saw and then with spots on prescription drug costs and the high cost of health care.

While we were advertising in those five states, we were polling there. Stan Greenberg and Anna Greenberg were doing the polling for us. They also helped us invent our market and Web tests. They and other pollsters were also working for The Media Fund and for America Coming Together [ACT] and polling in the other battleground states in which we weren't advertising. So, during the course of the primary campaign, we were able to compare the impact of early anti-Bush advertising on the electorate in a battleground state against the absence of such advertising in other battleground states. We had very clear evidence that in those five states where we had been advertising against Bush, his numbers were significantly lower than in battleground states in which there had been no advertising against Bush.

We took that evidence to Erik [Smith, President of the Media Fund], Harold Ickes, his colleague at The Media Fund, and Steve Rosenthal at the Americans Coming Together. We argued in late February and immediately after the primary in March that early advertising would be effective. There were other people arguing that we should save all of the money that was being raised and use it at the end. This strategic disagreement was a critical one on the Democratic side. We believe the right decision was made by committing to early advertising as Erik [Smith]'s presentation indicated. We were able to keep Bush's lead from getting too far ahead of Kerry, and in fact after two months of advertising in 17 battleground states, in March and April and into early May, we actually had Kerry ahead. So the first phase of our work, December, January, and February, we saw as successful in bringing Bush's numbers down and successful in demonstrating that they could be kept down in the next phase of the campaign, which began immediately after March 2.

After March 2, "Worker" was one of the first spots we ran.

TV Advertisement—"Worker"

ANNOUNCER: Times are tough till you work overtime to make ends meet. Then you find out George Bush wants to eliminate overtime pay for 8 million workers. Two million jobs lost, jobs going overseas, and now, no overtime pay. When it comes to choosing between corporate values and family values, face it, George Bush is not on our side. MoveOn PAC is responsible for the content of this advertisement.

Beginning on March 3, the Bush campaign launched two advertising campaigns running side by side, one positive and one negative. The negative spots laid the groundwork for calling John Kerry a flip-flopper and positioning him as more liberal than the electorate. The positive spots were positive. I don't really remember the content; they were boring. Then after three weeks, Bush pulled the positive spots off the air. It was clear from our polling that the Bush campaign pulled those positive spots off the air because they weren't moving his numbers up. You put positive spots on the air to raise your numbers, and you put negative spots on the air to lower the other guy's numbers. The polling numbers are gathered by different pollsters, but presumably they're reasonably close to each other. The polling indicated that, despite the three weeks of positive advertising, Bush's positives weren't going up. We assumed that was because of our negative advertising against Bush. So strategically we were serving the purpose that we had set out to achieve, to keep Bush from building up a lead.

Of course Bush's negative campaign was working, and Kerry's numbers were going down. This was at a time when Kerry had little money for advertising because he was just coming out of the primary. So strategically, what we were achieving in collaboration with The Media Fund, and ACT and the AFL, was placing a limit on how high Bush could go. All of us were operating under the assumption at that time that if we held an incumbent president below 50 percent all the way up to the election that would augur well because in most previous elections when that occurred, and when the incumbent's approval rating was as low as Bush's was, when the country wanted to move in a different direction, incumbents usually lose. Those assumptions did not prove to be correct, even though strategically we achieved our purpose of preventing Bush from getting to 50. During this time, the content of our advertising was focused on the economy. Starting in late May and June that began to shift. But before we get to that shift, let me discuss another economic ad that we ran, the "Burger" spot.

TV Advertisement—"Burger"

ANNOUNCER: You put in 30 years at the company. You get good pay, health care. Then they send your job overseas and under George Bush, the company actually gets a tax break for doing it. Now, Bush says we're in recovery. Then after a year, you finally land another job and you wonder, is this what you worked your whole life for? We're not being led; we're being misled.

MoveOn PAC is responsible for the content of this advertisement.

Starting in late May, we began to shift our advertising such that in addition to economic themes we began to work in themes involving the war in Iraq. We focused not only on how the war was being prosecuted, but also on some of the corporate corruption scandals that were plaguing the White House at that time. We were also then changing our targeting. By late May and June, we had given up on West Virginia and Missouri. We had also (I'm speaking now only of MoveOn, not of The Media Fund) pulled out of Florida. We started to focus more narrowly on Ohio, Nevada, and Oregon. We had always thought that Ohio would be the linchpin. We anticipated that we could carry Pennsylvania again; we thought that we would lose Florida even if we had won by a small margin, as we think we did in 2000. So Ohio became the critical state that we had to take away from Bush, and that was true from beginning to end. In this phase we started making spots that included something about Iraq in addition to economic issues. I'm going to focus on a pair of spots that we produced in this phase and again. One of them worked very well in our testing program, the other didn't work at all. They are called "Corporate Headquarters" and "Wrong Direction."

TV Advertisements—"Corporate Headquarters"

ANNOUNCER: Instead of protecting pensions, George Bush supported a bill giving Enron huge new tax breaks. Instead of giving seniors new prescription drug benefits, Bush gave drug companies billions in his Medicare bill. Instead of fighting corporation, George Bush gave no-bid contracts to Halliburton, a company caught overcharging for fuel and food for our soldiers in Iraq. George Bush: He's turned the White House into corporate headquarters. MoveOn PAC is responsible for the content of this advertisement.

"Wrong Direction"

ANNOUNCER: Every time George Bush has had a decision to make, he's gone the wrong way, leading us down the road to joblessness, higher health care costs, and huge deficits. We're not being led; we're being misled. MoveOn PAC is responsible for the content of this advertisement.

The second one was certainly more amusing, but the first one was the one that worked. I thought the first one was over the top. Putting a corporate headquarters sign on top of the White House is a little extreme. But the public reacted oppositely. They thought that that was exactly what was happening. This was especially true among independent voters. They didn't like the second one because it belittled the president and the presidency by turning him into a South Park-like cartoon character. So that spot was rejected, and we never aired it. These spots give you an idea of the kind of material we were airing at the time and also suggest the importance of testing; there are always surprises. People like me are smart enough to make spots, but not smart enough to know how they're going to go down when they're shown to undecided and independent voters.

MoveOn began to wind down its efforts in June and July. We continued to do a modest amount of advertising but not on a scale large enough to have an impact on too many voters. Then in August in the period between the Democratic and Republican conventions, we ramped up again. As you'll recall, the candidates received public money to support their campaign immediately after they received the nomination of their party at convention. So Kerry received his 75 million dollars in public money at the end of July but Bush didn't get his until the end of August. What happens to spending in August? If Kerry spends his money in August, he'll have less than Bush in September and October. So Kerry made the decision not to spend any of his public money during August so that he could go toe-to-toe with Bush in September and October. That meant that those of us working outside the Kerry campaign had to fill that gap because obviously Bush would continue advertising during August. We did a lot of advertising in collaboration with the other 527s during August to keep Kerry's numbers up. "Platter" is one of the spots we used then.

TV Advertisement—"Platter"

ANNOUNCER: The Bush administration gave Dick Cheney's old company no-bid contracts for Iraq on a silver platter. Then the Pentagon caught Halliburton overcharging $61 million for gasoline. Worse, they billed over $100 million for meals for our troops that they never delivered and George Bush is still doing business with them. George Bush: a failure of leadership. MoveOn PAC is responsible for the content of this advertisement.

Within a week or so of that ad playing, the Swift Boat [Swift Boat Veterans for Truth] attack on Kerry began. The Kerry campaign elected not to respond directly, so we responded with the "Kerry/Bush" spot.

TV Advertisement—"Kerry/Bush"

ANNOUNCER: It is said of war that it sometimes brings out the best in a man and sometimes the very worst. Two men: the first went to Vietnam—a lieutenant—in a boat riding up the Mekong River—nowhere to hide—a harrowing escape—then the more harrowing realization that one man was left wounded in the water. The lieutenant chose to go back through the gunfire because he couldn't leave even one man behind. The second man sailed to the top of a list on his father's name—was trained as a pilot but failed to show up for a required physical. He was grounded, wasn't seen for months, and then was released eight months early to go to Harvard Business School. This election is about character. It's between John Kerry who left no man behind and George Bush who simply left. MoveOn PAC is responsible for the content of this advertisement.

Unfortunately we were unable to play that ad as widely as the Swift Boat people played theirs, but we did get it on the air shortly after their campaign began.

This takes us up to the Republican convention. During the Republican convention we ran a series of ads showing Republican voters who were switching. These were talking heads spots that were shot for us by Errol Morris who had done the Apple iPod switcher campaign, and had also done the documentary film *Fog of War*. In that film, former Secretary of Defense Robert McNamara repudiated the policies that he had developed when he was in charge of prosecuting the war in Vietnam. In these spots four or five Republicans, one in each spot, would explain why they had voted for Bush in 2000 and become disappointed in him and were now voting against him.

After the convention, MoveOn ceased operations for the most part as a voter fund and went forward as a political action committee, a PAC. That change meant that all of the money that we raised and spent came in small donations from our members. The contributions were no longer supplemented by large donors like George Soros. Even though we had a diminished role, we continued advertising extensively in Ohio and Nevada. The focus of our spots shifted toward Iraq. In late September and early October there were many breaking news stories coming out of Iraq, most of them detrimental to the Bush administration. You'll remember the most dramatic of those stories focused on the ammunition missing from a large ammo dump outside Baghdad. At that point the content of the campaign began to shift toward Iraq, not only on our part but on the part of many of the other players. We made several spots having to do with Iraq. One was called "Quagmire."

TV Advertisement—"Quagmire"

ANNOUNCER: George Bush misled us into war with Iraq sending poorly equipped soldiers into battle. He said, mission accomplished, yet almost every day, more soldiers die. Going it alone, George Bush has spent $150 billion—money we need for schools and health care. Now facing a growing insurgency, he has no real plan to end the war. George Bush got us into this quagmire; it will take a new president to get us out. MoveOn PAC is responsible for the content of this advertisement.

So, to sum up, what did we achieve? Let me begin by saying we failed. We failed to win. There's no question about that and there's no backing away from that. We spent a great deal of time, effort, money, and energy, and we lost. On the other hand, we did accomplish a few things, none of which make up for that loss but all of which have some significance. We kept Bush from seizing an early lead in key primary states. We raised economic issues and forced them into the debate on both sides. We prevented Bush from opening up a big lead while he was attacking Kerry very effectively during the spring campaign. And ultimately we took away from the Bush campaign their primary strategy, which was to come out of the Republican convention with a 10-point lead and coast to victory. They came out of the Republican convention in a tied race, and they had a very difficult time winning.

During the course of this effort, the membership of MoveOn.org, which had been at 300,000 prior to the invasion of Iraq, grew to 2.8 million—an unprecedented number of people involved in a single political organization with the capacity to have two-way instantaneous communication between leadership and membership. All told, we raised and spent about 25 million dollars. We hope that we have empowered grass roots activism in the course of our work and that it will play a much greater role in the Democratic party of the future and we hope that these efforts are just the beginning and not an end.

David Jones

David W. Jones is president of DWJ Consulting Inc., a fundraising and strategic consulting firm. His clients have included Senator Max Baucus, former House Minority Leader Richard Gephardt, Rep. Charles Rangel, the International AIDS Trust Inc., Vice President Gore's presidential campaign, the Democratic National Committee, the Democratic Congressional Campaign Committee, and the Service Employees International Union. Jones was a member of the national finance board for President Clinton's 1996 reelection campaign and served on the staff of the president's 1993 inaugural committee. From 1990 to 1992, he worked on the senatorial and presidential campaigns of Sen. Tom Harkin.

The 527 that I founded was a lot different from those of my two colleagues. What they did was much larger, much better funded, and it was much broader. What we did was very, very specific, very targeted. We were born on November 3, 2003, and we didn't exactly die on February 19, but that was the day that Howard Dean dropped out of the presidential campaign. So I guess that was the day we effectively ended our activity.

In the summertime of 2003, it looked like this was a done deal; in some places, Howard Dean was drawing 30 percent leads over his closest opponents. His national polls were putting him at 5–20 percent up. He was looking like he was sailing to the nomination. Ten thousand people were showing up at his rallies at the Sleepless Summer tour. Joe Trippi had put together an Internet operation, rivaled only by MoveOn's operation. They went from 300 known supporters on the Internet in early 2003 to over I guess 700,000 Internet supporters later in the year around November and December. So it was an amazing, amazing revolutionary run that Governor Dean led with the help of his consultants, Joe Trippi and Steve McMahon. Our goal was to knock Governor Dean out of the Democratic primaries.

Now, when you're a 527, you're not really supposed to say that. You're not supposed to say, express advocacy—vote for, vote against, elect, or defeat. And we never did. We never used those words in our advertising. But don't let anybody ever tell you that the goal of a 527 is not express advocacy. It is. The goal for Swift Boats was to knock John Kerry out and to help George Bush. They never said that. That was the goal. So don't let anybody propagate the farce that 527s are not involved in express advocacy. They just don't say words that amount to express advocacy in

David Jones

advertisements, which I have to say because my lawyers made me. We never engage in any express advocacy in our advertisements.

Although Dean was a very strong candidate, our polling and research conducted by Paul Harstad from Colorado found two major vulnerabilities. Number one, Dean was a fairly moderate to conservative governor in Vermont. He was not the liberal, progressive, antiwar firebrand that the media and that his supporters thought he was. If you look at his record, Howard Dean is a moderate. He captured the mood of the Democratic Party, an antiwar mood, and that gained him traction. You recall in February 2003, he went in front of the DNC and he said, "I represent the Democratic wing of the Democratic Party."

He took that antiwar traction, which MoveOn also capitalized on, and rode it through the summer and fall to gain 20-point leads. What we found is when liberal, progressive Iowa caucus attendees were given information about where he actually stood on the issues, they turned away from him. The three issues we found were: number one, Medicare funding, which Governor Dean had expressed support for cutting; NAFTA (Governor Dean was at the signing ceremony at the White House signing NAFTA and obviously a large number of Iowa voters who

CHART 32. HARSTAD POLLING

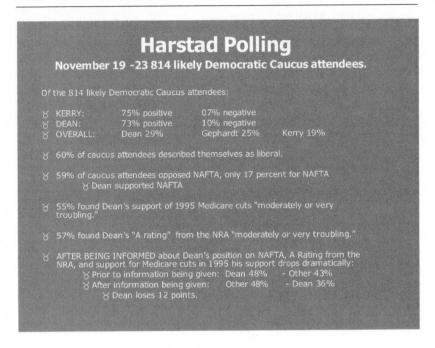

Harstad Polling

November 19 -23 814 likely Democratic Caucus attendees.

Of the 814 likely Democratic Caucus attendees:

    ☒ KERRY: 75% positive   07% negative
    ☒ DEAN: 73% positive   10% negative
    ☒ OVERALL: Dean 29%   Gephardt 25%   Kerry 19%

    ☒ 60% of caucus attendees described themselves as liberal.

    ☒ 59% of caucus attendees opposed NAFTA, only 17 percent for NAFTA
        ☒ Dean supported NAFTA

    ☒ 55% found Dean's support of 1995 Medicare cuts "moderately or very troubling."

    ☒ 57% found Dean's "A rating" from the NRA "moderately or very troubling."

    ☒ AFTER BEING INFORMED about Dean's position on NAFTA, A Rating from the NRA, and support for Medicare cuts in 1995 his support drops dramatically:
        ☒ Prior to information being given: Dean 48%   - Other 43%
        ☒ After information being given: Other 48%   - Dean 36%
           ☒ Dean loses 12 points.

were against NAFTA); and thirdly, gun restrictions. The liberal Iowa caucus attendees were for those restrictions; you wouldn't believe it, but they actually were. Howard Dean got an A rating eight times from the NRA and really was out of step with Iowa voters.

Public polls obviously showed a lot of concern about Governor Dean's inability to be elected against George W. Bush and about his lack of foreign policy experience. This is just a summary.

I want to show you the Kerry numbers specifically. Kerry was never back as far as everybody thought he was. Kerry always had the wherewithal to break through as he eventually did because he seemed the most electable candidate. This is what our polling [numbers] showed from November 19 to 23 (see Chart 32). Kerry had a 75 percent positive among Iowa caucus goers; Dean had 73 and we can see at that time Kerry was only 10 percent back. The other statistics just show you that Iowa voters did not like the fact that Dean supported NAFTA, that he supported Medicare cuts, and that he got eight A ratings from the NRA. When all that information was given to voters, they switched. Dean versus Kerry, Dean versus Gephardt. Dean lost 12 points when this information was given to them.

So our strategy was fairly simple: peel off the liberal, Democratic, progressive vote from Howard Dean that he already had by informing these voters of his moderate stands on the issues. Second, we were trying to get those considering supporting Howard Dean at that point because of his stand on the war to think again. Our message was, this guy is not who you think he is, please think again. We started the first ad we ran on December 5.

Television Advertisement—"Two Barrels Plain"

ANNOUNCER: These two men have been given "top grades" by the National Rifle Association. One is George Bush . . . the other might surprise you. It's Howard Dean. That's right. In Vermont, Dean was endorsed eight times by the National Rifle Association—and Dean got an A rating from the NRA because he joined them in opposing common sense gun safety laws. So, if you thought Howard Dean had a progressive record, check the facts—and please think again.

GRAPHIC: www.progressivevalues.com Paid for by Americans for Jobs, Healthcare and Progressive Values.

Obviously we're trying to peel off people who may consider him as their candidate. The second ad which ran in a rotation with this brought in all three issues that we were concerned about.

Television Advertisement—"Facts"

ANNOUNCER: Just the facts. Howard Dean backed the Republican plan in Congress to cut Medicare by over 250 billion dollars. Howard Dean and George Bush stood together and supported the unfair NAFTA trade agreement. And in Vermont, Howard Dean was endorsed eight times by the National Rifle Association—the NRA even gave Dean an "A" rating—an A!

So, if you thought Howard Dean had a progressive record . . . check the facts . . . and please think again.

GRAPHIC: www.progressivevalues2.com Paid for by Americans for Jobs, Healthcare and Progressive Values.

We ran about 600,000 dollars behind these two ads in the Des Moines and Cedar Rapids media markets, which covered about 80 percent of the caucus attendees in Iowa. Six hundred thousand dollars, as was mentioned before, in some states can't get you anything. That amount in Iowa can get you pretty heavy coverage for two weeks, and that's what we did.

For the third ad that we ran, we had no money left. I had about $22,000–23,000 in the bank. We decided to throw a long ball and address the third issue, Dean's electability against George Bush. Most Democratic polls were showing that was the main concern. We wanted to address it by addressing the fact that he had zero foreign policy experience in a year where foreign policy/military experience looked like it was going to be the top issue. Remember, this was all in December of 2003. We wound up spending very little money on this ad but it got a tremendous amount of attention. Of the $23,000 in the bank, I put $14,000 behind this ad.

Television Advertisement—"Cannot"

ANNOUNCER: We live in a very dangerous world.

GRAPHIC: Time Magazine cover with picture of Osama bin Laden.

ANNOUNCER: And there are those who wake up every morning determined to destroy western civilization . . .

Americans want a president who can face the dangers ahead. But Howard Dean has no military or foreign policy experience. And Howard Dean just cannot compete with George Bush on foreign policy. It's time for Democrats to think about that . . . and think about it now.

GRAPHIC: www.progressivevalues.com Paid for by Americans for Jobs, Healthcare and Progressive Values.

That ad got more attention than I could really believe. We put about 600,000 behind the first two ads; we put 14,000 dollars behind the final ad. We put it in Manchester, New Hampshire, and Columbia, South Carolina. New Hampshire and South Carolina were the next two primaries coming up. The reason we did it was because we wanted to get our belief that Dean was unelectable out into the public domain.

Nobody had used Osama bin Laden in an ad, and, obviously, the fact that Osama bin Laden was in this ad was incredibly controversial.

Unlike the other 527s, we went Democrat on Democrat. This was an internal Democratic Party fight. I'm a lifelong Democrat. All of our supporters were Democrats. I worked for a number of Democratic candidates, including President Clinton and Vice President Gore. So this was a Democrat on Democrat attack through a 527.

We started this Osama ad on the 12th of December. It got zero attention. Why? Because the next day, Saddam Hussein was captured. So, we thought, well, we just flushed that money down the toilet. We lost that money. Saddam Hussein was captured. Fortunately for us, CNN picked up the Osama ad on the 15th, which was Monday, and ran a spot on it. Howard Dean gave a speech, you might recall, saying that the world is not safer and the United States is not safer with Saddam Hussein in prison. Now I agreed with Governor Dean on that, but it really wasn't the time for Governor Dean to be coming out and say that right after our country had had a large victory. Dean caught a lot of flack for that.

Our ad caught fire that week, for four solid days. Jim Rutenberg at the *New York Times* wrote a piece, "Democratic Group Finances Republican Style Attack on Dean." And then our biggest gift of all. Joe Trippi, Howard Dean's campaign manager, now a friend of mine, actually called on all the Democratic candidates to condemn the ad. Thank you, Joe. When he did that, the media people did what they were supposed to do, which was ask, what is this ad he is talking about, we haven't seen it. When he sent out a letter condemning the ad, then newspaper, television folks came to us. What is the ad? We gave it out. Joe had done us a favor, as had Governor Dean. Over the next four days, I don't have the exact numbers because we didn't have enough money to track any of this, the ad was featured on almost every cable and network news show and dozens and dozens of newspaper articles all over the country. All of this fed right into what was ultimately Dean's own downfall because the following week, Dean had said Osama bin Laden, despite what he had done, deserved a fair and free trial, which was another mistake.

On December 20, we ended all ads because of the disclosure rule. We would have had to disclose all of our donors on December 21 if we continued to run these ads. I did not want to do that considering the amount of pressure we were under, at that point, to disclose our donors. So we did not disclose our donors. We wound up raising another 400,000 dollars in January 2004 because of these ads, but we never used that money because Dean by that point was falling fairly rapidly.

Just a few things, I've handed out an article in which Steve McMahon, one of Governor Dean's top spokespeople, called us a drive-by shooting, which I thought was a fairly accurate description. What we tried to do was affect the primary race; we did in a small way, with a very small amount of money. Unlike the hundreds of thousands MoveOn.org had, we had about 20 or 22 donors who funded the whole thing. So it was really a small operation that was up and down in a matter of two to three months, and it was fairly successful.

Discussion

Question: My name is Meg Kinnard and I write for NationalJournal
.com's Ad Spotlights section. I have a question about ad sharing. Erik,
you and Bill both talked about coordination among the 527 groups. . . .
Could you address that and talk about production coming from one
group and another group picking that idea up and thinking that's such
a good thing that we would like to run that and put some more money
behind it.

BILL ZIMMERMAN:

"87 Billion" was run by both organizations, as were several of the other
spots. "Platter" was run by both organizations, "Pills," and "Scary" that
Erik showed you, that The Media Fund produced, was run by MoveOn
at some times. When we did this, everything was fully disclosed to the
FEC. The production expenses were made as either in-kind contributions or money was transferred in the form of a purchase or a licensing
agreement between one organization and the other. Each organization
that ran a particular spot took public responsibility for production costs.

ERIK SMITH:

We did a lot of that. We bought or received spots from other groups and
we also sold spots to a lot of other groups. We had a commercial very
similar to the "87 Billion" spot. Their commercial tested much better. I
don't remember if we bought that one or you [MoveOn] gave that one
to us. There were some groups out there, groups such as Strong America
Now that formed a little late. They had a lot of money, but didn't have
any creative team at all. We sold them some stuff. There were groups
like the Detroit project, which had creative but no money. They had a
great ad on oil prices and gasoline prices that we tested. We had a Web
test going with three commercials and we had an empty slot for a fourth.
So we figured as a favor to Detroit Project, we'd throw their ad in and it
tested through the roof. We were looking for a spot at that time for
Nevada. Gas prices in Nevada were really through the roof, and that ad
just worked.

BILL ZIMMERMAN:

It's important to understand that all of this is driven by the testing program. You probably heard that MoveOn ran a contest at one point, and
asked its members to make their own spots. Much to our surprise, 1,500

spots were submitted. We ran two in full-blown advertising campaigns against undecided voters. This past fall, a lot of Hollywood and New York commercial directors wanted to make their own ads. We told them to make as many ads as you want, they're all going to go into the same testing program, and it doesn't matter if your name is Rob Reiner or somebody else. Your ads are going to be tested along with everyone else's. In fact, Reiner did make a spot that tested pretty well and we did run it. We rejected spots by numerous other very well-known directors because they didn't test well.

Question: Good afternoon, Major Garrett at Fox News. First of all, Erik [Smith] and the other gentlemen, are there any ads that you produced that you didn't run that you wish you had, maybe tougher ones, things that didn't test well but in retrospect you might have thought better to run? And is there anything too seductive about the testing process? It seems the earlier panel, I think it's fair to say, had ads that reinforced a larger ideological theme that Republicans ran on. Do you believe that your ads, even though they tested well, fit within a larger party ideology, that is to say, reinforced things that voters needed to know and would make the ultimate decision on Election Day?

ERIK SMITH:

I'll answer your first part quickly because I think the second part is more interesting. Media Fund tested more than 350 commercials. Is there anything that I would have run; no, I think we ran stuff that tested well. Is there something that made me feel good that I wish I could have thrown out there? Sure, but if it doesn't work, it doesn't work.

You're getting at something in that second part which is really interesting. One of the advantages that the other side had that we didn't have was the consistent message frame that you saw through all their commercials. There was a consistent message frame that complemented the Bush-Cheney advertising, which is, there's what John Kerry says and there's what John Kerry does and you can't trust him as commander-in-chief. That was their frame.

The Democratic groups didn't have that clear or consistent or disciplined a message frame that we were all using. We tried. We just didn't get there. One of the problems was just the fact that we were the non-incumbent party. And Bill [Zimmerman]'s group and mine, to some extent, were advertising before the Kerry campaign was advertising. We weren't benefiting as the Republican groups were from months and months of experience. The Republican groups were able to watch for months what the Bush-Cheney campaign was doing and build on and complement that. We just had to use our own research and our own gut and our own ideas.

BILL ZIMMERMAN:

I'd just add one thing to that, which is that we had thought that the best frame was the economic populist frame and the priorities message that was most clearly delivered in that spot called "87 Billion Dollars." By starting advertising early, we were trying to convince the other players in the field, including the Kerry campaign, that that was the best message for beating Bush. We didn't succeed in part because of breaking events in Iraq during September/October. Absent those breaking events, I think the Kerry campaign would have moved more effectively to the economic populist message. And I think, had they done so, they would have won.

ERIK SMITH:

I agree with everything you said, but I think what we're talking about is a kind of the tail wagging the dog scenario there. The ideal situation, which is what the Republicans have, is a strong clear message being sent to groups like ours as far as what the message is and what the frame is. Because we had a primary process that went into March, that didn't happen.

Question: Steve Weissman with the Campaign Finance Institute. This is for David Jones. My recollection is that a number of the donors, the twenty or twenty-two, were people who were sympathetic to other candidates in the primary, particularly Dick Gephardt, whom you used to be associated with in fundraising. Was there any concern by the donors or yourself that these ads could backfire on people some of your donors might have preferred? And the other part to this question, I was just curious when you mentioned that you ended the ads because you didn't want disclosure. What was the problem with disclosures? These other groups that we've heard today seemed not to mind disclosure and ran ads during their 30-, 60-day periods.

DAVID JONES:

The first issue was, as I said, taking down Howard Dean . . . Howard Dean was far ahead in most public polls and even in some of our private polls . . . Senator Bradley, Vice President Gore, Senator Harkin, and President Carter all thought he was going to be the nominee as well and endorsed him. So it looked like a cakewalk for him. The second thing was more of a personal decision. We had to go down because of Christmas. We felt that we could not run those ads, especially the Osama bin Laden ad, during Christmastime. We felt as if that would be over the top. We made a strategic decision. If we were going to go up and disclose the donors, we were going to do it about January 5. By that time, I had another 450,000 dollars, which would have gone a long way in those two media markets in Des Moines and Cedar Rapids. Dean had fallen so far during that time period, even before the scream, that it really looked like it was not necessary. We felt it was too dangerous to bring up the donors, most of whom were associated with Dick Gephardt or John Kerry. There was only one donor associated with General Clark, and General Clark was not competing in Iowa. So we thought that close to the election it would have been too dangerous to disclose and we didn't need to because Dean had fallen so far by that time.

Question: Tom Curry with MSNBC. Question for Mr. Zimmerman. Did MoveOn run any ads about Abu Ghraib and if not, why not? The other one was, do you think voters misunderstood Kerry's 1971 testimony? We saw how it was used by the Swift Boat group, but what's your view—how important an issue that was and how voters understood it?

BILL ZIMMERMAN:

We did run one ad on Abu Ghraib, but it was not run for voters. It was run here in D.C. and in New York to try to drive press coverage of that event. As it turned out we needn't have bothered since that event got enormous press coverage. But we got on the air very quickly after the story broke with a spot that ran here locally.

On your second question about the impact of Kerry's 1971 testimony: clearly that testimony was distorted in the Swift Boat advertising. Kerry never said that all soldiers in Vietnam committed atrocities and Kerry didn't claim to have seen those atrocities firsthand. That testimony grew out of an event that occurred in Detroit called the Winter Soldier hearings in 1971 in which dozens and dozens of U.S. military veterans testified that they had personally committed atrocities or had witnessed others committing atrocities. Kerry had helped convene those hearings to bring the issue to the fore. When he himself testified later in the U.S. Senate, he was describing testimony that he had heard others give.

Clearly that story was not presented to the American people by the opposition advertising or in any great depth by the press covering that advertising. The extent to which it hurt Kerry and played an influence in the campaign? Hard to say. These events are still part of a larger cultural war which has been raging since the end of Vietnam as to whether or not that war was justified and whether or not it was fought as it should have been. The two sides in that debate tend to fall on both sides of many other ideological questions that affect our political structure, so I'm not sure whether the specific content was what influenced voters or whether the general effect of those cultural wars was increased and helped to polarize people along those cultural lines. We've heard a lot after the campaign about the importance of guns, gays, and God in driving the Republican vote. That is just another way of invoking these cultural war issues that have been plaguing this country since the end of Vietnam.

Note

1. On July 15, 2004, Wes Boyd of MoveOn.org Voter Fund stated that the five core battleground states on which to focus were Ohio, Florida, Missouri, Nevada, and West Virginia (http://www.Moveon.org/voter fund/news/impact.html).

Participants

The contributors to this volume were discussants in the conference on campaign decision-making held at the Annenberg School for Communication, University of Pennsylvania, on December 3, 2004. A list of the participants at this debriefing appears below.

Peter Agree, University of Pennsylvania Press

Lemi Baruh, Annenberg School

Eran Ben-Porath, Annenberg School

David Birdsell, Baruch College

Mary Bock, Annenberg School

Jacqueline Boulden, Annenberg Public Policy Center

Mary Beth Cahill, Kerry-Edwards campaign

Joseph Cappella, Annenberg School

Matt Carlson, Annenberg School

Craig Carnaroli, University of Pennsylvania

Alex Castellanos, Bush-Cheney campaign

Lorena Chambers, Kerry-Edwards campaign

Elizabeth Cheney, Bush-Cheney campaign

Ana Maria Cobo, University of Pennsylvania

Michael Delli Carpini, Annenberg School

Nicolle Devenish, Bush-Cheney campaign

Michael Donilon, Kerry-Edwards campaign

Matthew Dowd, Bush-Cheney campaign

Kathryn Engebretson, The William Penn Foundation

Jennifer Ernst, Annenberg Public Policy Center

Tucker Eskew, Bush-Cheney campaign

Martin Fishbein, Annenberg School

Nicole Franklin, Annenberg Public Policy Center

Derek Freres, Annenberg School

Joyce Garczynski, Annenberg Public Policy Center

Joshua Gesell, Annenberg Public Policy Center

Seth Goldman, Annenberg Public Policy Center

Susan Haas, Annenberg School

Michael Hagen, Temple University

Mark Hannah, Kerry-Edwards campaign

Bill Herman, Annenberg School

Lee Humphreys, Annenberg School

Brooks Jackson, Annenberg Public Policy Center

Lela Jacobsohn, Annenberg School

Kathleen Hall Jamieson, Annenberg Public Policy Center

Patrick Jamieson, Annenberg Public Policy Center

Richard Johnston, University of British Columbia

Talia Jomini, Annenberg School

Henry Kenski, University of Arizona

Kate Kenski, Annenberg School

Margaret Kenski, Arizona Opinion

Donald Kettl, University of Pennsylvania

Bill Knapp, Kerry-Edwards campaign

Laura Kordiak, Annenberg Public Policy Center

Shiloh Krieger, Annenberg Public Policy Center

Klaus Krippendorff, Annenberg School

Antonio Lambino, Annenberg School

Kelli Lammie, Annenberg School

Jocelyn Landau, Annenberg School

Joe Lockhart, Kerry-Edwards campaign

Carolyn Marvin, Annenberg School

Mark McKinnon, Bush-Cheney campaign

Mark Mellman, Kerry-Edwards campaign

Kim Meltzer, Annenberg School

Jack Nagel, University of Pennsylvania

Jeffrey Niederdeppe, Annenberg School

Nathan Persily, University of Pennsylvania

Annette Price, Annenberg Public Policy Center

Vincent Price, Annenberg School

Susana Ramirez, Annenberg School

Karen Riley, Annenberg Public Policy Center

Nicole Rodgers, Annenberg School

Dan Romer, Annenberg Public Policy Center

Carol Scheman, University of Pennsylvania

Katherine Sender, Annenberg School

Lee Shaker, Annenberg School

Bob Shrum, Kerry-Edwards campaign

Alex Slater, Kerry-Edwards campaign

Rogers Smith, University of Pennsylvania

Robin Stanback Stevens, Annenberg School

Deborah Stinnett, Annenberg Public Policy Center

Russ Tisinger, Annenberg School

Lokman Tsui, Annenberg School

Miriam White, Annenberg Public Policy Center

Wendy White, University of Pennsylvania

Ken Winneg, Annenberg Public Policy Center

Magdalena Wojciezak, Annenberg School

Stanton Wortham, University of Pennsylvania

Danna Goldthwaite Young, Annenberg School

Undergraduate Participants

Julie S. Adler
Johanna Abil
Swati Bagaria
Beth Becker
Kyle M. Bell
Lindsay F. Berger
Michelle A. Berkowitz
Daniel Berstein
Rhea A. Bhandare
Ezra L. Billinkoff
Amber R. Birtcher
Jariel R. Bortnick
Meredith V. Bourne
Laura E. Brookover
David E. Burrick
Stefan E. Byrd-Krueger
Edward S. Byun
Kevin J. Castellano
Ali A. Causer
Joyce J. Chang
Raluca-Ioana Ciochina
Reuben H. Cohen
Kevin W. Collins
Brendan O. Darrow
Dominique C. De Armond
Daniel P. De Rosa
Brynna E. Deaver
Lauren R. Dooley
Michelle L. Dubert
Andrew S. Dulberg
Jonathan H. Dunn
Richard B. Eisenberg
Hershel S. Eisenberger
Alexander R. Eppstein
Kaitlin M. Farmer
Rachel A. Feintzeig
Lauren I. Fisher
Lesley J. Freiman
Michael J. Galligan
Lauren N. Gillespie
Evan B. Goldin

Megan E. Gompf
Matthew G. Gorski
Jordan M. Grossman
Nathaniel J. Hake
Edward Han
Adam L. Hellman
Michael R. Hogg
Christopher G. Johnson
Aaron M. Johnston
Eli R. Kaplan
Marnie B. Kaplan
Sloane K. Kaplan
Gena H. Katz
Byron M. Kho
Jooyean Kim
Maxwell A. Kosman
David J. Kovalchik
Melody J. Kramer
Jillian C. Kuhn
Sebastian E. Kurian
Renee C. Lam
Judy J. Lavi
Josephine Julia E. Leriche
Jason Letts
Sara B. Levine
Chenkay Li
Devon K. Mackenzie
Shannon J. Madden
Ralph E. Malmgren-Samuel
Bharadwaj S. Mannepalli
Marqui C. Mapp
Brendan T. Marnell
Ruth Martin
Brittany L. Merrill
Jacqueline P. Merzer
Lauren R. Mirowitz
Beth S. Mlynarczyk
Stephen R. Morse
Nancy M. Ngo
Garrett F. O'Dwyer
Jennifer J. Pan

Innae Park
Claudio J. Pavia
Sabina D. Pendse
Danielle E. Perlman
Michael D. Pertnoy
Brian M. Phillips
Anamaria S. Pop
Michelle A. Price
Benjamin K. Racine
Keith W. Randall
Jennifer W. Reiss
Sebastian Mozart Richards
Matthew W. Rosenbaum
Alvin I. Rosenblum
Brian A. Rosenwald
Adam B. Rothblatt
Amy D. Rublin
Karen D. Rutzick
Max W. Schapiro
Spencer J. Schrage
Jeff M. Shafer
David S. Shapiro
Jaime L. Shapiro
Haley N. Shapley
Scarlet R. Shore
Terry Shu

Stacey L. Siporin
Amanda M. Smith
Karen B. Smith
Jessica A. Smyth
Alexis A. Sohrakoff
Noah D. Solowiejczyk
Elizabeth R. Spector
Mindy P. Sprung
Amanda L. Stackman
Christina M. Starkweather
Jonathan M. Tannenwald
Schuyler L. Thompson
Daniel A. Treglia
Caroline L. Varin
Joel Ilan Weismer
Stefanie E. Williams
Benjamin P. Winter
Amber R. Woodward
Cynthia L. Wright
Peggy P. Yang
Alain Yassin
Hannah G. Yi
Joshua I. Zakim
Thomas N. Zelma
Michael Zubrow

Index

Italics indicate photographs.